TAX HEAVEN OR HELL

Eve Evans & Alan Fox

VACATION
PUBLICATIONS
HOUSTON

TAX HEAVEN OR HELL

Art Direction and Cover Design: Fred W. Salzmann

Research Manager: Suny Shin

Research Associates: Karen Northridge, Elizabeth Armstrong,
Jill Boxrud, Kim Orsak

Publisher's Note: This book contains information from many sources. Every effort has been made to verify the accuracy and authenticity of the information contained in this book. Although care and diligence have been used in preparation and review, the material is subject to change. It is published for general reference and the publisher does not guarantee the accuracy of the information.

Published by Vacation Publications, Inc.
1502 Augusta Drive, Suite 415
Houston, TX 77057

Library of Congress Catalog Card Number: 96-60037
ISBN 0-9644216-5-8

Printed in the United States of America

TAX HEAVEN OR HELL

CONTENTS

INTRODUCTION

If you plan to move to another state to retire, examine the tax burden you'll face when you arrive. Your retirement dreamland could be a tax heaven — or hell.

Taxes are increasingly important to everyone, but retirees have extra cause for concern since their income may be fixed. In a survey by *Where to Retire* magazine, readers cited a low overall tax rate as one of the five most important factors in choosing a place to retire.

Retirees' interest in the tax scene and the lack of readily available information about tax burdens in specific locations prompted us to undertake a unique — and massive — project: to compare the tax burdens in 149 cities in all 50 states.

That's *total* tax burden — all state and local taxes, fees and assessments — including state and local income tax, property tax, personal property tax, sales tax, auto licensing fees and fees or assessments for things like garbage pickup, street and storm drain maintenance and more.

Nowhere else have we seen information as extensive and specific as what is presented in this book. Rather than base our data on the "average" retired couple, we've calculated the tax liabilities for 9 different couples, using three income levels and six home values. Most relocating retirees will find that their income and home value fall near those of one of our couples.

For each city, you will find a chart detailing and tallying the taxes due from our couples. Our figures are based on married couples filing jointly who are age 65 or older. We've included tax breaks related to age in our calculations. These additional deductions and exemptions are widespread and frequently quite significant. We suspect that rankings based on tax burdens of residents under the age of 65 could be dramatically different from those herein. All couples are assumed to be relocating across state lines.

Our three income levels — $24,281, $34,275 and $68,098 in gross income — are drawn from the Consumer Expenditure Survey of people age 65 and older, issued by the U.S. Department of Labor, Bureau of Labor Statistics (BLS). The BLS survey also tracks spending habits of this age group. From those specific expenditure figures, we've estimated the sales taxes for each income level in each city.

We've determined the amount due in state income tax from the rates provided to us by the individual states, taking into account appropriate exemptions, deductions and credits.

Some cities levy a local income tax, although the type of income subject to the tax differs. We have included local income taxes in our calculations.

We have calculated property taxes for six home values ranging from $50,000 to $250,000. For each income, we cite three home values. Since our detailed breakdowns include home value and income level, you can more closely identify your own tax burden. For instance, if you expect to earn about $35,000 a year in retirement, you can look up your estimated tax bill according to whether you will live in a home valued at $75,000, $100,000 or $150,000.

Don't plan on moving to a home valued at $100,000 or less in cities such as Los Angeles, San Francisco, New York or Honolulu. Most homes at that price wouldn't be fit to live in. We've included these home values in our charts to be consistent, but we've also calculated taxes on homes valued at $300,000, $350,000 and $400,000 in order to give a more realistic view of what retirees might expect to pay there.

Personal property taxes are not uncommon, although most cities don't impose a personal property tax on individuals. Items that are taxed vary from city to city. In cities where there are personal property taxes on automobiles or household furnishings, we have calculated these taxes and they appear in the chart.

Finally, registering a vehicle is one cost relocators might overlook. We found that the fees can vary dramatically, so we've broken down automobile registration and renewal fees by gathering the information for two specific cars.

FACT FINDING

All of the tax rates, assessment rates, deductions, exemptions, rebates, credits and related facts and data included in this book were supplied to us by local and/or state tax authorities. The same authorities were asked to review our calculations.

The great majority of these public officials were informed and willing to help. In a few cases, however, tax authorities at the local level refused to take or return our calls or respond to letters or faxes. Rather than drop these cities from the study, we have noted any unverified rates and prepared our best estimate of total tax burden.

It's important to note here that the data-gathering part of this study began in the first half of 1995 and continued well into 1996. In fact, it took five researchers more than ten months to collect and verify the information contained in this report. We based our work on the tax year 1994, the latest year for which every state and municipality could supply complete information. Tax rates and qualifiers change frequently, and

Published by *Where to Retire* magazine and Vacation Publications, Inc., 1502 Augusta Drive – Suite 415, Houston, TX 77057, (713) 974-6903. Copyright© 1996 by Vacation Publications, Inc. All rights reserved. No part of this publication may be reproduced without the written consent of Vacation Publications, Inc.

A city's tax climate may not be uniformly favorable or unfavorable across all income levels. Helena, MT, for example, has higher-than-average total tax burdens for higher incomes and lower-than-average total tax burdens for lower incomes.

some of the data herein may already have changed. Nonetheless, this is our third study of tax burdens over the past four years, and while there is fluctuation and a general tendency for rates to increase over time, rankings have remained remarkably consistent. Still, you should use our calculations as a rough guide only, and be sure to inquire about planned tax hikes before you relocate.

Many of the cities featured are locations favored for retirement, while others are urban areas from which large numbers of retirees migrate. Geographically, we cover at least two cities in each state, plus Washington, DC.

BOOK LAYOUT

Our book begins with a brief synopsis of the kinds of taxes you can expect to pay. Next, we've alphabetized our report by state and then by city within the state. The applicable taxes for each city are described in detail. Our comprehensive charts tally it all up and tell you where each city stands in our rankings.

At the end, you'll find our exclusive list of Tax Heavens and Tax Hells, plus nine separate rankings of all cities, one for each of our income/home value categories. A rank of #1 means that city has the lowest total tax burden. The average total tax burden for each category is also shown.

As we neared completion of this project and our rankings began to take shape, we found more than a few surprises. Perhaps the most significant of these is the fact that a city's tax climate may not be uniformly favorable or unfavorable across all income levels. Helena, MT, for example, has higher-than-average total tax burdens for higher incomes and lower-than-average total tax burdens for lower incomes. Also, note that in some cities only the low-priced homes in each income category earn favor-

able rankings; in other cities, it may be midpriced homes or high-priced homes that net better rankings.

Perhaps the greatest paradox of all is the fact that many cities widely known for a high cost of living do not have high tax *rates*. New York City, for example, has total tax burdens ranging from lower than average to about average. It appears that inflated real estate prices and high personal salaries have made it unnecessary to raise tax rates in order to collect more taxes.

STATE INCOME TAX

Many retirees use the presence or absence of a state income tax as a litmus test for a retirement destination. This is a serious miscalculation, as higher sales and property taxes can more than offset the lack of a state income tax, particularly for retirees with little or no earned income. The lack of a state income tax doesn't necessarily ensure a low total tax burden.

Only a handful of states don't tax personal income. The others levy some sort of income tax, although the

taxable income varies. One state may tax only interest and dividends, while another bases its income tax on adjusted gross income calculated for the federal tax return.

Most states allow exemptions to reduce gross income. For instance, some states tax Social Security benefits subject to federal taxation, while other states allow your full monthly check to escape taxation.

Some states allow residents to exempt all or part of federal, state or private pensions, while others don't exclude any pension income from taxation.

Of course, tax rates vary from state to state. Some states have graduated rates; for instance, the first $20,000 in taxable income might be taxed at a rate of 5% while the next $5,000 would be taxed at a rate of 6%. Other states tax all income at the same flat rate.

Most states have standard deductions, although these deductions vary. Some are the same deductions offered on the federal return, while other states offer additional deductions that may be based on age or income.

Most states offer income tax credits or rebates as well. The most common is credit for income taxes paid to other states. We've assumed our couples do not owe income taxes to any other states. Other credits are often based on low income, for which our couples would not be eligible. In several states, there are a host of credits available which might apply to your situation. We do not attempt to list all of them.

If you're considering several states for retirement, contact state tax offices and request a tax form to determine the full tax bite in each state.

In order to calculate state and local income tax, it is necessary to make a large number of assumptions about

When inquiring about the presence of a local income tax, word your question to include any local tax, assessment or fee applied to any of your income. Some municipalities go to extremes to avoid calling their tax an income tax.

our couples and the nature and source of their income. We will not list these assumptions here, due to space considerations, except for the following:

1) Our couples are age 65, file jointly, and take standard deductions rather than itemizing. In some states and under certain circumstances, retirees might reduce their state income tax by filing separately or itemizing deductions.

2) We use three representative household income levels which are detailed in the BLS survey: $24,281, $34,275 and $68,098. In the survey, income consists of: wages and salaries; self-employment income; Social Security, private and government retirement; interest, dividends, rental income and other property income; and other income.

3) We do not include the effect of the Alternative Minimum Tax Calculation in our analysis of income taxes due.

LOCAL INCOME TAX

Retirees who relocate to certain U.S. cities may be surprised to learn that they owe income taxes not only to the state but also to the local government.

Cities call local income taxes by different names, such as wage taxes or occupational license fees. Just as their names are different, local income taxes are assessed in varying ways.

Some cities tax only earned income. Other cities impose taxes based on a percentage of the amount of state income tax due. Still others tax all income, offering exemptions and deductions like those at the state level.

When inquiring about the presence of a local income tax, word your question to include any local tax, assessment or fee applied to any of your income. Some municipalities go to extremes to avoid calling their tax an income tax.

We have used the same local income tax assumptions as were used in calculating state income tax.

SALES TAX

In all but a handful of states, residents pay some form of sales tax on their purchases. In a few states, a sales tax is replaced by a general excise tax or gross receipts tax on businesses. Since these taxes are also passed on to the consumer, we treat them herein as sales taxes.

Usually, a base sales tax rate is determined by the state. Often, local governments add to that base rate, sometimes more than doubling the percentage.

Our sales tax calculations are based on the BLS survey, which estimates how much people age 65 and over in each of the three income levels spend each year on certain items.

We estimate the sales tax burden in each city by applying local and state sales taxes to each of the following categories named in the BLS survey: Food at home; food away from home; household operations and housekeeping supplies; household furnishings and equipment; apparel and services; transportation; medical services; drugs; medical supplies; entertainment; personal care products and services; and miscellaneous.

We assume that certain categories — shelter, health insurance, cash contributions and personal insurance and pensions — are universally exempt from sales tax.

We exclude sales tax on utilities from our calculations altogether because it is often difficult to distinguish the basic rate from fees and taxes. Frequently, there are markups in utility bills which we believe are hidden taxes. We recommend that retirees inquire about the typical utility bill for the typical home before relocating.

Generally, residents of a city pay the same sales tax rate on most purchases. However, it is common to find certain items taxed at a different rate. For instance, groceries or drugs may be taxed at a lower rate than clothing, or exempt altogether. Or, there may be an additional tax on food away from home. We've incorporated the applicable varying tax rates in our calculations if the items were included in the BLS survey as a separate category.

In most cases, if any items within a category are taxed, we assume that the whole category is taxed since the BLS survey does not break out all potential components of a category. For example, some cities exempt services from tax but do tax apparel. We assume the entire category of "apparel and services" is taxable. Therefore, we may overstate sales tax burdens in some cities, but this method is consistently applied to all cities.

The most common items exempt from sales tax are drugs, groceries and medical services.

PROPERTY TAX AND OTHER FEES

Property taxes differ widely from state to state and between cities within the same state. Sometimes property taxes vary from neighborhood to neighborhood or even street to street within the same city.

Property taxes may consist of components from several different taxing entities, including the city, county, school district, fire district and others. Property tax rates change annually in many communities.

In most states the property tax is determined by multiplying a property tax rate by an assessed value. Assessment rates are decided either by the state or by local governments. Homes are assessed at such widely varying rates as 1% to 125% of market value, but a low assessment percentage does not translate into lower

The costs of registering a vehicle and annually renewing license plates are often overlooked by relocators, but these fees can add up (and do, in several states).

taxes, as the tax rate may be adjusted to make up the difference.

Some cities appraise property annually, but once every two, three or four years is more common. We assume that the appraised value equals the market value of the home.

In a few cases, municipalities tax homes and the land on which they are built at different rates. We have assumed that the home (or improvement) value is 80% and the land value is 20% of the total market value. Actual allocations will vary significantly depending on the location in question.

Many cities offer tax-saving breaks from the amount of property taxes due, often exempting a certain dollar amount from the home's assessed value. Other exemptions or deductions may be statewide and may be based on age or income. In cities where our couples qualified for these tax breaks, we have included them in our property tax calculations. Some homestead exemptions or credits require one or more years residency. We assume our couples meet these residency requirements, because we believe it is more useful to reflect ongoing, long-term tax burdens than those of year one.

In some cities, services such as garbage pickup, street maintenance and storm drain utility fees are included in your property tax bill. In other locations, residents pay these fees separately. To make our numbers comparable, we have added these additional fees where applicable, and they are included with the property tax amounts in our charts. We do not include fees to register or own pets.

★ ★ ★

It is necessary to make many assumptions about our couples and their age and income in order to complete property tax calculations. We will not list these assumptions here, except for the following:

1) We selected three home values for each of the income categories used in the income tax analysis. For income of $24,281, we look at property tax burdens for homes valued at $50,000, $75,000 and $100,000. For income of $34,275, the home values we use are $75,000, $100,000 and $150,000. For income of $68,098, we figure property tax bills for home values of $150,000, $200,000 and $250,000.

2) We assume a freestanding site-built home and lot. The current national median home price is approximately $109,000. We selected a range of homes we believe reflect home-buying capabilities as determined by incomes shown above.

AUTO LICENSING FEES

The costs of registering a vehicle and annually renewing license plates are often overlooked by relocators, but these fees can add up (and do, in several states). So we contacted every city's Department of Motor Vehicles and asked for all fees related to registration or renewal of an automobile.

In order to show the wide range of vehicle registration costs in different cities, we've given our couples two cars — a 1992 Chrysler New Yorker Salon Sedan and a 1991 Oldsmobile Cutlass Supreme Sedan. Their current market values — $12,225 for the Chrysler and $8,750 for the Oldsmobile — are based on average retail prices in the January 1995 issue of the *NADA Official Used Car Guide*.

At the time of registration, relocators can expect to pay for a state title, which generally ranges from $5 to $50. Other common expenses are plate and inspection fees.

In many states, registration fees are based on the value of the car, but the method for determining value varies from state to state. Some states base their fees on the automobile's weight or model. You should know

this specific information about your car before calling to find out registration fees in a particular city.

New residents may also face a tax on automobiles brought into the state. For instance, the Kentucky sales tax rate is 6%. Relocators to that state who paid a sales tax of 6% or greater on their vehicle in another state at the time of purchase are not subject to additional tax. However, people who paid a sales tax of less than 6% to another state are required to pay the difference on the current market value of the car to Kentucky, in the form of a road usage tax.

Florida recently abolished one very unpopular surprise for newcomers — a $295 impact fee per automobile brought into the state. There's still a one-time $100 additional-wheels-on-the-road fee paid by everyone registering a car.

Annual license plate renewal fees also vary. In many states, the costs decrease as the car depreciates. Other states have a flat renewal fee, regardless of the type or year of the vehicle.

It's important to note here that even though we discuss initial registration fees in our text, our charts reflect the ongoing annual or annualized fees, for the first year after registration.

Finally, in many cities, auto licensing fees resemble personal property taxes in size and method of calculation. In most cases, if the tax is verified and assessed by the Department of Motor Vehicles we discuss it with other auto registration-related taxes. Otherwise, you'll find it noted in the paragraph devoted to personal property taxes.

PERSONAL PROPERTY TAX

In addition to a property tax, many local governments tax the personal property of individuals.

> *Because (intangibles) tax is not well-known outside the handful of states that levy it, relocating retirees are often shocked to discover its existence after moving, when the first payment is due.*

Items that are taxed vary, even among cities within the same state. Items that are most often taxed are vehicles, including automobiles, boats, motorcycles, motor homes and mobile homes. However, some cities levy a personal property tax on household furnishings, which may even include jewelry and clothing.

Usually, but not always, the personal property tax rate in a city or area is the same as the property tax rate there, and items subject to the tax are usually assessed at the same rate as homes.

Several cities levy personal property tax only on mobile homes or mobile home attachments (carports, etc.). We assume our couples do not own these items.

If a city's personal property tax applies only to property owned by an individual and used in the operation of a business, we state that the city has no personal property tax on individuals.

A few cities levy what they refer to as a personal property tax on stocks, bonds and other investments. This type of tax is also known as an intangible personal property tax or intangibles tax, and we do not include it in our calculations regardless of what it is called by local governments. However, the tax can be significant and merits discussion below as well as careful consideration prior to moving.

INTANGIBLES TAX

An intangibles tax is a tax imposed on the value of investments that many retirees depend on for income. Because this tax is not well-known outside the handful of states that levy it, relocating retirees are often shocked to discover its existence after moving, when the first payment is due. That's particularly frustrating because some careful portfolio management might have reduced the tax, had they known about it in advance.

Six states either collect an intangibles tax or allow cities to collect the tax: Florida, Georgia, Kentucky, Michigan, Pennsylvania and West Virginia. Michigan is phasing out its tax; it will be eliminated by January 1, 1998. North Carolina recently repealed its intangibles tax, at least partially in response to a lawsuit challenging its constitutionality.

Investments subject to the tax and the tax rate itself vary from state to state. Some states tax all of your money, including that held in passbook savings accounts and safe-deposit boxes. Others tax only stocks, bonds and notes. States may exempt certain assets, such as shares of stocks or bonds from corporations based in that state, or bonds or notes issued by that state or the federal government.

Michigan currently taxes either the value of the intangible property or the interest and dividends earned from it, whichever produces a greater tax.

Another state, Kansas, allows its counties to collect what they refer to as an intangibles tax; however, it's actually a local income tax because the tax is applied to the interest and dividend income earned from investments and not to the investments themselves. (Note: Neither of the Kansas counties in this book levies an intangibles tax.)

In most cases, the intangibles tax is a county ad valorem tax, and while you may file a return with the state, the money is usually redistributed to the county in which you reside.

If you're considering a move to any of the six states listed, call the state tax office to request an intangibles tax return to determine how you would be affected.

HOW TO USE THIS BOOK

Unless you are personally involved in local or state taxation or have an academic interest in the national taxation picture, you probably won't read this book cover to cover. Instead, a good place to start is the table of contents, where you can identify cities of interest and find their location in the book.

For each city covered, we have described both the state and local tax picture as it relates to retirees. At the end of this description, we reveal whether the city's total tax burdens are higher than average, lower than average or about average. We define "about average" as the actual average tax burden for all cities, plus or minus 10%.

In a table above this description, we estimate tax components and total tax burdens for nine different couples. Find the income and home value that most closely resembles your financial situation, and pay closest attention to the tax estimates for that category. At the far right of the table, you can see how this city ranks against all others in total tax burden placed on retirees. Ranking #1 is best (lowest tax burden), and #149 is worst (highest tax burden).

If you don't find a city you're interested in, see if we cover a nearby city of similar size. Usually, but not always, same-state cities of similar size will have similar tax burdens.

Perhaps you're undecided as to your ultimate retirement destination and want to get a quick glance at tax-friendly cities for retirees with your income and expected home value. You may wish to turn immediately to our list of tax heavens and hells on pages 122-123. Or, if you're interested in a particular area of the country, check out our map on pages 124-125 for your best regional options. Finally, for an idea of how 149 cities match up for retirees in your income/home value category, turn to the rankings on pages 113-121.

Is your prospective retirement destination a tax heaven or a tax hell? Read on to find out.

ALABAMA

Income	Home Value	Property Tax & Other Fees	Personal Property Tax & Auto Fees	Sales Tax	Local Income Tax	State Income Tax	Total Tax	Rank From #1–#149
FAIRHOPE								
$24,281	$50,000	$82	$182	$786	–	$96	$1,146	#11
	75,000	82	182	786	–	96	1,146	#7
	100,000	82	182	786	–	96	1,146	#6
$34,275	$75,000	$334	$182	$1,037	–	$309	$1,862	#12
	100,000	424	182	1,037	–	309	1,952	#10
	150,000	604	182	1,037	–	309	2,132	#8
$68,098	$150,000	$604	$182	$1,514	–	$1,344	$3,644	#6
	200,000	784	182	1,514	–	1,344	3,824	#5
	250,000	964	182	1,514	–	1,344	4,004	#5
GULF SHORES								
$24,281	$50,000	$120	$151	$1,178	–	$96	$1,545	#41
	75,000	120	151	1,178	–	96	1,545	#15
	100,000	120	151	1,178	–	96	1,545	#10
$34,275	$75,000	$297	$151	$1,555	–	$309	$2,312	#46
	100,000	362	151	1,555	–	309	2,377	#23
	150,000	492	151	1,555	–	309	2,507	#13
$68,098	$150,000	$492	$151	$2,271	–	$1,344	$4,258	#17
	200,000	622	151	2,271	–	1,344	4,388	#9
	250,000	752	151	2,271	–	1,344	4,518	#6

Alabama has a state income tax and a state sales tax.

The state income tax rate is graduated from 2% to 5%, depending upon income bracket. For married couples filing jointly the rate is 2% on the first $1,000 of taxable income; the rate is 4% on the next $5,000 of taxable income; and the rate is 5% on taxable income above $6,000.

In calculating the tax, there is a deduction from adjusted gross income for federal income tax paid. Federal pensions are exempt. State of Alabama pensions are exempt. Private pensions that qualify as a "defined benefit plan" are exempt. Social Security benefits are exempt. There is a $3,000 exemption from adjusted gross income for married couples filing jointly and a standard deduction of 20% of total adjusted gross income not to exceed $4,000 for married couples filing jointly.

Major tax credits or rebates include: Credit for income taxes paid to other states. Our couples do not qualify for this program.

The state sales tax rate is 4% but local governments can add to this amount.

Our couples relocating to the cities listed below must pay a $24.25 tag fee to register each automobile and $18.00 per automobile for a title. Thereafter, on an annual basis, our couples will pay a tag fee per automobile in addition to a road use fee based on year and market value of each automobile.

FAIRHOPE

Fairhope has no local income tax but does levy a local sales tax.

Most purchases are taxed at a rate of 6%. Major consumer categories taxed at a different rate: None. Major consumer categories which are exempt from sales tax include: Drugs and medical services.

Within the city limits of Fairhope, the property tax rate is .0425. Homes are assessed at 10% of market value. There are four categories of homestead exemptions available. Property tax does not cover garbage pickup; the additional fee is approximately $82 per year.

Fairhope has no personal property tax for individuals.

★Total tax burdens in Fairhope are lower than average overall. Fairhope is a tax heaven in 7 of 9 income/home value categories.

GULF SHORES

Gulf Shores has no local income tax but does levy a local sales tax.

Most purchases are taxed at a rate of 9%. Major consumer categories taxed at a different rate: None. Major consumer categories which are exempt from sales tax include: Drugs and medical services.

Within the city limits of Gulf Shores, the property tax rate is .0325. Homes are assessed at 10% of market value. There are four categories of homestead exemptions available. Property tax does not cover garbage pickup; the additional fee is approximately $120 per year.

Gulf Shores has no personal property tax for individuals.

★Total tax burdens in Gulf Shores are lower than average overall. Gulf Shores is a tax heaven in 3 of 9 income/ home value categories.

ALASKA

Income	Home Value	Property Tax & Other Fees	Personal Property Tax & Auto Fees	Sales Tax	Local Income Tax	State Income Tax	Total Tax	Rank From #1–#149
ANCHORAGE								
$24,281	$50,000	$180	$2	–	–	–	$182	#1
	75,000	180	2	–	–	–	182	#1
	100,000	180	2	–	–	–	182	#1
$34,275	$75,000	$180	$2	–	–	–	$182	#1
	100,000	180	2	–	–	–	182	#1
	150,000	180	2	–	–	–	182	#1
$68,098	$150,000	$180	$2	–	–	–	$182	#1
	200,000	754	2	–	–	–	756	#1
	250,000	1,327	2	–	–	–	1,329	#1
JUNEAU								
$24,281	$50,000	$299	–	–	–	–	$299	#2
	75,000	299	–	–	–	–	299	#2
	100,000	299	–	–	–	–	299	#2
$34,275	$75,000	$299	–	–	–	–	$299	#2
	100,000	299	–	–	–	–	299	#2
	150,000	299	–	–	–	–	299	#2
$68,098	$150,000	$299	–	–	–	–	$299	#2
	200,000	1,000	–	–	–	–	1,000	#2
	250,000	1,701	–	–	–	–	1,701	#2

Alaska has no state income tax and no state sales tax.

Major tax credits or rebates include: Property tax exemption for persons age 65 or older and renters rebate program. Our couples qualify for the property tax exemption.

Since car registration and renewal fees differ within the state, see city information for details.

ANCHORAGE

Anchorage has no local income tax and no sales tax.

In the Hillside area of Anchorage, the property tax rate is .01147. Homes are assessed at 100% of market value. People age 65 and older are exempt from property taxes on up to $150,000 of home value. Property tax does not cover garbage pickup; the additional fee is approximately $180 per year.

Anchorage has a personal property tax rate of .01147 within the Hillside area. Personal property is assessed at 100% of average Blue Book value. Items subject to the tax include mobile homes, snow machines, boats, motors, trailbikes, aircraft and tractors. The tax does not apply to automobiles. We've assumed our couples do not own any of the items subject to the personal property tax.

Our couples relocating to Anchorage pay $5 per automobile for an Alaska title, plus a $1 emissions fee per automobile at the time of registration. Thereafter, on an annual basis, our couples will pay a $1 emissions fee per automobile.

★Total tax burdens in Anchorage are lower than average overall. Anchorage is the top-rated tax heaven in all 9 income/home value categories.

JUNEAU

Juneau has no local income tax but does levy a sales tax.

Most purchases are taxed at a rate of 4%. Major consumer categories taxed at a different rate: None. Major consumer categories which are exempt from sales tax include: Drugs and medical services. Residents age 65 and older are exempt from all sales tax except for tax on liquor. We've assumed our couples do not buy liquor.

In downtown Juneau, the property tax rate is .01402. Homes are assessed at 100% of market value. People age 65 and older are exempt from property taxes on up to $150,000 of home value. Property tax does not cover garbage pickup; the additional fee is approximately $299 per year.

Juneau has no personal property tax.

Our couples relocating to Juneau pay $5 per automobile for an Alaska title. There are no annual fees thereafter.

★Total tax burdens in Juneau are lower than average overall. Juneau is a tax heaven in all 9 income/home value categories.

ARIZONA

Income	Home Value	Property Tax & Other Fees	Personal Property Tax & Auto Fees	Sales Tax	Local Income Tax	State Income Tax	Total Tax	Rank From #1–#149
FLAGSTAFF								
$24,281	$50,000	$523	$486	$712	–	$24	$1,745	#67
	75,000	743	486	712	–	24	1,965	#54
	100,000	962	486	712	–	24	2,184	#47
$34,275	$75,000	$743	$486	$960	–	$313	$2,502	#61
	100,000	962	486	960	–	313	2,721	#52
	150,000	1,402	486	960	–	313	3,161	#34
$68,098	$150,000	$1,402	$486	$1,487	–	$1,507	$4,882	#36
	200,000	1,842	486	1,487	–	1,507	5,322	#24
	250,000	2,282	486	1,487	–	1,507	5,762	#20
PHOENIX								
$24,281	$50,000	$652	$486	$721	–	$24	$1,883	#89
	75,000	903	486	721	–	24	2,134	#73
	100,000	1,154	486	721	–	24	2,385	#64
$34,275	$75,000	$903	$486	$969	–	$313	$2,671	#79
	100,000	1,154	486	969	–	313	2,922	#73
	150,000	1,656	486	969	–	313	3,424	#57
$68,098	$150,000	$1,656	$486	$1,497	–	$1,507	$5,146	#48
	200,000	2,159	486	1,497	–	1,507	5,649	#43
	250,000	2,661	486	1,497	–	1,507	6,151	#30
PRESCOTT								
$24,281	$50,000	$640	$486	$683	–	$24	$1,833	#79
	75,000	893	486	683	–	24	2,086	#68
	100,000	1,147	486	683	–	24	2,340	#60
$34,275	$75,000	$893	$486	$915	–	$313	$2,607	#75
	100,000	1,147	486	915	–	313	2,861	#65
	150,000	1,655	486	915	–	313	3,369	#53
$68,098	$150,000	$1,655	$486	$1,399	–	$1,507	$5,047	#40
	200,000	2,162	486	1,399	–	1,507	5,554	#35
	250,000	2,670	486	1,399	–	1,507	6,062	#28
SCOTTSDALE								
$24,281	$50,000	$567	$486	$740	–	$24	$1,817	#76
	75,000	782	486	740	–	24	2,032	#61
	100,000	998	486	740	–	24	2,248	#51
$34,275	$75,000	$782	$486	$991	–	$313	$2,572	#72
	100,000	998	486	991	–	313	2,788	#58
	150,000	1,430	486	991	–	313	3,220	#41 (tie)
$68,098	$150,000	$1,430	$486	$1,514	–	$1,507	$4,937	#37
	200,000	1,862	486	1,514	–	1,507	5,369	#27
	250,000	2,293	486	1,514	–	1,507	5,800	#21
TUCSON								
$24,281	$50,000	$740	$486	$742	–	$24	$1,992	#99
	75,000	1,111	486	742	–	24	2,363	#103
	100,000	1,481	486	742	–	24	2,733	#99
$34,275	$75,000	$1,111	$486	$997	–	$313	$2,907	#98
	100,000	1,481	486	997	–	313	3,277	#102
	150,000	2,221	486	997	–	313	4,017	#90 (tie)
$68,098	$150,000	$2,221	$486	$1,541	–	$1,507	$5,755	#74
	200,000	2,961	486	1,541	–	1,507	6,495	#74
	250,000	3,702	486	1,541	–	1,507	7,236	#74 (tie)

Income	Home Value	Property Tax & Other Fees	Personal Property Tax & Auto Fees	Sales Tax	Local Income Tax	State Income Tax	Total Tax	Rank From #1–#149
YUMA								
$24,281	$50,000	$584	$486	$768	–	$24	$1,862	#84 (tie)
	75,000	876	486	768	–	24	2,154	#78
	100,000	1,168	486	768	–	24	2,446	#69
$34,275	$75,000	$876	$486	$1,028	–	$313	$2,703	#82
	100,000	1,168	486	1,028	–	313	2,995	#78
	150,000	1,752	486	1,028	–	313	3,579	#66
$68,098	$150,000	$1,752	$486	$1,569	–	$1,507	$5,314	#53
	200,000	2,336	486	1,569	–	1,507	5,898	#54
	250,000	2,920	486	1,569	–	1,507	6,482	#46

Arizona has a state income tax and a state sales tax.

The state income tax is graduated from 3.25% to 6.90% depending upon income bracket. For married couples filing jointly the rate is 3.25% on the first $20,000 of taxable income; the rate is 4.0% on the next $30,000 of taxable income; the rate is 5.05% on the next $50,000 of taxable income; the rate is 6.4% on the next $200,000 of taxable income; and the rate is 6.9% on taxable income above $300,000.

In calculating the tax, there is no deduction for federal income tax paid. Federal, state and local pensions are exempt up to $2,500. Private pensions are not exempt. Social Security benefits are exempt. There is a $7,000 standard deduction from adjusted gross income for married couples filing jointly. There is a $4,200 exemption from adjusted gross income for married couples filing jointly. There is a $2,100 exemption from adjusted gross income for each person age 65 or older.

Major tax credits or rebates include: Credit for income taxes paid to other states and property tax credit. Our couples do not qualify for these programs.

The state sales tax rate is 5% but local governments can add to this amount.

Our couples relocating to the cities listed below must pay a motor vehicle license tax based on year and MSRP of each automobile at the time of registration. The tax is $327 for the Chrysler and $222 for the Oldsmobile. Our couples also pay a registration fee of $8 per automobile, a title fee of $4 per automobile and an air quality fee of $2 per automobile. In Phoenix,

there is an additional $20 emissions fee per automobile. Thereafter, on an annual basis, our couples will pay a motor vehicle license tax, registration fee and air quality fee, per automobile.

FLAGSTAFF

Flagstaff has no local income tax but does levy a sales tax.

Most purchases are taxed at a rate of 6.5%. Major consumer categories taxed at a different rate include: Food away from home, which is taxed at a rate of 8.5%. Major consumer categories which are exempt from sales tax include: Drugs, groceries and medical services.

Within the city limits of Flagstaff, the property tax rate is .104629. Homes are assessed at 10% of market value. There is a state aid to education deduction for all homeowners. Property tax does not cover garbage pickup; the additional fee is approximately $83 per year.

Flagstaff has a personal property tax rate of .10455. Personal property is assessed at 10% of MSRP. Items subject to the tax include mobile homes. We've assumed our couples do not own any of the items subject to the personal property tax.

★Total tax burdens in Flagstaff are about average for the $24,281 income category and lower than average for the $34,275 and $68,098 income categories.

PHOENIX

Phoenix has no local income tax but does levy a sales tax.

Most purchases are taxed at a rate of 6.8%. Major consumer categories taxed at a different rate: None. Major consumer categories which are

exempt from sales tax include: Drugs, groceries and medical services.

In the Puerta Vieja 4 area of Phoenix, the property tax rate is .111586. Homes are valued at 90% of market value and then assessed at 10% of that value. There is a state aid to education deduction for all homeowners. Property tax does not cover garbage pickup; the additional fee is approximately $150 per year.

In the Puerta Vieja 4 area, there is a personal property tax rate of .127707. Personal property is assessed at 10% of MSRP. Items subject to the tax include mobile homes. We've assumed our couples do not own any of the items subject to the personal property tax.

★Total tax burdens in Phoenix are about average for the $24,281 and $34,275 income categories and lower than average for the $68,098 income category.

PRESCOTT

Prescott has no local income tax but does levy a sales tax.

During the 12-month period covered by this study, the sales tax rate changed from 6% to 6.5%. Our estimates for sales tax are based on a weighted average of these rates. Major consumer categories taxed at a different rate include: Groceries, which are taxed at the rate of 1%. Major consumer categories which are exempt from sales tax include: Drugs and medical services.

Within the city limits of Prescott, the property tax rate is .1015. Homes are assessed at 10% of market value. There is a state aid to education deduction for all homeowners. There is a state property tax refund for homeowners age 65 or older with a gross income of less than $5,500. Property tax does not cover garbage pickup; the additional fee is approximately $132 per year.

Prescott has a personal property tax rate of .109752. Personal property is assessed at 10% of MSRP. Items subject to the tax include mobile homes. We've assumed our couples do not own any of the items subject to the personal property tax.

★Total tax burdens in Prescott are about average for the $24,281 and $34,275 income categories and lower than average for the $68,098 income category.

SCOTTSDALE

Scottsdale has no local income tax but does levy a sales tax.

Most purchases are taxed at a rate of 6.7%. Major consumer categories taxed at a different rate include: Groceries, which are taxed at the rate of 1.2%. Major consumer categories which are exempt from sales tax include: Drugs and medical services.

In the Scottsdale Area Code 481400, the property tax rate is .095919. Homes are valued at 90% of market value and then assessed at 10% of that value. There is a state aid to education deduction for all homeowners. Property tax does not cover garbage pickup; the additional fee is approximately $135 per year.

In the Scottsdale Area Code 4890,

there is a personal property tax rate of .104755. Personal property is assessed at 10% of MSRP. Items subject to the tax include mobile homes. We've assumed our couples do not own any of the items subject to the personal property tax.

★Total tax burdens in Scottsdale are about average for the $24,281 and $34,275 income categories and lower than average for the $68,098 income category.

TUCSON

Tucson has no local income tax but does levy a sales tax.

Most purchases are taxed at a rate of 7%. Major consumer categories taxed at a different rate: None. Major consumer categories which are exempt from sales tax include: Drugs, groceries and medical services.

In the Harold Bell Wright subdivision of Tucson, the property tax rate is .148067. Homes are assessed at 10% of market value. There is a state aid to education deduction for all homeowners. Property tax includes garbage pickup.

Tucson has a personal property tax rate of .161213 within the Harold Bell Wright subdivision. Personal property is assessed at 10% of MSRP. Items subject to the tax include mobile homes. We've assumed our couples do not own any of the items subject to the personal property tax.

★Total tax burdens in Tucson are about average overall.

YUMA

Yuma has no local income tax but does levy a sales tax.

During the 12-month period covered by this study, the sales tax rate changed from 6.5% to 7%. Our estimates for sales tax are based on a weighted average of these rates. Major consumer categories taxed at a different rate include: Groceries, which were taxed at the rate of 1% for part of the period and 1.5% for part of the period. Major consumer categories which are exempt from sales tax include: Drugs and medical services.

In the Yuma Area Code 0130, the property tax rate is .11678. Homes are assessed at 10% of market value. There is a state aid to education deduction for all homeowners. Property tax includes garbage pickup.

In the Foothills area, there is a personal property tax rate of .11178. Personal property is assessed at 10% of MSRP. Items subject to the tax include mobile homes. We've assumed our couples do not own any of the items subject to the personal property tax.

★Total tax burdens in Yuma are about average for the $24,281 and $34,275 income categories and lower than average for the $68,098 income category.

ARKANSAS

Income	Home Value	Property Tax & Other Fees	Personal Property Tax & Auto Fees	Sales Tax	Local Income Tax	State Income Tax	Total Tax	Rank From #1–#149
HOT SPRINGS								
$24,281	$50,000	$509	$214	$886	–	$137	$1,746	#68
	75,000	703	214	886	–	137	1,940	#52
	100,000	897	214	886	–	137	2,134	#40 (tie)
$34,275	$75,000	$703	$214	$1,174	–	$583	$2,674	#80
	100,000	897	214	1,174	–	583	2,868	#67
	150,000	1,286	214	1,174	–	583	3,257	#46
$68,098	$150,000	$1,286	$214	$1,723	–	$2,736	$5,959	#81 (tie)
	200,000	1,675	214	1,723	–	2,736	6,348	#65
	250,000	2,064	214	1,723	–	2,736	6,737	#57
LITTLE ROCK								
$24,281	$50,000	$827	$331	$809	–	$137	$2,104	#113
	75,000	1,162	331	809	–	137	2,439	#111
	100,000	1,496	331	809	–	137	2,773	#105
$34,275	$75,000	$1,162	$331	$1,072	–	$583	$3,148	#118
	100,000	1,496	331	1,072	–	583	3,482	#109
	150,000	2,164	331	1,072	–	583	4,150	#101 (tie)
$68,098	$150,000	$2,164	$331	$1,569	–	$2,736	$6,800	#114
	200,000	2,832	331	1,569	–	2,736	7,468	#106
	250,000	3,501	331	1,569	–	2,736	8,137	#98
MOUNTAIN HOME								
$24,281	$50,000	$448	$199	$851	–	$137	$1,635	#56
	75,000	625	199	851	–	137	1,812	#39
	100,000	801	199	851	–	137	1,988	#29
$34,275	$75,000	$625	$199	$1,123	–	$583	$2,530	#65
	100,000	801	199	1,123	–	583	2,706	#50
	150,000	1,154	199	1,123	–	583	3,059	#27
$68,098	$150,000	$1,154	$199	$1,640	–	$2,736	$5,729	#72
	200,000	1,507	199	1,640	–	2,736	6,082	#55
	250,000	1,860	199	1,640	–	2,736	6,435	#42

Arkansas has a state income tax and a state sales tax.

The state income tax rate is graduated from 1% to 7% depending upon income bracket. For all filers the rate is 1% on the first $2,999 of taxable income; the rate is 2.5% on the next $3,000 of taxable income; the rate is 3.5% on the next $3,000 of taxable income; the rate is 4.5% on the next $6,000 of taxable income; the rate is 6% on the next $10,000 of taxable income; and the rate is 7% on taxable income above $25,000.

In calculating the tax, there is no deduction for federal income tax paid. Federal and state pensions are not exempt. The first $6,000 of private pensions are exempt. Social Security benefits are exempt. There is a standard deduction of 10% off ad-

justed gross income up to a maximum of $1,000 for married couples filing jointly. There is a $40 credit against tax for married couples filing jointly and a $20 credit against tax per person for each person age 65 or older.

Major tax credits or rebates include: Credit for income taxes paid to other states, child care credit and a special credit for persons age 65 or older who don't claim the $6,000 per year exemption for private pensions. Our couples do not qualify for these programs.

The state sales tax rate is 4.5% but local governments can add to this amount.

Our couples relocating to the cities listed below must pay a registration fee of $25 per automobile and a title fee of $5 per automobile at the

time of registration. Thereafter, on an annual basis, our couples will pay a registration fee per automobile.

HOT SPRINGS

Hot Springs has no local income tax but does levy a sales tax.

Most purchases are taxed at a rate of 6.5%. Major consumer categories taxed at a different rate include: Food away from home, which is taxed at 9.5%. Major consumer categories which are exempt from sales tax include: Drugs and medical services.

In Hot Springs School District #6, the property tax rate is .03887. Homes are assessed at 20% of market value. There is a homestead relief refund of $50 to $250 for homeowners age 62 or older with a household income of up to $15,000. Property tax does not cover garbage pickup; the additional fee is approximately $120 per year. Residents within School District No. 6 may also live within certain Improvement Districts and be subject to additional taxes.

In Hot Springs School District #6, the personal property tax rate is .03887. Personal property is assessed at 20% of market value. Items subject to the tax include automobiles, boats, campers, motors and RVs.

★Total tax burdens in Hot Springs are lower than average for the $24,281 income category and about average for the $34,275 and $68,098 income categories.

LITTLE ROCK

Little Rock has no local income tax but does levy a sales tax.

Most purchases are taxed at a rate of 6%. Major consumer categories taxed at a different rate include: Food away from home, which is taxed at 8%. Major consumer categories which are exempt from sales tax include: Drugs and medical services.

Within the city limits of Little Rock, the property tax rate is .066834. Homes are assessed at 20% of market value. There is a homestead relief refund of $50 to $250 for homeowners age 62 or older with a household income of up to $15,000. Property tax does not cover garbage pickup; the additional fee is approximately $159 per year.

Little Rock has a personal property tax rate of .066834. Personal property is assessed at 20% of market value. Items subject to the tax include automobiles, boats, campers, motors and RVs.

★Total tax burdens in Little Rock are higher than average overall.

MOUNTAIN HOME

Mountain Home has no local income tax but does levy a sales tax.

Most purchases are taxed at a rate of 6.5%. Major consumer categories taxed at a different rate: None. Major consumer categories which are exempt from sales tax include: Drugs and medical services.

Within the city limits of Mountain Home, the property tax rate is .0353. Homes are assessed at 20% of market value. There is a homestead relief refund of $50 to $250 for homeowners age 62 or older with a household income of up to $15,000. Property tax does not cover garbage pickup; the additional fee is approximately $95 per year.

Mountain Home has a personal property tax rate of .0353. Personal property is assessed at 20% of market value. Items subject to the tax include automobiles, boats, campers, motors and RVs.

★Total tax burdens in Mountain Home are lower than average overall.

CALIFORNIA

Income	Home Value	Property Tax & Other Fees	Personal Property Tax & Auto Fees	Sales Tax	Local Income Tax	State Income Tax	Total Tax	Rank From #1–#149
BARSTOW								
$24,281	$50,000	$741	$584	$822	–	–	$2,147	#118
	75,000	997	584	822	–	–	2,403	#110
	100,000	1,254	584	822	–	–	2,660	#92 (tie)
$34,275	$75,000	$997	$584	$1,104	–	$50	$2,735	#87
	100,000	1,254	584	1,104	–	50	2,992	#76 (tie)
	150,000	1,767	584	1,104	–	50	3,505	#60
$68,098	$150,000	$1,767	$584	$1,707	–	$1,669	$5,727	#71
	200,000	2,280	584	1,707	–	1,669	6,240	#60
	250,000	2,792	584	1,707	–	1,669	6,752	#59
LOS ANGELES								
$24,281	$50,000	$733	$586	$875	–	–	$2,194	#126
	75,000	991	586	875	–	–	2,452	#113
	100,000	1,249	586	875	–	–	2,710	#97
$34,275	$75,000	$991	$586	$1,175	–	$50	$2,802	#92
	100,000	1,249	586	1,175	–	50	3,060	#83
	150,000	1,765	586	1,175	–	50	3,576	#65
$68,098	$150,000	$1,765	$586	$1,817	–	$1,669	$5,837	#76
	200,000	2,281	586	1,817	–	1,669	6,353	#66
	250,000	2,797	586	1,817	–	1,669	6,869	#64
	$300,000	$3,313	$586	$1,817	–	$1,669	$7,385	Not Ranked
	350,000	3,829	586	1,817	–	1,669	7,901	Not Ranked
	400,000	4,345	586	1,817	–	1,669	8,417	Not Ranked
MONTEREY								
$24,281	$50,000	$577	$584	$689	–	–	$1,850	#81
	75,000	830	584	689	–	–	2,103	#69
	100,000	1,082	584	689	–	–	2,355	#62
$34,275	$75,000	$830	$584	$926	–	$50	$2,390	#53
	100,000	1,082	584	926	–	50	2,642	#45
	150,000	1,587	584	926	–	50	3,147	#31
$68,098	$150,000	$1,587	$584	$1,431	–	$1,669	$5,271	#52
	200,000	2,092	584	1,431	–	1,669	5,776	#48
	250,000	2,597	584	1,431	–	1,669	6,281	#38
	$300,000	$3,102	$584	$1,431	–	$1,669	$6,786	Not Ranked
	350,000	3,607	584	1,431	–	1,669	7,291	Not Ranked
	400,000	4,112	584	1,431	–	1,669	7,796	Not Ranked
ONTARIO								
$24,281	$50,000	$621	$584	$822	–	–	$2,027	#104
	75,000	874	584	822	–	–	2,280	#91 (tie)
	100,000	1,127	584	822	–	–	2,533	#85 (tie)
$34,275	$75,000	$874	$584	$1,104	–	$50	$2,612	#77
	100,000	1,127	584	1,104	–	50	2,865	#66
	150,000	1,634	584	1,104	–	50	3,372	#54
$68,098	$150,000	$1,634	$584	$1,707	–	$1,669	$5,594	#67
	200,000	2,140	584	1,707	–	1,669	6,100	#56
	250,000	2,647	584	1,707	–	1,669	6,607	#51
PALM SPRINGS								
$24,281	$50,000	$712	$588	$822	–	–	$2,122	#116
	75,000	991	588	822	–	–	2,401	#109
	100,000	1,269	588	822	–	–	2,679	#95
$34,275	$75,000	$991	$588	$1,104	–	$50	$2,733	#86
	100,000	1,269	588	1,104	–	50	3,011	#80
	150,000	1,826	588	1,104	–	50	3,568	#63
$68,098	$150,000	$1,826	$588	$1,707	–	$1,669	$5,790	#75
	200,000	2,383	588	1,707	–	1,669	6,347	#64
	250,000	2,940	588	1,707	–	1,669	6,904	#67

Income	Home Value	Property Tax & Other Fees	Personal Property Tax & Auto Fees	Sales Tax	Local Income Tax	State Income Tax	Total Tax	Rank From #1–#149
SAN DIEGO								
$24,281	$50,000	$510	$582	$762	–	–	$1,854	#83
	75,000	807	582	762	–	–	2,151	#77
	100,000	1,103	582	762	–	–	2,447	#70
$34,275	$75,000	$807	$582	$1,024	–	$50	$2,463	#59
	100,000	1,103	582	1,024	–	50	2,759	#55
	150,000	1,696	582	1,024	–	50	3,352	#50
$68,098	$150,000	$1,696	$582	$1,583	–	$1,669	$5,530	#63
	200,000	2,289	582	1,583	–	1,669	6,123	#57
	250,000	2,882	582	1,583	–	1,669	6,716	#56
	$300,000	$3,475	$582	$1,583	–	$1,669	$7,309	Not Ranked
	350,000	4,068	582	1,583	–	1,669	7,902	Not Ranked
	400,000	4,661	582	1,583	–	1,669	8,495	Not Ranked
SAN FRANCISCO								
$24,281	$50,000	$669	$586	$901	–	–	$2,156	#119
	75,000	960	586	901	–	–	2,447	#112
	100,000	1,251	586	901	–	–	2,738	#101
$34,275	$75,000	$960	$586	$1,211	–	$50	$2,807	#93
	100,000	1,251	586	1,211	–	50	3,098	#85
	150,000	1,832	586	1,211	–	50	3,679	#72
$68,098	$150,000	$1,832	$586	$1,872	–	$1,669	$5,959	#81 (tie)
	200,000	2,414	586	1,872	–	1,669	6,541	#77
	250,000	2,995	586	1,872	–	1,669	7,122	#70
	$300,000	$3,577	$586	$1,872	–	$1,669	$7,704	Not Ranked
	350,000	4,158	586	1,872	–	1,669	8,285	Not Ranked
	400,000	4,740	586	1,872	–	1,669	8,867	Not Ranked

California has a state income tax and a state sales tax.

The state income tax rate is graduated from 1% to 11% depending upon income bracket. For married couples filing jointly with taxable income up to $9,444, the rate is 1%; for taxable income of over $9,444 and up to $22,384, the tax is $94.44 plus 2% of the amount above $9,444; for taxable income of over $22,384 and up to $35,324, the tax is $353.24 plus 4% of the amount above $22,384; for taxable income of over $35,324 and up to $49,038, the tax is $870.84 plus 6% of the amount above $35,324; for taxable income of over $49,038 and up to $61,974, the tax is $1,693.68 plus 8% of the amount above $49,038; for taxable income of over $61,974 and up to $214,928, the tax is $2,728.56 plus 9.3% of the amount above $61,974; for taxable income of over $214,928 and up to $429,858, the tax is $16,953.28 plus 10% of the amount above $214,928; and for taxable income above $429,858, the tax is $38,446.28 plus 11% of the amount above $429,858.

In calculating the tax, there is no deduction for federal income tax paid. Federal, state and private pensions are not exempt. Social Security benefits are exempt. There is a $4,862 standard deduction from adjusted gross income for married couples filing jointly. There is a $130 credit against tax for married couples filing jointly and a $65 credit against tax per person for persons age 65 or older. Personal exemption credits are reduced by $12 per $2,500 of taxable income over $214,929 for joint filers.

Major tax credits or rebates include: Credit for income taxes paid to other states and credit for senior head of household. Our couples do not qualify for these programs.

The state sales tax rate is 6% but local governments can add to this amount.

Our couples relocating to the cities listed below must pay a vehicle license fee per automobile of 2% of the vehicle's assessed value. The license fee is approximately $302 for the Chrysler and $212 for the Oldsmobile. Our couples also must pay a registration fee of $27 per automobile, county fees of $5 to $8 per automobile, a service fee of $10 per automobile and a CHP fee of $1 per automobile at the time of registration. Most automobiles brought into the state do not meet California emissions standards and are subject to a $300 smog impact fee. Thereafter, on an annual basis, our couples will pay a vehicle license fee, registration fee, CHP fee and county fees, per automobile.

BARSTOW

Barstow has no local income tax but does levy a sales tax.

Most purchases are taxed at a rate of 7.75%. Major consumer categories taxed at a different rate: None. Major consumer categories which are exempt from sales tax include: Drugs, groceries and medical services.

Within the Silverado Estates area of Barstow, the property tax rate is .010257. Homes are assessed at either 100% of market value or purchase price plus 2% per year, whichever is lower. There is a homeowner's exemption of $7,000 off assessed value of the home available to all homeowners. Property tax does not cover garbage pickup; the additional fee is approximately $270 per year. There is a parks and recreation assessment of approximately $30 per year.

Barstow has a personal property tax rate of .010257 within the Silverado Estates area. Personal property is assessed at 100% of market value. Items subject to the tax include aircraft, mobile homes and boats. We've assumed our couples do not own any of the items subject to the tax.

★Total tax burdens in Barstow are higher than average for the $24,281 income category and about average for the $34,275 and $68,098 income categories.

LOS ANGELES

Los Angeles has no local income tax but does levy a sales tax.

Most purchases are taxed at a rate of 8.25%. Major consumer categories taxed at a different rate: None. Major consumer categories which are exempt from sales tax include: Drugs, groceries and medical services.

Between the Beverly Hills and Westwood areas of Los Angeles, a property tax rate is .0103202. Homes are assessed at either 100% of market value or purchase price plus 2% per year, whichever is lower. There is a homeowner's exemption of $7,000 off assessed value of the home available to all homeowners. Additional fees, including garbage pickup, average about $289 per year.

Los Angeles has a personal property tax rate of .01025979 between the Beverly Hills and Westwood areas. Personal property is assessed at 100% of market value. Items subject to the tax include aircraft, boats, mobile homes and race horses. We've assumed our couples do not own any of the items subject to the tax.

★Total tax burdens in Los Angeles are higher than average for the $24,281 income category and about average for the $34,275 and $68,098 income categories.

MONTEREY

Monterey has no local income tax

but does levy a sales tax.

Most purchases are taxed at a rate of 6.5%. Major consumer categories taxed at a different rate: None. Major consumer categories which are exempt from sales tax include: Drugs, groceries and medical services.

Within the city limits of Monterey, the property tax rate is .010099. Homes are assessed at either 100% of market value or purchase price plus 2% per year, whichever is lower. There is a homeowner's exemption of $7,000 off assessed value of the home available to all homeowners. Property tax does not cover garbage pickup; the additional fee is approximately $131 per year. There is an ambulance/911 fee of approximately $12 per year.

Monterey has a personal property tax rate of .010099. Personal property is assessed at 100% of market value. Items subject to the tax include airplanes, mobile homes and boats. We've assumed our couples do not own any of the items subject to the tax.

★Total tax burdens in Monterey are about average for the $24,281 income category and lower than average for the $34,275 and $68,098 income categories.

ONTARIO

Ontario has no local income tax but does levy a sales tax.

Most purchases are taxed at a rate of 7.75%. Major consumer categories taxed at a different rate: None. Major consumer categories which are exempt from sales tax include: Drugs, groceries and medical services.

For most residents within the city limits of Ontario, the property tax rate is .010131. Homes are assessed at either 100% of market value or purchase price plus 2% per year, whichever is lower. There is a homeowner's exemption of $7,000 off assessed value of the home available to all homeowners. Property tax does not cover garbage pickup; the additional fee is approximately $177 per year. There is a water standby fee of approximately $8 per year.

Ontario has a personal property tax rate of .010131 for most residents. Personal property is assessed at 100% of market value. Items subject to the

tax include airplanes, boats and mobile homes. We've assumed our couples do not own any of the items subject to the tax.

★Total tax burdens in Ontario are about average for the $24,281 and $34,275 income categories and lower than average for the $68,098 income category.

PALM SPRINGS

Palm Springs has no local income tax but does levy a sales tax.

Most purchases are taxed at a rate of 7.75%. Major consumer categories taxed at a different rate: None. Major consumer categories which are exempt from sales tax include: Drugs, groceries and medical services.

Within the city limits of Palm Springs, the property tax rate is .01114. Homes are assessed at either 100% of market value or purchase price plus 2% per year, whichever is lower. There is a homeowner's exemption of $7,000 off assessed value of the home available to all homeowners. Property tax does not cover garbage pickup; the additional fee is approximately $233 per year. Some residents may also live within special assessment districts, such as flood control, and may be subject to additional taxes.

Palm Springs has a personal property tax rate of .01114. Personal property is assessed at 100% of current market value. Items subject to the tax include airplanes and boats. We've assumed our couples do not own any of the items subject to the tax.

★Total tax burdens in Palm Springs are higher than average for the $24,281 income category and about average for the $34,275 and 68,098 income categories.

SAN DIEGO

San Diego has no local income tax but does levy a sales tax.

During the 12-month period covered by this study, the sales tax rate changed from 7.75% to 7%. Our estimates for sales tax are based on a weighted average of these rates. Major consumer categories taxed at a different rate: None. Major consumer categories which are exempt from sales tax include: Drugs, groceries and medical services.

Within the San Diego City/County and Unified School District, the property tax rate is .011861. Homes are assessed at either 100% of market value or purchase price plus 2% per year, whichever is lower. There is a homeowner's exemption of $7,000 off assessed value of the home available to all homeowners. Property tax includes garbage pickup.

San Diego has a personal property tax rate of .011861 within the San Diego City/County and Unified School District. Personal property is assessed at 100% of market value. Items subject to the tax include airplanes, mobile homes and boats. We've assumed our couples do not own any of these items subject to the tax.

★Total tax burdens in San Diego are about average overall.

SAN FRANCISCO

San Francisco has no local income tax but does levy a sales tax.

Most purchases are taxed at a rate of 8.5%. Major consumer categories taxed at a different rate: None. Major consumer categories which are exempt from sales tax include: Drugs, groceries and medical services.

Within the city limits of San Francisco, the property tax rate is .01163. Homes are assessed at either 100% of market value or purchase price plus 2% per year, whichever is lower. There is a homeowner's exemption of $7,000 off assessed value of the home available to all homeowners. Property tax does not cover garbage pickup; the additional fee is approximately $112 per year. There is also an earthquake/school tax of approximately $46 per year and a special assessment averaging $11 per year.

San Francisco has a personal property tax rate of .0115. Personal property is assessed at 100% of market value. Items subject to the tax include airplanes, mobile homes and boats. We've assumed our couples do not own any of the items subject to the tax.

★Total tax burdens in San Francisco are higher than average for the $24,281 income category and about average for the $34,275 and $68,098 income categories.

COLORADO

Income	Home Value	Property Tax & Other Fees	Personal Property Tax & Auto Fees	Sales Tax	Local Income Tax	State Income Tax	Total Tax	Rank From #1–#149
COLORADO SPRINGS								
$24,281	$50,000	$527	$201	$657	–	–	$1,385	#25
	75,000	737	201	657	–	–	1,595	#22
	100,000	946	201	657	–	–	1,804	#14
$34,275	$75,000	$737	$201	$883	–	$151	$1,972	#19
	100,000	946	201	883	–	151	2,181	#16
	150,000	1,366	201	883	–	151	2,601	#15
$68,098	$150,000	$1,366	$201	$1,365	–	$1,641	$4,573	#29
	200,000	1,785	201	1,365	–	1,641	4,992	#17
	250,000	2,204	201	1,365	–	1,641	5,411	#17
FORT COLLINS								
$24,281	$50,000	$671	$201	$692	–	–	$1,564	#47
	75,000	956	201	692	–	–	1,849	#44
	100,000	1,241	201	692	–	–	2,134	#40 (tie)
$34,275	$75,000	$956	$201	$923	–	$151	$2,231	#39
	100,000	1,241	201	923	–	151	2,516	#34
	150,000	1,811	201	923	–	151	3,086	#28
$68,098	$150,000	$1,811	$201	$1,393	–	$1,641	$5,046	#39
	200,000	2,381	201	1,393	–	1,641	5,616	#39
	250,000	2,951	201	1,393	–	1,641	6,186	#32

Colorado has a state income tax and a state sales tax.

The state income tax rate is 5% applied to modified federal taxable income.

In calculating the tax, there is no deduction for federal income tax paid. Pensions and Social Security benefits subject to federal tax are not exempt. However, the first $20,000 in taxable pensions and Social Security benefits is exempt for each taxpayer age 55 and older. There is a $2,450 personal exemption per person from adjusted gross income. There is a $7,850 standard deduction from adjusted gross income for married couples filing jointly when both are age 65 or older.

Major tax credits or rebates include: Credit for income taxes paid to other states and low-income property tax/rent/heat credit. Our couples do not qualify for these programs.

The state sales tax rate is 3% but local governments can add to this amount.

Our couples relocating to the cities listed below must pay a personal property tax based on the year and MSRP of each automobile, which is assessed and collected through the Department of Motor Vehicles. Our couples also pay a license fee per automobile based on the weight of each automobile and a title fee of $5.50 per automobile. The personal property tax is $156.20 for the Chrysler and $72.17 for the Oldsmobile. The license fee is $26.80 for the Chrysler and $26.80 for the Oldsmobile. Thereafter, on an annual basis, our couples will pay a personal property tax and a license fee, per automobile.

COLORADO SPRINGS

Colorado Springs has no local income tax but does levy a sales tax.

Most purchases are taxed at a rate of 6.2%. Major consumer categories taxed at a different rate: None. Major consumer categories which are exempt from sales tax include: Drugs, groceries and medical services.

In the area of Villages at Skyline, the property tax rate is .065199. Homes are assessed at 12.86% of market value. Property tax does not cover garbage pickup; the additional fee is approximately $108 per year.

Colorado Springs has a personal property tax on automobiles, discussed above.

★Total tax burdens in Colorado Springs are lower than average overall.

FORT COLLINS

Fort Collins has no local income tax but does levy a sales tax.

Most purchases are taxed at a rate of 6%. Major consumer categories taxed at a different rate include: Groceries, which are taxed at a rate of 2.25%. Major consumer categories which are exempt from sales tax include: Drugs and medical services.

In the Poudre School District, the property tax rate is .088655. Homes are assessed at 12.86% of market value. Property tax does not cover garbage pickup; the additional fee is approximately $101 per year.

Fort Collins has a personal property tax on automobiles, discussed above.

★Total tax burdens in Fort Collins are lower than average overall.

CONNECTICUT

Income	Home Value	Property Tax & Other Fees	Personal Property Tax & Auto Fees	Sales Tax	Local Income Tax	State Income Tax	Total Tax	Rank From #1–#149
HARTFORD								
$24,281	$50,000	$181	$584	$579	–	–	$1,344	#21
	75,000	555	584	579	–	–	1,718	#33
	100,000	907	584	579	–	–	2,070	#35
$34,275	$75,000	$1,172	$584	$779	–	$11	$2,546	#68
	100,000	1,563	584	779	–	11	2,937	#75
	150,000	2,344	584	779	–	11	3,718	#74
$68,098	$150,000	$2,344	$584	$1,210	–	$2,165	$6,303	#93 (tie)
	200,000	3,126	584	1,210	–	2,165	7,085	#92
	250,000	3,907	584	1,210	–	2,165	7,866	#90
NEW HAVEN								
$24,281	$50,000	$1,131	$992	$579	–	–	$2,702	#144
	75,000	1,696	992	579	–	–	3,267	#141
	100,000	2,262	992	579	–	–	3,833	#138
$34,275	$75,000	$1,885	$992	$779	–	$11	$3,667	#136
	100,000	2,513	992	779	–	11	4,295	#137
	150,000	3,769	992	779	–	11	5,551	#135
$68,098	$150,000	$3,769	$992	$1,210	–	$2,165	$8,136	#134
	200,000	5,026	992	1,210	–	2,165	9,393	#136
	250,000	6,282	992	1,210	–	2,165	10,649	#136

Connecticut has a state income tax and a state sales tax.

The state income tax rate is 4.5% of Connecticut taxable income for all filers. There is a credit against income taxes due of up to 75% depending upon filing status and income bracket. For married couples filing jointly with adjusted gross income of $24,001 to $30,000, the credit is 75%; from $30,001 to $40,000, the credit is 35%; from $40,001 to $50,000, the credit is 15%; from $50,001 to $96,000, the credit is 10%; and above $96,000, there is no credit.

In calculating the tax, there is no deduction for federal income tax paid. Federal, state and private pensions are subject to tax if the pension is subject to tax at the federal level. Social Security benefits are subject to tax if subject to tax at the federal level. There is a personal exemption of up to $24,000 from adjusted gross income for married couples filing jointly.

Major tax credits or rebates include: Credit for income taxes paid to other states. Our couples do not qualify for this program.

The state sales tax rate is 6%.

Our couples relocating to the cities listed below must pay a registration fee of $70 for two years per automobile, a title fee of $25 per automobile, a safety plate fee of $5 per automobile, a safety inspection fee of $25 per automobile and an emissions inspection fee of $20 per automobile for two years, at the time of registration. Thereafter, every two years, our couples will pay a registration fee, a clean air fee and an emissions inspection fee, per automobile.

HARTFORD

Hartford has no local income tax and does not levy an additional sales tax.

Most purchases are taxed at the state rate of 6%. Major consumer categories taxed at a different rate: None. Major consumer categories which are exempt from sales tax include: Drugs, groceries, medical services and entertainment.

In the Avery Heights area of Hartford, the property tax rate is .022327. Homes are assessed at 70% of 1989 market value. Property taxes are based on both market value and assessed value of the home. There is a $500 credit against tax for homeowners age 65 or older with an adjusted gross income of less than $27,600. There is a graduated credit subject to certain minimum and maximum amounts, of 10% to 50% against tax for homeowners age 65 or older with an adjusted gross income of less than $26,100. Property tax includes garbage pickup.

In the Avery Heights area of Hartford, there is a personal property tax rate of .0334. Personal property is assessed at 70% of NADA retail. Items subject to the tax include motor vehicles.

★Total tax burdens in Hartford are lower than average for the $24,281 income category and about average for the $34,275 and $68,098 income categories.

NEW HAVEN

New Haven has no local income tax and does not levy an additional sales tax.

Most purchases are taxed at the state rate of 6%. Major consumer categories taxed at a different rate: None. Major consumer categories which are exempt from sales tax include: Drugs, groceries, medical services and entertainment.

Within the city limits of New Haven, the property tax rate is .06114. Homes are assessed at 41.1% of market value. There is a graduated credit subject to certain minimum and maximum amounts, of 10% to 50% against tax for homeowners age 65 or older with an adjusted gross income of less than $26,100. Property tax includes garbage pickup.

New Haven has a personal property tax rate of .06114. Personal property is assessed at 70% of fair market value. Items subject to the tax include motor vehicles.

★Total tax burdens in New Haven are higher than average overall. New Haven is a tax hell in 2 of 9 income/home value categories.

DELAWARE

Income	Home Value	Property Tax & Other Fees	Personal Property Tax & Auto Fees	Sales Tax	Local Income Tax	State Income Tax	Total Tax	Rank From #1–#149
DOVER								
$24,281	$50,000	$579	$40	–	–	–	$619	#6
	75,000	869	40	–	–	–	909	#6
	100,000	1,158	40	–	–	–	1,198	#7
$34,275	$75,000	$869	$40	–	–	$551	$1,460	#6
	100,000	1,158	40	–	–	551	1,749	#6
	150,000	1,737	40	–	–	551	2,328	#9
$68,098	$150,000	$1,737	$40	–	–	$2,789	$4,566	#28
	200,000	2,316	40	–	–	2,789	5,145	#21
	250,000	2,895	40	–	–	2,789	5,724	#19
WILMINGTON								
$24,281	$50,000	$373	$40	–	$55	–	$468	#3
	75,000	577	40	–	55	–	672	#5
	100,000	782	40	–	55	–	877	#5
$34,275	$75,000	$613	$40	–	$120	$551	$1,324	#5
	100,000	817	40	–	120	551	1,528	#5
	150,000	1,225	40	–	120	551	1,936	#5
$68,098	$150,000	$1,225	$40	–	$377	$2,789	$4,431	#24
	200,000	1,634	40	–	377	2,789	4,840	#16
	250,000	2,042	40	–	377	2,789	5,248	#15

Delaware has a state income tax but no state sales tax.

The state income tax rate is graduated from 3.2% to 7.7% depending upon income bracket. All filers pay no tax on the first $2,000 of taxable income; the rate is 3.2% on the next $3,000 of taxable income; the rate is 5% on the next $5,000 of taxable income; the rate is 6% on the next $10,000 of taxable income; the rate is 6.6% on the next $5,000 of taxable income; the rate is 7% on the next $5,000 of taxable income; the rate is 7.6% on the next $10,000 of taxable income; and the rate is 7.7% on taxable income above $40,000.

In calculating the tax, there is no deduction for federal income tax paid. Federal, state and private pensions are not exempt, but there is a $3,000 exemption from pension income per person for persons age 60 or older and a $2,000 exemption from pension income per person for persons under age 60. Social Security benefits are exempt. There is a $1,600 standard deduction from adjusted gross income for married couples filing jointly and a $2,000 standard deduction from adjusted gross income for married couples filing jointly when both are age 65 or older. There is a

$1,250 exemption from adjusted gross income per person and a $1,250 exemption from adjusted gross income per person for persons age 60 or older. There is also a $4,000 exclusion from adjusted gross income for married couples filing jointly when both are age 60 or older and total earned income is less than $5,000 and Delaware adjusted gross income does not exceed $20,000.

Major tax credits or rebates include: Credit for income taxes paid to other states, child care credit and Delaware investment credit. Our couples do not qualify for these programs.

Our couples relocating to the cities listed below must pay a document fee per automobile, based on the NADA trade-in value of the automobile. The document fee is $275 for the Chrysler and $193 for the Oldsmobile. Our couples must also pay a registration fee of $20 per automobile and a title fee of $15 per automobile at the time of registration. Thereafter, on an annual basis, our couples will pay a registration fee per automobile.

DOVER

Dover has no local income tax and does not levy a sales tax.

In the Capital School District of

Dover, the property tax rate is .0193. Homes are assessed at 60% of market value. There are various deductions from assessed home value for the city and county portions of the property tax. Property tax includes garbage pickup.

Dover has no personal property tax for individuals.

★Total tax burdens in Dover are lower than average overall. Dover is a tax heaven in 6 of 9 income/home value categories.

WILMINGTON

Wilmington has a local income tax but does not levy a sales tax.

The local income tax rate is 1.25% of wages, salaries and self-employment income. Federal, state and private pensions are exempt. Social Security benefits are exempt.

Note: The Wilmington tax assessor's office declined to provide property tax estimates or verify our calculations. Rates shown were provided for an earlier edition of this publication and may no longer be valid. In the Rockford Park area of Wilmington, the property tax rate is .010211. Homes are assessed at 80% of market value. There are various deductions from assessed home value for the city and county portions of the property tax. Property tax includes garbage pickup.

Wilmington has no personal property tax for individuals.

★Total tax burdens in Wilmington are lower than average overall. Wilmington is a tax heaven in 6 of 9 income/home value categories.

FLORIDA

Income	Home Value	Property Tax & Other Fees	Personal Property Tax & Auto Fees	Sales Tax	Local Income Tax	State Income Tax	Total Tax	Rank From #1–#149
BOCA RATON								
$24,281	$50,000	$731	$70	$636	–	–	$1,437	#30 (tie)
	75,000	1,278	70	636	–	–	1,984	#57
	100,000	1,826	70	636	–	–	2,532	#84
$34,275	$75,000	$1,278	$70	$855	–	–	$2,203	#37
	100,000	1,826	70	855	–	–	2,751	#54
	150,000	2,920	70	855	–	–	3,845	#82
$68,098	$150,000	$2,920	$70	$1,321	–	–	$4,311	#21
	200,000	4,015	70	1,321	–	–	5,406	#30
	250,000	5,109	70	1,321	–	–	6,500	#49
FORT LAUDERDALE								
$24,281	$50,000	$995	$70	$636	–	–	$1,701	#61 (tie)
	75,000	1,669	70	636	–	–	2,375	#104
	100,000	2,342	70	636	–	–	3,048	#118
$34,275	$75,000	$1,669	$70	$855	–	–	$2,594	#74
	100,000	2,342	70	855	–	–	3,267	#100
	150,000	3,689	70	855	–	–	4,614	#111
$68,098	$150,000	$3,689	$70	$1,321	–	–	$5,080	#43
	200,000	5,036	70	1,321	–	–	6,427	#68
	250,000	6,383	70	1,321	–	–	7,774	#87
GAINESVILLE								
$24,281	$50,000	$889	$70	$636	–	–	$1,595	#52
	75,000	1,608	70	636	–	–	2,314	#99
	100,000	2,327	70	636	–	–	3,033	#116
$34,275	$75,000	$1,608	$70	$855	–	–	$2,533	#66
	100,000	2,327	70	855	–	–	3,252	#96 (tie)
	150,000	3,766	70	855	–	–	4,691	#114
$68,098	$150,000	$3,766	$70	$1,321	–	–	$5,157	#49
	200,000	5,205	70	1,321	–	–	6,596	#78
	250,000	6,644	70	1,321	–	–	8,035	#92
JACKSONVILLE								
$24,281	$50,000	$554	$70	$689	–	–	$1,313	#19
	75,000	1,108	70	689	–	–	1,867	#47
	100,000	1,663	70	689	–	–	2,422	#67
$34,275	$75,000	$1,108	$70	$926	–	–	$2,104	#28
	100,000	1,663	70	926	–	–	2,659	#47
	150,000	2,771	70	926	–	–	3,767	#78
$68,098	$150,000	$2,771	$70	$1,431	–	–	$4,272	#18
	200,000	3,879	70	1,431	–	–	5,380	#28
	250,000	4,988	70	1,431	–	–	6,489	#47 (tie)
LAKELAND								
$24,281	$50,000	$631	$70	$636	–	–	$1,337	#20
	75,000	1,154	70	636	–	–	1,860	#46
	100,000	1,677	70	636	–	–	2,383	#63
$34,275	$75,000	$1,154	$70	$855	–	–	$2,079	#26
	100,000	1,677	70	855	–	–	2,602	#41
	150,000	2,724	70	855	–	–	3,649	#70
$68,098	$150,000	$2,724	$70	$1,321	–	–	$4,115	#14
	200,000	3,770	70	1,321	–	–	5,161	#22
	250,000	4,816	70	1,321	–	–	6,207	#33

Income	Home Value	Property Tax & Other Fees	Personal Property Tax & Auto Fees	Sales Tax	Local Income Tax	State Income Tax	Total Tax	Rank From #1–#149
MIAMI								
$24,281	$50,000	$938	$70	$701	–	–	$1,709	#63 (tie)
	75,000	1,715	70	701	–	–	2,486	#116
	100,000	2,493	70	701	–	–	3,264	#124
$34,275	$75,000	$1,715	$70	$943	–	–	$2,728	#85
	100,000	2,493	70	943	–	–	3,506	#111
	150,000	4,049	70	943	–	–	5,062	#123
$68,098	$150,000	$4,049	$70	$1,459	–	–	$5,578	#66
	200,000	5,604	70	1,459	–	–	7,133	#95
	250,000	7,160	70	1,459	–	–	8,689	#115
NAPLES								
$24,281	$50,000	$513	$70	$636	–	–	$1,219	#13
	75,000	857	70	636	–	–	1,563	#16
	100,000	1,202	70	636	–	–	1,908	#21
$34,275	$75,000	$857	$70	$855	–	–	$1,782	#11
	100,000	1,202	70	855	–	–	2,127	#13
	150,000	1,891	70	855	–	–	2,816	#21
$68,098	$150,000	$1,891	$70	$1,321	–	–	$3,282	#5
	200,000	2,581	70	1,321	–	–	3,972	#6
	250,000	3,270	70	1,321	–	–	4,661	#7
OCALA								
$24,281	$50,000	$770	$70	$636	–	–	$1,476	#36
	75,000	1,351	70	636	–	–	2,057	#65
	100,000	1,931	70	636	–	–	2,637	#91
$34,275	$75,000	$1,351	$70	$855	–	–	$2,276	#41
	100,000	1,931	70	855	–	–	2,856	#63 (tie)
	150,000	3,092	70	855	–	–	4,017	#90 (tie)
$68,098	$150,000	$3,092	$70	$1,321	–	–	$4,483	#25
	200,000	4,252	70	1,321	–	–	5,643	#41 (tie)
	250,000	5,413	70	1,321	–	–	6,804	#63
ORLANDO								
$24,281	$50,000	$702	$70	$636	–	–	$1,408	#27
	75,000	1,243	70	636	–	–	1,949	#53
	100,000	1,783	70	636	–	–	2,489	#76
$34,275	$75,000	$1,243	$70	$855	–	–	$2,168	#34
	100,000	1,783	70	855	–	–	2,708	#51
	150,000	2,864	70	855	–	–	3,789	#80
$68,098	$150,000	$2,864	$70	$1,321	–	–	$4,255	#16
	200,000	3,945	70	1,321	–	–	5,336	#26
	250,000	5,026	70	1,321	–	–	6,417	#41
ST. PETERSBURG								
$24,281	$50,000	$881	$70	$742	–	–	$1,693	#59 (tie)
	75,000	1,543	70	742	–	–	2,355	#102
	100,000	2,206	70	742	–	–	3,018	#114
$34,275	$75,000	$1,543	$70	$997	–	–	$2,610	#76
	100,000	2,206	70	997	–	–	3,273	#101
	150,000	3,531	70	997	–	–	4,598	#109
$68,098	$150,000	$3,531	$70	$1,541	–	–	$5,142	#47
	200,000	4,856	70	1,541	–	–	6,467	#72
	250,000	6,181	70	1,541	–	–	7,792	#88

Income	Home Value	Property Tax & Other Fees	Personal Property Tax & Auto Fees	Sales Tax	Local Income Tax	State Income Tax	Total Tax	Rank From #1–#149
SARASOTA								
$24,281	$50,000	$794	$70	$742	–	–	$1,606	#53
	75,000	1,321	70	742	–	–	2,133	#72
	100,000	1,848	70	742	–	–	2,660	#92 (tie)
$34,275	$75,000	$1,321	$70	$997	–	–	$2,388	#52
	100,000	1,848	70	997	–	–	2,915	#72
	150,000	2,902	70	997	–	–	3,969	#89
$68,098	$150,000	$2,902	$70	$1,541	–	–	$4,513	#26
	200,000	3,956	70	1,541	–	–	5,567	#36
	250,000	5,010	70	1,541	–	–	6,621	#52
TAMPA								
$24,281	$50,000	$872	$70	$689	–	–	$1,631	#55
	75,000	1,552	70	689	–	–	2,311	#98
	100,000	2,232	70	689	–	–	2,991	#112
$34,275	$75,000	$1,552	$70	$926	–	–	$2,548	#70
	100,000	2,232	70	926	–	–	3,228	#92
	150,000	3,592	70	926	–	–	4,588	#108
$68,098	$150,000	$3,592	$70	$1,431	–	–	$5,093	#45
	200,000	4,952	70	1,431	–	–	6,453	#71
	250,000	6,312	70	1,431	–	–	7,813	#89

Florida has no state income tax but does have a state sales tax.

Major tax credit or rebates: None.

The state sales tax rate is 6%, but local governments can add to this amount.

Our couples relocating to the cities listed below must pay a registration fee of $45.05 per automobile, a title fee of $29.25 per automobile, a $100 additional-wheels-on-the-road fee per automobile and some counties also have a $10 emissions inspection fee per automobile. Thereafter, on an annual basis, our couples will pay a registration fee per automobile.

BOCA RATON

Boca Raton has no local income tax and does not levy an additional sales tax.

Most purchases are taxed at the state rate of 6%. Major consumer categories taxed at a different rate: None. Major consumer categories which are exempt from sales tax include: Drugs, groceries and medical services.

For most residents within the city limits of Boca Raton, the property tax rate is .0218896. Homes are assessed at 100% of market value. There is a homestead exemption of $25,000 off assessed value available to all homeowners who own and live on the property before Jan. 1 of the previous tax year. Property tax does not cover garbage pickup; the additional fee is approximately $157 per year. There is a drainage maintenance fee of approximately $27 per year.

Boca Raton has a personal property tax rate of .0218896. Personal property is assessed at 100% of market value. Items subject to the tax include mobile home attachments. We've assumed our couples do not own any items subject to the tax.

★Total tax burdens in Boca Raton are about average for the $24,281 income category and lower than average for the $34,275 and $68,098 income categories.

FORT LAUDERDALE

Fort Lauderdale has no local income tax and does not levy an additional sales tax.

Most purchases are taxed at the state rate of 6%. Major consumer categories taxed at a different rate: None. Major consumer categories which are exempt from sales tax include: Drugs, groceries and medical services.

For most residents within the city limits of Fort Lauderdale, the property tax rate is .0269381. Homes are assessed at 100% of market value. There is a homestead exemption of $25,000 off assessed value available to all homeowners who own and live on the property before Jan. 1 of the previous tax year. Property tax does not cover garbage pickup; the additional fee is approximately $322 per year.

Fort Lauderdale has no personal property tax for individuals.

★Total tax burdens in Fort Lauderdale are higher than average for the $24,281 income category and about average for the $34,275 and $68,098 income categories.

GAINESVILLE

Gainesville has no local income tax and does not levy an additional sales tax.

Most purchases are taxed at the state rate of 6%. Major consumer categories taxed at a different rate: None. Major consumer categories which are exempt from sales tax include: Drugs, groceries and medical services.

In the St. John's Water District of Gainesville, the property tax rate is .0287799. Homes are assessed at 100% of market value. There is a homestead exemption of $25,000 off assessed value available to all homeowners who own and live on the property before Jan. 1 of the previous tax year. Property tax does not cover garbage pickup; the additional fee is approximately $169 per year.

Gainesville has no personal property tax for individuals.

★Total tax burdens in Gainesville are about average overall.

JACKSONVILLE

Jacksonville has no local income tax but does levy a sales tax.

Most purchases are taxed at a rate of 6.5%. Major consumer categories taxed at a different rate: None. Major consumer categories which are exempt from sales tax include: Drugs, groceries and medical services.

In the General Services area of Jacksonville, the property tax rate is .0221678. Homes are assessed at 100% of market value. There is a homestead exemption of $25,000 off assessed value available to all homeowners who own and live on the property before Jan. 1 of the previous tax year. Property tax includes garbage pickup.

Jacksonville has no personal property tax for individuals.

★Total tax burdens in Jacksonville are lower than average overall.

LAKELAND

Lakeland has no local income tax and does not levy an additional sales tax.

Most purchases are taxed at the state rate of 6%. Major consumer categories taxed at a different rate: None. Major consumer categories which are exempt from sales tax include: Drugs, groceries and medical services.

In the Dranes 2nd Edition area of Lakeland, the property tax rate is .020926. Homes are assessed at 100% of market value. There is a homestead exemption of $25,000 off assessed value available to all homeowners who own and live on the property before Jan. 1 of the previous tax year. Property tax does not cover garbage pickup; the additional fee is approximately $108 per year.

Lakeland has a personal property tax rate of .020926. Personal property is assessed at 100% of market value. Items subject to the tax include mobile home attachments. We've

assumed our couples do not own any items subject to the tax.

★Total tax burdens in Lakeland are lower than average overall.

MIAMI

Miami has no local income tax but does levy a sales tax.

Most purchases are taxed at a rate of 6.5%. Major consumer categories taxed at a different rate include: Food away from home, which is taxed at a rate of 7.5%. Major consumer categories which are exempt from sales tax include: Drugs, groceries and medical services.

In District 01 of Miami, the property tax rate is .0311095. Homes are assessed at 100% of market value. There is a homestead exemption of $25,000 off assessed value available to all homeowners who own and live on the property before Jan. 1 of the previous tax year. Property tax does not cover garbage pickup; the additional fee is approximately $160 per year.

Miami has no personal property tax for individuals.

★Total tax burdens in Miami are higher than average for the $24,281 and $34,275 income categories and about average for the $68,098 income category.

NAPLES

Naples has no local income tax and does not levy an additional sales tax.

Most purchases are taxed at the state rate of 6%. Major consumer categories taxed at a different rate: None. Major consumer categories which are exempt from sales tax include: Drugs, groceries and medical services.

In District 4 of Naples, the property tax rate is .0137872. Homes are assessed at 100% of full just value. There is a homestead exemption of $25,000 off assessed value available to all homeowners who own and live on the property before Jan. 1 of the previous tax year. Property tax does not cover garbage pickup; the additional fee is approximately $136 per year. There is also a landfill fee of approximately $32 per year.

Naples has a personal property tax rate of .0137872. Personal property is assessed at 100% of market value.

Items subject to the tax include mobile home attachments. We've assumed our couples do not own any items subject to the tax.

★Total tax burdens in Naples are lower than average overall. Naples is a tax heaven in 3 of 9 income/home value categories.

OCALA

Ocala has no local income tax and does not levy an additional sales tax.

Most purchases are taxed at the state rate of 6%. Major consumer categories taxed at a different rate: None. Major consumer categories which are exempt from sales tax include: Drugs, groceries and medical services.

For most residents within the city limits of Ocala, the property tax rate is .0232121. Homes are assessed at 100% of market value. There is a homestead exemption of $25,000 off assessed value available to all homeowners who own and live on the property before Jan. 1 of the previous tax year. Property tax does not cover garbage pickup; the additional fee is approximately $190 per year.

Ocala has no personal property tax for individuals.

★Total tax burdens in Ocala are about average for the $24,281 and $34,275 income categories and lower than average for the $68,098 income category.

ORLANDO

Orlando has no local income tax and does not levy an additional sales tax.

Most purchases are taxed at the state rate of 6%. Major consumer categories taxed at a different rate: None. Major consumer categories which are exempt from sales tax include: Drugs, groceries and medical services.

Within the city limits of Orlando, the property tax rate is .0216172. Homes are assessed at 100% of market value. There is a homestead exemption of $25,000 off assessed value available to all homeowners who own and live on the property before Jan. 1 of the previous tax year. Property tax does not cover garbage pickup; the additional fee is approximately $126 per year. There is a storm water utility assessment fee of approximately $36 per year.

Orlando has a personal property tax rate of .0216172. Personal property is assessed at 100% of market value. Items subject to the tax include mobile home attachments. We've assumed our couples do not own any items subject to the tax.

★Total tax burdens in Orlando are about average for the $24,281 income category and lower than average for the $34,275 and $68,098 income categories.

ST. PETERSBURG

St. Petersburg has no local income tax but does levy a sales tax.

Most purchases are taxed at a rate of 7%. Major consumer categories taxed at a different rate: None. Major consumer categories which are exempt from sales tax include: Drugs, groceries and medical services.

Within the city limits of St. Petersburg, the property tax rate is .0265003. Homes are assessed at 100% of market value. There is a homestead exemption of $25,000 off assessed value available to all homeowners who own and live on the property before Jan. 1 of the previous tax year. Property tax does not cover garbage pickup; the additional fee is approximately $218 per year.

St. Petersburg has no personal property tax for individuals.

★Total tax burdens in St. Petersburg are about average overall.

SARASOTA

Sarasota has no local income tax but does levy a sales tax.

Most purchases are taxed at a rate of 7%. Major consumer categories taxed at a different rate: None. Major consumer categories which are exempt from sales tax include: Drugs, groceries and medical services.

Within the city limits of Sarasota, the property tax rate is .0210796. Homes are assessed at 100% of market value. There is a homestead exemption of $25,000 off assessed value available to all homeowners who own and live on the property before Jan. 1 of the previous tax year. Property tax does not cover garbage pickup; the additional fee is approximately $233 per year. There is a storm water assessment fee of approximately $34 per year.

Sarasota has a personal property tax rate of .0210796. Personal property is assessed at 100% of market value. Items subject to the tax include mobile home attachments. We've assumed our couples do not own any items subject to the tax.

★Total tax burdens in Sarasota are about average for the $24,281 and $34,275 income categories and below average for the $68,098 income category.

TAMPA

Tampa has no local income tax but does levy a sales tax.

Most purchases are taxed at a rate of 6.5%. Major consumer categories taxed at a different rate: None. Major consumer categories which are exempt from sales tax include: Drugs, groceries and medical services.

In the Colbreth Isles area of Tampa, the property tax rate is .0272019. Homes are assessed at 100% of market value. There is a homestead exemption of $25,000 off assessed value available to all homeowners who own and live on the property before Jan. 1 of the previous tax year. Property tax does not cover garbage pickup; the additional fee is approximately $192 per year.

Tampa has no personal property tax for individuals.

★Total tax burdens in Tampa are about average overall.

GEORGIA

Income	Home Value	Property Tax & Other Fees	Personal Property Tax & Auto Fees	Sales Tax	Local Income Tax	State Income Tax	Total Tax	Rank From #1–#149
ATLANTA								
$24,281	$50,000	$461	$474	$786	–	–	$1,721	#65
	75,000	969	474	786	–	–	2,229	#88
	100,000	1,476	474	786	–	–	2,736	#100
$34,275	$75,000	$969	$474	$1,037	–	$67	$2,547	#69
	100,000	1,476	474	1,037	–	67	3,054	#82
	150,000	2,491	474	1,037	–	67	4,069	#94
$68,098	$150,000	$2,500	$474	$1,514	–	$1,584	$6,072	#86
	200,000	3,514	474	1,514	–	1,584	7,086	#93
	250,000	4,529	474	1,514	–	1,584	8,101	#95
SAVANNAH								
$24,281	$50,000	$343	$442	$786	–	–	$1,571	#48
	75,000	546	442	786	–	–	1,774	#36
	100,000	923	442	786	–	–	2,151	#43
$34,275	$75,000	$546	$442	$1,037	–	$67	$2,092	#27
	100,000	923	442	1,037	–	67	2,469	#31
	150,000	1,926	442	1,037	–	67	3,472	#59
$68,098	$150,000	$3,067	$442	$1,514	–	$1,584	$6,607	#105
	200,000	4,099	442	1,514	–	1,584	7,639	#112
	250,000	5,130	442	1,514	–	1,584	8,670	#114

Georgia has a state income tax and a state sales tax.

The state income tax rate is graduated from 1% to 6% depending upon income bracket. For married couples filing jointly the rate is 1% on the first $1,000 of taxable income; the rate is 2% on the next $2,000 of taxable income; the rate is 3% on the next $2,000 of taxable income; the rate is 4% on the next $2,000 of taxable income; the rate is 5% on the next $3,000 of taxable income; and the rate is 6% on taxable income above $10,000.

In calculating the tax, there is no deduction for federal income tax paid. There is a retirement income exclusion of up to $11,000 for people age 62 or older. Retirement income includes all unearned income and the first $4,000 of earned income for each person age 62 or older. There is a $3,000 deduction from adjusted gross income for married couples filing jointly. There is a $1,500 exemption per person and a $700 exemption per person for residents age 65 or older. Social Security benefits are exempt.

Major tax credits or rebates include: Low income tax credit. Our couples do not qualify for this program.

The state sales tax rate is 4% but local governments can add to this amount.

Our couples relocating to the cities listed below must pay an impact fee per automobile based on the value of the vehicle. The impact fee is $100 for the Chrysler and $100 for the Oldsmobile. Our couples also must pay a tag fee of $20 per automobile and a title fee of $18 per automobile at the time of registration. Thereafter, on an annual basis, our couples must pay a tag fee per automobile.

ATLANTA

Atlanta has no local income tax but does levy a sales tax.

Most purchases are taxed at a rate of 6%. Major consumer categories taxed at a different rate: None. Major consumer categories which are exempt from sales tax include: Drugs and medical services.

In Fulton County, the property tax rate is .05073. Homes are assessed at 40% of market value. There are various exemptions off the different components of the property tax. Property tax does not cover garbage pickup; the additional sanitary service charge is approximately $180 per year.

Fulton County has a personal property tax rate of .05173. Personal property is assessed at 40% of depreciated value for boats, planes, RVs and campers; automobiles are assessed at 40% of NADA retail value. We've assumed automobiles are the only items our couples own that are subject to the personal property tax. ★Total tax burdens in Atlanta are about average overall.

SAVANNAH

Savannah has no local income tax but does levy a sales tax.

Most purchases are taxed at a rate of 6%. Major consumer categories taxed at a different rate: None. Major consumer categories which are exempt from sales tax include: Drugs and medical services.

Within the city limits of Savannah, the property tax rate is .05157. Homes are assessed at 40% of market value. There are various exemptions off the different components of the property tax. Property tax does not cover garbage pickup; the additional fee is approximately $180 per year.

Savannah has a personal property tax rate of .05187 for aircraft, boats and motors, which are assessed at 40% of depreciated market value.

There is a personal property tax rate of .04788 for automobiles, which are assessed at 40% of NADA retail value. We've assumed automobiles are the only items our couples own that are subject to the personal property tax.

★Total tax burdens in Savannah are lower than average for the $24,281 and $34,275 income categories and higher than average for the $68,098 income category.

HAWAII

Income	Home Value	Property Tax & Other Fees	Personal Property Tax & Auto Fees	Sales Tax	Local Income Tax	State Income Tax*	Total Tax	Rank From #1–#149
HONOLULU								
$24,281	$50,000	$100	$198	$559	–	($246)	$611	#5
	75,000	100	198	559	–	(246)	611	#4
	100,000	100	198	559	–	(246)	611	#4
$34,275	$75,000	$100	$198	$725	–	$253	$1,276	#4
	100,000	100	198	725	–	253	1,276	#4
	150,000	172	198	725	–	253	1,348	#3
$68,098	$150,000	$172	$198	$1,048	–	$2,885	$4,303	#20
	200,000	360	198	1,048	–	2,885	4,491	#12
	250,000	548	198	1,048	–	2,885	4,679	#8
	$300,000	$736	$198	$1,048	–	$2,885	$4,867	Not Ranked
	350,000	924	198	1,048	–	2,885	5,055	Not Ranked
	400,000	1,112	198	1,048	–	2,885	5,243	Not Ranked
KAHULUI								
$24,281	$50,000	$120	$155	$559	–	($246)	$588	#4
	75,000	120	155	559	–	(246)	588	#3
	100,000	130	155	559	–	(246)	598	#3
$34,275	$75,000	$120	$155	$725	–	$253	$1,253	#3
	100,000	130	155	725	–	253	1,263	#3
	150,000	305	155	725	–	253	1,438	#4
$68,098	$150,000	$305	$155	$1,048	–	$2,885	$4,393	#22
	200,000	480	155	1,048	–	2,885	4,568	#14
	250,000	655	155	1,048	–	2,885	4,743	#10

*Medical and food/excise tax credits are issued as a reduction of income tax due or as a refund if the credit is greater than the tax liability.

Hawaii has a state income tax and a state excise tax (sales tax).

The state income tax rate is graduated from 2% to 10% depending upon income bracket. For married couples filing jointly the rate is 2% on the first $3,000 of taxable income; the rate is 4% on the next $2,000 of taxable income; the rate is 6% on the next $2,000 of taxable income; the rate is 7.25% on the next $4,000 of taxable income; the rate is 8% on the next $10,000 of taxable income; the rate is 8.75% on the next $10,000 of taxable income; the rate is 9.5% on the next $10,000 of taxable income; and the rate is 10% on taxable income above $41,000.

In calculating the tax, there is no deduction for federal tax paid. Federal and state pensions are exempt. Private pensions are exempt if they do not include employee contributions. Social Security benefits are exempt. There is a $1,900 exemption from adjusted gross income for married couples filing jointly. There is a $1,040 personal exemption from adjusted gross income per person

and a $1,040 personal exemption from adjusted gross income per person age 65 or older.

Major tax credits or rebates include: Credit for income taxes paid to other states, which our couples do not qualify for; food/excise tax credit, which our couples do qualify for; and medical services excise tax credit, which our couples do qualify for.

The state excise tax rate is 4%. Although this tax is imposed on the seller (unlike a sales tax, which is imposed on the buyer), businesses customarily pass the tax on to the buyer.

Since car registration and renewal fees differ within the state, see city information for details.

HONOLULU

Honolulu has no local income tax and does not levy an additional excise tax.

Most purchases include the 4% state excise tax. Major consumer categories taxed at a different rate: None. Major consumer categories which are

exempt from excise tax include: Drugs.

Within the city limits of Honolulu, the property tax rate is .00392 on buildings and .00312 on land. Homes and land are assessed at 100% of market value. All properties are subject to a minimum tax of $100 per year. There is a homeowner's exemption that increases by age. For homeowners age 65-69, the exemption is $100,000. The exemption is applied first to the house value, but if the amount of the exemption exceeds the house value, the amount remaining is applied to the land. Property tax includes garbage pickup.

Honolulu has no personal property tax for individuals.

Our couples relocating to Honolulu must pay several fees per automobile at the time of registration, some of which are based on the weight of the vehicle. The total fee is approximately $104 for the Chrysler and $104 for the Oldsmobile. Thereafter, on an annual basis, our couples will pay a renewal fee per automobile.

★Total tax burdens in Honolulu are lower than average overall. Honolulu is a tax heaven in 7 of 9 income/home value categories.

KAHULUI

Kahului has no local income tax and does not levy an additional excise tax.

Most purchases include the 4% state excise tax. Major consumer categories taxed at a different rate: None. Major consumer categories which are exempt from excise tax include: Drugs.

Within the city limits of Kahului, the property tax rate is .00350. Homes are assessed at 100% of market value. All properties are subject to a minimum tax of $60 per year. There is a homeowner's exemption that increases by age. For homeowners age 60-69, the exemption is $80,000. Property tax does not cover garbage pickup; the additional fee is approximately $60 per year.

Kahului has no personal property tax for individuals.

Our couples relocating to Kahului must pay several fees per automobile at the time of registration, some of which are based on the weight of the vehicle. The total fee is approximately $75 for the Chrysler and $75 for the Oldsmobile. Thereafter, on an annual basis, our couples will pay a renewal fee per automobile.

★Total tax burdens in Kahului are lower than average overall. Kahului is a tax heaven in 7 of 9 income/home value categories.

IDAHO

Income	Home Value	Property Tax & Other Fees	Personal Property Tax & Auto Fees	Sales Tax	Local Income Tax	State Income Tax	Total Tax	Rank From #1–#149
BOISE								
$24,281	$50,000	$689	$109	$655	–	$46	$1,499	#37
	75,000	986	109	655	–	46	1,796	#38
	100,000	1,283	109	655	–	46	2,093	#38
$34,275	$75,000	$986	$109	$864	–	$570	$2,529	#64
	100,000	1,283	109	864	–	570	2,826	#62
	150,000	2,075	109	864	–	570	3,618	#67
$68,098	$150,000	$2,075	$109	$1,261	–	$3,060	$6,505	#102 (tie)
	200,000	3,064	109	1,261	–	3,060	7,494	#109
	250,000	4,054	109	1,261	–	3,060	8,484	#107
COEUR D'ALENE								
$24,281	$50,000	$750	$74	$655	–	$46	$1,525	#39
	75,000	1,068	74	655	–	46	1,843	#43
	100,000	1,385	74	655	–	46	2,160	#44
$34,275	$75,000	$1,068	$74	$864	–	$570	$2,576	#73
	100,000	1,385	74	864	–	570	2,893	#70
	150,000	2,231	74	864	–	570	3,739	#75
$68,098	$150,000	$2,231	$74	$1,261	–	$3,060	$6,626	#108
	200,000	3,288	74	1,261	–	3,060	7,683	#114
	250,000	4,345	74	1,261	–	3,060	8,740	#116

Idaho has a state income tax and a state sales tax.

The state income tax rate is graduated from 2% to 8.2% depending upon income bracket. For married couples filing jointly the rate is 2% on the first $2,000 of taxable income; the rate is 4% on the next $2,000 of taxable income; the rate is 4.5% on the next $2,000 of taxable income; the rate is 5.5% on the next $2,000 of taxable income; the rate is 6.5% on the next $2,000 of taxable income; the rate is 7.5% on the next $5,000 of taxable income; the rate is 7.8% on the next $25,000 of taxable income; and the rate is 8.2% on taxable income above $40,000.

In calculating the tax, there is no deduction for federal income tax paid. Federal pensions are not exempt; however, married couples filing jointly both age 65 or older qualify for up to a $20,304 deduction, minus any Social Security or Railroad retirement benefits, from their federal pension income. State and private pensions are not exempt. Social Security benefits are exempt. There is a $7,850 standard deduction from adjusted gross income for married couples filing jointly when both are age 65 or older and a $2,450 personal exemption per person from adjusted gross income.

There is a $10 excise tax per state income tax return.

Major tax credits or rebates include: Credit for income taxes paid to other states, grocery credit and credit for maintaining a home for someone over 65. Our couples qualify for the grocery credit but do not qualify for the other programs.

The state sales tax rate is 5%.

Since car registration and renewal fees differ within the state, see city information for details.

BOISE

Boise has no local income tax and does not levy an additional sales tax.

Most purchases are taxed at the state rate of 5%. Major consumer categories taxed at a different rate: None. Major consumer categories which are exempt from sales tax include: Drugs and medical services.

In the River's Run and Sea Pines areas of Boise, the property tax rate is .019795953. Homes are assessed at 100% of market value. There is a homeowner's exemption of 50% up to $50,000 off assessed value of home, not including the land value. Property tax does not include garbage pickup; the additional fee is approximately $95 per year.

Boise has a personal property tax rate of .019795953 in the River's Run and Sea Pines areas. Personal property is assessed at 100% of fair market value. Items subject to the tax include mobile homes. We've assumed our couples do not own any of the items subject to the personal property tax.

Our couples relocating to Boise must pay a registration fee of $36.48 for the Chrysler and $33.48 for the Oldsmobile, a title fee of $11 per automobile, a plate fee of $6 per automobile, miscellaneous fees of $3.25 per automobile, and county fees of $20 for the Chrysler and $18 for the Oldsmobile, at the time of registration. Thereafter, on an annual basis, our couples will pay a registration fee, county fee and miscellaneous fees, per automobile.

★Total tax burdens in Boise are lower than average for the $24,281 income category, about average for the $34,275 income category and higher than average for the $68,098 income category.

COEUR D'ALENE

Coeur d'Alene has no local income

tax and does not levy an additional sales tax.

Most purchases are taxed at the state rate of 5%. Major consumer categories taxed at a different rate: None. Major consumer categories which are exempt from sales tax include: Drugs and medical services.

In the downtown area of Coeur d'Alene, the property tax rate is .021146577. Homes are assessed at 100% of market value. There is a homeowner's exemption of 50% up to $50,000 off assessed value of home, not including the land value. Prop-

erty tax does not include garbage pickup; the additional fee is approximately $36 per year. Homeowners must also pay a solid waste fee of approximately $80 per year.

Coeur d'Alene has a personal property tax rate of .021146577 in the downtown area. Personal property is assessed at 100% of fair market value. Items subject to the tax include mobile homes. We've assumed our couples do not own any of the items subject to the personal property tax.

Our couples relocating to Coeur d'Alene must pay a registration fee of

$43.27 for the Chrysler and $40.02 for the Oldsmobile, a title fee of $8 per automobile, an inspection fee of $3 per automobile and a plate fee of $6 per automobile at the time of registration. Thereafter, on an annual basis, our couples will pay a registration fee per automobile.

★Total tax burdens in Coeur d'Alene are lower than average for the $24,281 income category, about average for the $34,275 income category and higher than average for the $68,098 income category.

ILLINOIS

Income	Home Value	Property Tax & Other Fees	Personal Property Tax & Auto Fees	Sales Tax	Local Income Tax	State Income Tax*	Total Tax	Rank From #1–#149
CHICAGO								
$24,281	$50,000	$918	$216	$999	–	$74	$2,207	#127
	75,000	1,701	216	999	–	35	2,951	#134
	100,000	2,484	216	999	–	–	3,699	#136
$34,275	$75,000	$1,701	$216	$1,334	–	$268	$3,519	#134
	100,000	2,484	216	1,334	–	229	4,263	#135
	150,000	4,051	216	1,334	–	150	5,751	#140
$68,098	$150,000	$4,051	$216	$2,030	–	$1,044	$7,341	#122
	200,000	5,617	216	2,030	–	966	8,829	#127
	250,000	7,183	216	2,030	–	888	10,317	#132
DECATUR								
$24,281	$50,000	$1,083	$96	$799	–	$74	$2,052	#106
	75,000	1,771	96	799	–	39	2,705	#122
	100,000	2,460	96	799	–	5	3,360	#127
$34,275	$75,000	$1,771	$96	$1,069	–	$272	$3,208	#120
	100,000	2,460	96	1,069	–	238	3,863	#125 (tie)
	150,000	3,837	96	1,069	–	169	5,171	#126
$68,098	$150,000	$3,837	$96	$1,635	–	$1,063	$6,631	#109
	200,000	5,214	96	1,635	–	994	7,939	#117
	250,000	6,591	96	1,635	–	925	9,247	#122

* Credit for property tax paid is issued as a reduction of income tax due.

Illinois has a state income tax and a state sales tax.

The state income tax rate is 3%. In calculating the tax, there is no deduction for federal income tax paid. Federal, state and private pensions are exempt. Social Security benefits are exempt. There is a $1,000 personal exemption from adjusted gross income per person and a $1,000 exemption from adjusted gross income per person for residents age 65 or older.

Major tax credits or rebates include: Credit for income taxes paid to other states, which our couples do not qualify for, and property tax credit, which our couples do qualify for.

The state sales tax rate is 6.25% but local governments can add to this amount.

Since car registration and renewal fees differ within the state, see city information for details.

CHICAGO

Chicago has no local income tax but does levy a sales tax.

Most purchases are taxed at a rate of 8.75%. Major consumer categories taxed at a different rate include: Drugs, which are taxed at a rate of 2%; food away from home, which is taxed at a rate of 9.75%; and groceries, which are taxed at a rate of 2%. Major consumer categories which are exempt from sales tax include: Medical services.

For most residents within the city limits of Chicago, the property tax rate is .09264. Homes are assessed at 16% of market value then multiplied by a state equalization factor of 2.1135. There is a homestead exemption of $4,500 off assessed value of the home available to all resident homeowners and a senior citizens exemption of $2,500 off assessed value of the home available to resident homeowners age 65 or older. Property tax includes garbage pickup, but some residents may live within special assessment districts and be subject to additional taxes for alleys and streets.

Chicago has no personal property tax for individuals.

Our couples relocating to Chicago must pay a registration fee of $48 per automobile, a title transfer fee of $13 per automobile and a wheel tax of $60 per automobile at the time of registration. Thereafter, on an annual basis, our couples will pay a registra-

tion fee and wheel tax per automobile.

★Total tax burdens in Chicago are higher than average overall. Chicago is a tax hell in 1 of 9 income/home value categories.

DECATUR

Decatur has no local income tax but does levy a sales tax.

Most purchases are taxed at a rate of 7.25%. Major consumer categories taxed at a different rate include: Drugs, which are taxed at a rate of 1%; and groceries, which are taxed at a rate of 1%. Major consumer categories which are exempt from sales tax include: Medical services.

For most residents within the city limits of Decatur, the property tax rate is .08262. Homes are assessed at 33.3% of market value. There is a homestead exemption of $3,500 off assessed value of the home available to all homeowners and a senior citizens exemption of $2,000 off assessed value of the home available to homeowners age 65 or older. Property tax does not cover garbage pickup; the additional fee is approximately $160 per year. Some residents may live within special assessment districts and be subject to additional taxes for drainage and sewer.

Decatur has no personal property tax for individuals.

Our couples relocating to Decatur must pay a registration fee of $48 per automobile and a title transfer fee of $13 per automobile at the time of registration. Thereafter, on an annual basis, our couples will pay a registration fee per automobile.

★Total tax burdens in Decatur are higher than average overall.

INDIANA

Income	Home Value	Property Tax & Other Fees	Personal Property Tax & Auto Fees	Sales Tax	Local Income Tax	State Income Tax	Total Tax	Rank From #1–#149
BLOOMINGTON								
$24,281	$50,000	$234	$532	$530	$121	$413	$1,830	#78
	75,000	535	532	530	121	413	2,131	#71
	100,000	642	532	530	121	413	2,238	#50
$34,275	$75,000	$535	$532	$712	$210	$715	$2,704	#83
	100,000	642	532	712	210	715	2,811	#61
	150,000	1,127	532	712	210	715	3,296	#47
$68,098	$150,000	$1,127	$532	$1,101	$528	$1,796	$5,084	#44
	200,000	1,516	532	1,101	528	1,796	5,473	#33
	250,000	1,578	532	1,101	528	1,796	5,535	#18
INDIANAPOLIS								
$24,281	$50,000	$882	$532	$542	$85	$413	$2,454	#138
	75,000	1,307	532	542	85	413	2,879	#131
	100,000	1,732	532	542	85	413	3,304	#125
$34,275	$75,000	$1,307	$532	$729	$147	$715	$3,430	#128
	100,000	1,732	532	729	147	715	3,855	#123
	150,000	2,582	532	729	147	715	4,705	#115
$68,098	$150,000	$2,582	$532	$1,128	$370	$1,796	$6,408	#99
	200,000	3,432	532	1,128	370	1,796	7,258	#101
	250,000	4,282	532	1,128	370	1,796	8,108	#96

Indiana has a state income tax and a state sales tax.

The state income tax rate is 3.4%. In calculating the tax, there is no deduction for federal income tax paid. Federal pensions are exempt up to $2,000. State and private pensions are not exempt. Social Security benefits are exempt. There is a $1,000 exemption per person and an additional $1,000 exemption per person for persons age 65 or older.

Major tax credits or rebates include: Credit for income taxes paid to other states, credit for local taxes paid outside of state, unified tax credit for the elderly, renter's deduction, college credit, solar and wind energy carryover credit. Our couples do not qualify for these programs.

The state sales tax rate is 5%.

Our couples relocating to the cities listed below must pay an excise fee based on year and MSRP of each automobile and a surtax which is 10% of the excise fee per automobile. The excise fee is $312 for the Chrysler and $224 for the Oldsmobile. The surtax is $31.20 for the Chrysler and $22.40 for the Oldsmobile. Our couples also pay $12.75 per automobile for license plates and $5 per automo-bile for a title at the time of registration. Thereafter, on an annual basis, our couples will pay an excise fee, a surtax and a plate fee, per automobile.

BLOOMINGTON

Bloomington has a local income tax but does not levy an additional sales tax.

The local income tax rate is 1% of Indiana taxable income calculated on the state income tax return.

Most purchases are taxed at the state rate of 5%. Major consumer categories taxed at a different rate: None. Major consumer categories which are exempt from sales tax include: Drugs, groceries and medical services.

In the area of Bloomington Township, property taxes are determined in a complex calculation which takes into account discounted reproduction cost and depreciation. Note: The tax assessor's office declined to provide property tax estimates for our couples and independent calculation is not possible. Rates shown were provided for an earlier edition of this publication and may no longer be valid. There is a standard deduction of $1,000 off assessed value for homeowners having a mortgage of $1,000 or more. There is a homestead exemption of $2,000 off assessed value for homeowners, plus a variable homestead credit off the net tax due. There is an elderly exemption of $1,000 off assessed value for persons age 65 or older with a federal adjusted gross income of less than $15,000 and with property assessed at $19,000 or less. The standard deduction is not allowed if the elderly exemption is taken. Property tax does not cover garbage pickup; the additional fee is approximately $104 per year.

Bloomington has a personal property tax based on depreciated value set by the state of Indiana. Items subject to the tax include boats without motors, boat trailers over 3,000 pounds, trucks over 11,000 pounds, RVs, ATVs, truck campers, travel trailers and motor homes. The tax does not apply to automobiles. We've assumed our couples do not own any of the items subject to the personal property tax.

★Total tax burdens in Bloomington are about average for the $24,281 and $34,275 income categories and lower than average for the $68,098 income category.

INDIANAPOLIS

Indianapolis has a local income tax but does not levy an additional sales tax.

The local income tax rate is .7% of Indiana taxable income calculated on the state income tax return.

Most purchases are taxed at the state rate of 5%. Major consumer categories taxed at a different rate include: Food away from home, which is taxed at a rate of 6%. Major consumer categories which are exempt from sales tax: Drugs, groceries and medical services.

For most residents within the area of Lawrence Township, property taxes are determined in a complex calculation which takes into account dis-counted reproduction cost and depreciation. Property tax amounts shown are estimates from the assessor's office. There is a standard deduction of $1,000 off assessed value for all home-owners having a mortgage of $1,000 or more. There is a homestead exemption of $2,000 off assessed value for homeowners, plus a variable homestead credit off the net tax due. There is an elderly exemption of $1,000 off assessed value for persons age 65 or older with a federal adjusted gross income of less than $15,000 and with property assessed at $19,000 or less. The standard deduction is not allowed if the elderly exemption is taken. Property tax does not cover garbage pickup; the additional fee is approximately $32 per year.

Indianapolis has a personal property tax based on depreciated value set by the state of Indiana. Items subject to the tax include boats without motors, boat trailers over 3,000 pounds, trucks over 11,000 pounds, RVs, ATVs, truck campers, travel trailers, snowmobiles and motor homes. The tax does not apply to automobiles. We've assumed our couples do not own any of the items subject to the personal property tax.

★Total tax burdens in Indianapolis are higher than average for the $24,281 and $34,275 income categories and about average for the $68,098 income category.

IOWA

Income	Home Value	Property Tax & Other Fees	Personal Property Tax & Auto Fees	Sales Tax	Local Income Tax	State Income Tax	Total Tax	Rank From #1–#149
CEDAR RAPIDS								
$24,281	$50,000	$1,060	$365	$574	–	$444	$2,443	#136
	75,000	1,622	365	574	–	444	3,005	#137
	100,000	2,185	365	574	–	444	3,568	#132
$34,275	$75,000	$1,622	$365	$754	–	$974	$3,715	#137
	100,000	2,185	365	754	–	974	4,278	#136
	150,000	3,309	365	754	–	974	5,402	#133
$68,098	$150,000	$3,309	$365	$1,150	–	$3,406	$8,230	#135
	200,000	4,433	365	1,150	–	3,406	9,354	#135
	250,000	5,558	365	1,150	–	3,406	10,479	#133
DES MOINES								
$24,281	$50,000	$1,389	$365	$574	–	$444	$2,772	#146
	75,000	2,140	365	574	–	444	3,523	#147
	100,000	2,890	365	574	–	444	4,273	#147
$34,275	$75,000	$2,140	$365	$754	–	$974	$4,233	#147
	100,000	2,890	365	754	–	974	4,983	#147
	150,000	4,392	365	754	–	974	6,485	#146
$68,098	$150,000	$4,392	$365	$1,150	–	$3,406	$9,313	#144
	200,000	5,893	365	1,150	–	3,406	10,814	#144
	250,000	7,394	365	1,150	–	3,406	12,315	#143

Iowa has a state income tax and a state sales tax.

The state income tax rate is graduated from .40% to 9.98%, depending upon income bracket. For all filers the rate is .40% on the first $1,060 of taxable income; the rate is .80% on the next $1,060 of taxable income; the rate is 2.7% on the next $2,120 of taxable income; the rate is 5% on the next $5,300 of taxable income; the rate is 6.8% on the next $6,360 of taxable income; the rate is 7.2% on the next $5,300 of taxable income; the rate is 7.55% on the next $10,600 of taxable income; the rate is 8.8% on the next $15,900 of taxable income; and the rate is 9.98% on taxable income above $47,700.

In calculating the tax, there is a deduction from adjusted gross income for federal income tax paid. Federal, state and private pensions are not exempt. Social Security benefits subject to federal tax are not exempt. There is a $3,310 standard deduction from adjusted gross income for married couples filing jointly. There is a $40 credit against tax for married couples filing jointly and an additional $20 credit against tax for each person age 65 or older.

There is also an alternate method for income tax calculation which may yield a lower tax due for some taxpayers, particularly lower income taxpayers.

Major tax credits or rebates include: Credit for income taxes paid to other states, child-care credit, research activities credit, motor vehicle fuel credit, Iowa senior citizens and disabled persons rent reimbursement and Iowa senior citizens and disabled persons property tax credit claim. Our couples do not qualify for these programs.

The state sales tax rate is 5% but local governments can add to this amount.

Our couples relocating to the cities listed below must pay a registration fee based on year, make and model of each automobile. The registration fee is $201 for the Chrysler and $164 for the Oldsmobile. Our couples also pay $15 per automobile for a title at the time of registration. Thereafter, on an annual basis, our couples will pay a licensing renewal fee per automobile.

CEDAR RAPIDS

Cedar Rapids has no local income tax and does not levy an additional sales tax.

Most purchases are taxed at the state rate of 5%. Major consumer categories taxed at a different rate: None. Major consumer categories which are exempt from sales tax include: Drugs and groceries.

Within the Cedar Rapids School District, the property tax rate is .03305153. Homes are assessed at 68.0404% of market value. There is a homestead exemption of $4,850 off assessed value for all homeowners. Property tax does not cover garbage pickup; the additional fee is approximately $96 per year. Some residents may also live within special assessment districts and be subject to additional charges such as gravel, weed-cutting and paving.

Cedar Rapids has no personal property tax for individuals.

★Total tax burdens in Cedar Rapids are higher than average overall.

DES MOINES

Des Moines has no local income tax and does not levy an additional sales tax.

Most purchases are taxed at the state rate of 5%. Major consumer categories taxed at a different rate:

None. Major consumer categories which are exempt from sales tax include: Drugs and groceries.

Within the Des Moines School District, the property tax rate is .04412684. Homes are assessed at 68.0404% of market value. There is a homestead exemption of $4,850 off assessed value for all homeowners.

Property tax on new homes (not including land values) is abated for five years. We assumed our couples did not buy new homes. Property tax does not cover garbage pickup; the additional fee is approximately $102 per year. Some residents may also live within special assessment districts and be subject to additional charges such as gravel, weed-cutting and paving.

Des Moines has no personal property tax for individuals.

★Total tax burdens in Des Moines are higher than average overall. Des Moines is a tax hell in all 9 income/home value categories.

KANSAS

Income	Home Value	Property Tax & Other Fees	Personal Property Tax & Auto Fees	Sales Tax	Local Income Tax	State Income Tax	Total Tax	Rank From #1–#149
TOPEKA								
$24,281	$50,000	$1,108	$920	$860	–	$207	$3,095	#149
	75,000	1,595	920	860	–	207	3,582	#148
	100,000	2,082	920	860	–	207	4,069	#145
$34,275	$75,000	$1,595	$920	$1,114	–	$519	$4,148	#146
	100,000	2,082	920	1,114	–	519	4,635	#142
	150,000	3,057	920	1,114	–	519	5,610	#137
$68,098	$150,000	$3,057	$920	$1,612	–	$2,688	$8,277	#136
	200,000	4,031	920	1,612	–	2,688	9,251	#133
	250,000	5,006	920	1,612	–	2,688	10,226	#130
WICHITA								
$24,281	$50,000	$786	$689	$825	–	$207	$2,507	#139
	75,000	1,108	689	825	–	207	2,829	#129
	100,000	1,431	689	825	–	207	3,152	#120
$34,275	$75,000	$1,108	$689	$1,069	–	$519	$3,385	#125
	100,000	1,431	689	1,069	–	519	3,708	#118
	150,000	2,077	689	1,069	–	519	4,354	#105
$68,098	$150,000	$2,077	$689	$1,546	–	$2,688	$7,000	#118
	200,000	2,722	689	1,546	–	2,688	7,645	#113
	250,000	3,368	689	1,546	–	2,688	8,291	#104

Kansas has a state income tax and a state sales tax.

The state income tax rate is graduated from 3.5% to 6.45% depending upon income bracket. For married couples filing jointly with taxable income up to $30,000, the rate is 3.5%; up to $60,000 the tax is 6.25% of the amount above $30,000 plus $1,050; above $60,000, the tax is 6.45% of the amount above $60,000 plus $2,925.

In calculating the tax, there is no deduction for federal income tax paid. Federal and state pensions are exempt. Private pensions are not exempt. Social Security benefits subject to federal tax are not exempt. There is a $2,000 personal exemption per person from adjusted gross income. There is also a $6,200 standard deduction from adjusted gross income for married couples filing jointly when both are age 65 or older.

Major tax credits or rebates include: Credit for income taxes paid to other states, child-care credit and homestead and food sales act rebate. Our couples do not qualify for these programs.

The state sales tax rate is 4.9% but local governments can add to this amount.

Our couples relocating to the cities listed below must pay a registration fee of $27.25 per automobile and a title fee of $7.50 per automobile at the time of registration. Thereafter, on an annual basis, our couples will pay a registration fee per automobile.

TOPEKA

Topeka has no local income tax but does levy a sales tax.

Most purchases are taxed at a rate of 6.15%. Major consumer categories taxed at a different rate: None. Major consumer categories which are exempt from sales tax include: Drugs.

In the Topeka Public School District, the property tax rate is .169479. Homes are assessed at 11.5% of market value. Property tax does not cover garbage pickup; the additional fee is approximately $99 per year. There is also a storm water utility fee of approximately $34 per year.

Topeka has a personal property tax rate of .169479 on boats, RVs and campers within the Topeka Public School District. These items are assessed at 30% of market value. Topeka has a personal property tax rate of .144156 on automobiles, small trucks, motor homes and motorcycles. These items are assessed at 30% of

estimated dealer cost. The assessed value decreases by 16% each year until the item is 15 years old. The tax is then $12 per year.

★Total tax burdens in Topeka are higher than average overall. Topeka is a tax hell in 5 of 9 income/home value categories.

WICHITA

Wichita has no local income tax but does levy a sales tax.

Most purchases are taxed at a rate of 5.9%. Major consumer categories taxed at a different rate: None. Major consumer categories which are exempt from sales tax include: Drugs.

In the Wichita School District, the property tax rate is .112281. Homes are assessed at 11.5% of market value. Property tax does not cover garbage pickup; the additional fee is approximately $120 per year. There is also a storm water utility fee of approximately $20 per year.

Wichita has a personal property tax rate of .112281 on boats, RVs and campers within the Wichita School District. These items are assessed at 30% of market value. Wichita has a personal property tax rate of .105659 on automobiles, small trucks, motor homes and motorcycles. These items are assessed at 30% of estimated dealer cost. The assessed value decreases by 16% each year until the item is 15 years old. The tax is then $12 per year.

★Total tax burdens in Wichita are higher than average overall.

KENTUCKY

Income	Home Value	Property Tax & Other Fees	Personal Property Tax & Auto Fees	Sales Tax	Local Income Tax	State Income Tax	Total Tax	Rank From #1–#149
LEXINGTON								
$24,281	$50,000	$279	$266	$636	$57	$518	$1,756	#70
	75,000	527	266	636	57	518	2,004	#59
	100,000	775	266	636	57	518	2,252	#52
$34,275	$75,000	$527	$266	$855	$214	$1,142	$3,004	#109
	100,000	775	266	855	214	1,142	3,252	#96 (tie)
	150,000	1,270	266	855	214	1,142	3,747	#77
$68,098	$150,000	$1,270	$266	$1,321	$830	$3,051	$6,738	#112
	200,000	1,765	266	1,321	830	3,051	7,233	#99
	250,000	2,260	266	1,321	830	3,051	7,728	#86
MURRAY								
$24,281	$50,000	$409	$319	$636	–	$518	$1,882	#88
	75,000	676	319	636	–	518	2,149	#75
	100,000	943	319	636	–	518	2,416	#66
$34,275	$75,000	$676	$319	$855	–	$1,142	$2,992	#106 (tie)
	100,000	943	319	855	–	1,142	3,259	#99
	150,000	1,477	319	855	–	1,142	3,793	#81
$68,098	$150,000	$1,477	$319	$1,321	–	$3,051	$6,168	#90
	200,000	2,011	319	1,321	–	3,051	6,702	#82
	250,000	2,545	319	1,321	–	3,051	7,236	#74 (tie)

Kentucky has a state income tax and a state sales tax.

The state income tax rate is graduated from 2% to 6% depending upon income bracket. For all filers the rate is 2% on the first $3,000 of taxable income; the rate is 3% on the next $1,000 of taxable income; the rate is 4% on the next $1,000 of taxable income; the rate is 5% on the next $3,000 of taxable income; and the rate is 6% on taxable income above $8,000.

In calculating the tax, there is no deduction for federal income tax paid. Federal pensions are exempt. Kentucky state and local pensions are exempt. An exemption of private pensions is being phased in and by 1998 private pension income up to $35,000 will be exempt. Social Security benefits are exempt. There is a $650 standard deduction for married couples filing jointly, a $40 credit against tax for married couples filing jointly and a $40 credit against tax for each person of minimum age 65. There is a low income credit after all other tax credits have been deducted for persons with an adjusted gross income up to $25,000.

Major tax credits or rebates include: Credit for income taxes paid to other states, and child and dependent care credit. Our couples do not qualify for these programs.

The state sales tax rate is 6%.

Since car registration and renewal fees differ within the state, see city information for details.

LEXINGTON

Lexington has a local income tax but does not levy an additional sales tax.

The local income tax is composed of an occupational license fee of 2.5% and a school tax of .5%, each of which is applied to wages, salaries and self-employment income.

In calculating the tax, federal, state and private pensions are exempt. Social Security benefits are exempt.

In calculating the occupational license fee the first $3,000 of earned income is exempt for taxpayers age 65 or older.

Most purchases are taxed at the state rate of 6%. Major consumer categories taxed at a different rate: None. Major consumer categories which are exempt from sales tax include: Drugs, groceries and medical services.

Within the city limits of Lexington in District 1, the property tax rate is .009905. Homes are assessed at 100% of market value. There is a homestead exemption of $21,800 off assessed value for homeowners age 65 or older. Property tax includes garbage pickup.

Lexington has a personal property tax rate of .01123 in District 1. Personal property is assessed at 100% of fair cash value. Items subject to the tax include automobiles, boats, motorcycles and motor homes.

Our couples relocating to Lexington must pay a road usage tax on automobiles which is 6% of the current market value and is paid when a vehicle is initially registered in the state. If a vehicle owner paid a usage or sales tax in another state when the automobile was purchased which is equal to or greater than the Kentucky usage tax, there is no additional charge. If a vehicle owner paid a usage or sales tax to another state which is less than the Kentucky usage tax, they are required to pay the difference. We've assumed our couples have paid tax equal to or greater than the usage tax. Our couples also pay $17 for license plates per automobile, $6 per automobile for a title, $4 per automobile for a title application preparation fee and $3

per automobile for an inspection fee at the time of registration. Thereafter, on an annual basis, our couples will pay a plate fee per automobile.
★Total tax burdens in Lexington are about average overall.

MURRAY

Murray has no local income tax and does not levy an additional sales tax.

Most purchases are taxed at the state rate of 6%. Major consumer categories taxed at a different rate: None. Major consumer categories which are exempt from sales tax include: Drugs, groceries and medical services.

Within the city limits of Murray in the Murray Independent School District, the property tax rate is .01068.

Homes are assessed at 100% of market value. There is a homestead exemption of $21,800 off assessed value for homeowners age 65 or older. Property tax does not include garbage pickup; the additional fee for homeowners age 65 or older is approximately $108 per year.

Murray has a personal property tax rate of .013797 in the Murray Independent School District. Personal property is assessed at 100% of NADA average retail value. Items subject to the tax include automobiles, boats, motorcycles and motor homes.

Our couples relocating to Murray must pay a road usage tax on automobiles which is 6% of the current market value and is paid when a vehicle is initially registered in the state. If a

vehicle owner paid a usage or sales tax in another state when the automobile was purchased which is equal to or greater than the Kentucky usage tax, there is no additional charge. If a vehicle owner paid a usage or sales tax to another state which is less than the Kentucky usage tax, they are required to pay the difference. We've assumed our couples have paid tax equal to or greater than the usage tax. Our couples also pay $14 for license plates per automobile, $9 per automobile for a title and $3 per automobile for an inspection fee at the time of registration. Thereafter, on an annual basis, our couples will pay a plate fee per automobile.
★Total tax burdens in Murray are about average overall.

LOUISIANA

Income	Home Value	Property Tax & Other Fees	Personal Property Tax & Auto Fees	Sales Tax	Local Income Tax	State Income Tax	Total Tax	Rank From #1–#149
BATON ROUGE								
$24,281	$50,000	$112	$20	$1,038	–	–	$1,170	#12
	75,000	134	20	1,038	–	–	1,192	#8
	100,000	384	20	1,038	–	–	1,442	#8
$34,275	$75,000	$134	$20	$1,368	–	$58	$1,580	#7
	100,000	384	20	1,368	–	58	1,830	#8
	150,000	884	20	1,368	–	58	2,330	#10
$68,098	$150,000	$884	$20	$2,004	–	$799	$3,707	#7
	200,000	1,384	20	2,004	–	799	4,207	#7
	250,000	1,884	20	2,004	–	799	4,707	#9
NEW ORLEANS								
$24,281	$50,000	$172	$289	$1,090	–	–	$1,551	#43 (tie)
	75,000	199	289	1,090	–	–	1,578	#17
	100,000	600	289	1,090	–	–	1,979	#28
$34,275	$75,000	$199	$289	$1,443	–	$58	$1,989	#20
	100,000	600	289	1,443	–	58	2,390	#26
	150,000	1,403	289	1,443	–	58	3,193	#38
$68,098	$150,000	$1,403	$289	$2,153	–	$799	$4,644	#32
	200,000	2,206	289	2,153	–	799	5,447	#32
	250,000	3,009	289	2,153	–	799	6,250	#36

Louisiana has a state income tax and a state sales tax.

The state income tax rate is graduated from 2% to 6% depending upon income bracket. For married couples filing jointly the rate is 2% on the first $20,000 of taxable income; the rate is 4% on the next $80,000 of taxable income; and the rate is 6% on taxable income above $100,000.

In calculating the tax, there is a deduction for federal income tax paid. Federal, state of Louisiana and local government pensions are exempt. Social Security benefits are exempt. There is an exclusion of up to $6,000 of all other pension income for each person age 65 or older. There is a $9,000 standard deduction for married couples filing jointly and a $1,000 personal exemption per person, both applied to income subject to tax at 2% for persons age 65 or older.

Major tax credits or rebates include: Credit for income taxes paid to other states and credit for 10% of the allowable credits on the federal return. Our couples do not qualify for these programs.

The state sales tax rate is 4% but local governments can add to this amount.

Since car registration fees differ within the state, see city information for details.

BATON ROUGE

Baton Rouge has no local income tax but does levy a sales tax.

Most purchases are taxed at a rate of 8%. Major consumer categories taxed at a different rate include: Drugs, which are taxed at a rate of 3%; and groceries, which are taxed at a rate of 7%. Major consumer categories which are exempt from sales tax include: Medical services.

Within the city limits of Baton Rouge, the property tax rate is .10004. Homes are assessed at 10% of market value. There is a homestead exemption of $75,000 off market value which does not apply to the city portion of property taxes and which is available to all homeowners. Property tax does not include garbage pickup; the additional fee is approximately $68 per year.

Baton Rouge has no personal property tax for individuals.

Our couples relocating to Baton Rouge must pay a use tax based on 75% of the NADA current market value of each automobile. The tax rate is 8%, however, the state will give a credit to new residents of up to 4% based on sales tax previously paid to another state. We've assumed a 4% credit on the use tax since this is the most common credit given. The use tax would be approximately $367 for the Chrysler and $263 for the Oldsmobile. Our couples also pay $20 for plates per automobile, $19 per automobile for a title and $6 per automobile for a handling fee at the time of registration. Thereafter, every 2 years, our couples will pay a plate fee per automobile.

★Total tax burdens in Baton Rouge are lower than average overall. Baton Rouge is a tax heaven in 8 of 9 income/home value categories.

NEW ORLEANS

New Orleans has no local income tax but does levy a sales tax.

Most purchases are taxed at a rate of 9%. Major consumer categories taxed at a different rate include: Drugs and groceries, which are taxed at a rate of 4.5%. Major consumer categories which are exempt from sales tax include: Medical services.

For most residents within the city limits of New Orleans, the property tax rate is .16062. Homes are assessed at 10% of market value. There is a homestead exemption of $75,000 off market value which does not apply to the police and fire service portions of property taxes and which is available to all homeowners. Property tax does not include garbage pickup; the additional fee is approximately $120 per year.

New Orleans has a personal property tax rate of .1493. Personal property is assessed at 15% of the value calculated by the parish assessors. Items subject to the tax include automobiles, motorcycles and trucks.

Our couples relocating to New Orleans must pay a use tax based on 75% of the NADA current market value of each automobile. The tax rate is 9%, however, the state will give a credit to new residents of up to 4% based on sales tax previously paid to another state. We've assumed a 4% credit on the use tax since this is the most common credit given. The use tax would be approximately $458 for the Chrysler and $328 for the Oldsmobile. Our couples also pay $20 for plates per automobile, $19 per automobile for a title and $6 per automobile for a handling fee at the time of registration. Thereafter, every 2 years, our couples will pay a plate fee per automobile.

★Total tax burdens in New Orleans are lower than average overall.

MAINE

Income	Home Value	Property Tax & Other Fees	Personal Property Tax & Auto Fees	Sales Tax	Local Income Tax	State Income Tax	Total Tax	Rank From #1–#149
AUGUSTA								
$24,281	$50,000	$1,085	$449	$647	–	$82	$2,263	#131
	75,000	1,628	449	647	–	82	2,806	#127
	100,000	1,841	449	647	–	82	3,019	#115
$34,275	$75,000	$1,628	$449	$871	–	$377	$3,325	#123
	100,000	2,170	449	871	–	377	3,867	#128
	150,000	3,255	449	871	–	377	4,952	#121
$68,098	$150,000	$3,255	$449	$1,349	–	$2,693	$7,746	#129
	200,000	4,340	449	1,349	–	2,693	8,831	#128
	250,000	5,425	449	1,349	–	2,693	9,916	#126
CAMDEN								
$24,281	$50,000	$648	$449	$647	–	$82	$1,826	#77
	75,000	972	449	647	–	82	2,150	#76
	100,000	1,295	449	647	–	82	2,473	#73
$34,275	$75,000	$972	$449	$871	–	$377	$2,669	#78
	100,000	1,295	449	871	–	377	2,992	#76 (tie)
	150,000	1,942	449	871	–	377	3,639	#69
$68,098	$150,000	$1,942	$449	$1,349	–	$2,693	$6,433	#100
	200,000	2,589	449	1,349	–	2,693	7,080	#91
	250,000	3,236	449	1,349	–	2,693	7,727	#85

Maine has a state income tax and a state sales tax.

The state income tax rate is graduated from 2% to 8.5% depending upon income bracket. For married couples filing jointly, the rate is 2% on the first $8,250 of taxable income; the rate is 4.5% on the next $8,250 of taxable income; the rate is 7% on the next $16,500 of taxable income; and the rate is 8.5% on taxable income above $33,000.

In calculating the tax, there is no deduction for federal income tax paid. Federal, state and private pensions are not exempt. Social Security benefits are exempt. There is a $2,100 personal exemption per person from adjusted gross income. There is a $7,850 standard deduction from adjusted gross income for married couples filing jointly when both are age 65 or older.

Major tax credits or rebates include: Credit for income taxes paid to other states, retirement and disability credit, child care credit, elderly tax and rent refund program, and elderly low-cost drug program. Our couples do not qualify for these programs.

The state sales tax rate is 6%.

Maine has a personal property tax which is called a vehicle excise tax and the rate is based on the age of the vehicle. Vehicles are assessed at 100% of original factory list price. Items subject to the tax include autos, boats, mobile homes, RVs and trucks.

Our couples relocating to the cities listed below must pay a registration fee of $22 per automobile and a title fee of $10 per automobile at the time of registration. Thereafter, on an annual basis, our couples will pay a registration fee per automobile.

AUGUSTA

Augusta has no local income tax and does not levy an additional sales tax.

Most purchases are taxed at the state rate of 6%. Major consumer categories taxed at a different rate include: Food away from home, which is taxed at a rate of 7%. Major consumer categories which are exempt from sales tax include: Drugs, groceries and medical services.

Within the city limits of Augusta, the property tax rate is .02170. Homes are assessed at 100% of market value. There is a property tax rebate for homeowners with a household income of up to $25,800 based on amount of property taxes paid. Property tax includes garbage pickup.

★Total tax burdens in Augusta are higher than average overall.

CAMDEN

Camden has no local income tax and does not levy an additional sales tax.

Most purchases are taxed at the state rate of 6%. Major consumer categories taxed at a different rate include: Food away from home, which is taxed at a rate of 7%. Major consumer categories which are exempt from sales tax include: Drugs, groceries and medical services.

Within the city limits of Camden, the property tax rate is .01294. Homes are assessed at 100% of market value. There is a property tax rebate for homeowners with a household income of up to $25,800 based on amount of property taxes paid. According to assessor's office, there is no garbage pickup in Camden. Residents must take garbage to a transfer station for removal.

★Total tax burdens in Camden are about average overall.

MARYLAND

Income	Home Value	Property Tax & Other Fees	Personal Property Tax & Auto Fees	Sales Tax	Local Income Tax	State Income Tax	Total Tax	Rank From #1–#149
BALTIMORE								
$24,281	$50,000	$1,212	$70	$530	$27	$53	$1,892	#90 (tie)
	75,000	1,365	70	530	27	53	2,045	#64
	100,000	1,365	70	530	27	53	2,045	#32
$34,275	$75,000	$1,818	$70	$712	$272	$544	$3,416	#127
	100,000	2,265	70	712	272	544	3,863	#125 (tie)
	150,000	3,636	70	712	272	544	5,234	#127
$68,098	$150,000	$3,636	$70	$1,101	$1,092	$2,184	$8,083	#132
	200,000	4,848	70	1,101	1,092	2,184	9,295	#134
	250,000	6,060	70	1,101	1,092	2,184	10,507	#134
OCEAN CITY								
$24,281	$50,000	$628	$70	$530	$16	$53	$1,297	#17
	75,000	942	70	530	16	53	1,611	#23
	100,000	1,256	70	530	16	53	1,925	#24
$34,275	$75,000	$942	$70	$712	$163	$544	$2,431	#56
	100,000	1,256	70	712	163	544	2,745	#53
	150,000	1,884	70	712	163	544	3,373	#55
$68,098	$150,000	$1,884	$70	$1,101	$655	$2,184	$5,894	#78
	200,000	2,512	70	1,101	655	2,184	6,522	#75
	250,000	3,140	70	1,101	655	2,184	7,150	#72

Maryland has a state income tax and a state sales tax.

The state income tax rate is graduated from 2% to 6% depending upon income bracket. For married couples filing jointly, the rate is 2% on the first $1,000 of taxable income; the rate is 3% on the next $1,000 of taxable income; the rate is 4% on the next $1,000 of taxable income; the rate is 5% on the next $147,000 of taxable income; and the rate is 6% on taxable income above $150,000.

In calculating the tax, there is no deduction for federal income tax paid. There is a federal, state and private pension income exclusion of up to $13,600 for persons age 65 or older. Social Security benefits are exempt. There is a $1,200 personal exemption per person from adjusted gross income and a $1,000 personal exemption per person from adjusted gross income for people age 65 or older. There is a variable standard deduction from adjusted gross income for married couples filing jointly that is based on income. There is also a $1,200 two-income deduction for married couples filing jointly if any income, including interest income, is earned by both people.

Major tax credits or rebates include: Credit for income taxes paid to other states, earned income credit and child care subtraction modification. Our couples do not qualify for these programs.

The state sales tax rate is 5%.

Our couples relocating to the cities listed below may have to pay an excise titling tax per automobile depending on the amount of tax paid in the state in which the vehicle was purchased. If a vehicle owner paid a sales tax in another state when the automobile was purchased which is equal to or greater than the Maryland sales tax, the excise titling tax is $100. If a vehicle owner paid a sales tax to another state which is less than the Maryland sales tax, they are required to pay the difference, unless the vehicle is valued at less than $2,000, in which case the 5% rate will apply. Vehicles over 7 years old will be valued at a minimum of $500. Our couples also pay a registration fee of $70 per automobile and a title fee of $15 per automobile at the time of registration. Thereafter, our couples will pay a registration fee of $70 per automobile every two years.

BALTIMORE

Baltimore has a local income tax but does not levy an additional sales tax.

The local income tax is 50% of the state income tax due.

Most purchases are taxed at the state rate of 5%. Major consumer categories taxed at a different rate: None. Major consumer categories which are exempt from sales tax include: Drugs, medical services and groceries.

Within the city limits of Baltimore, the property tax rate is .0606. Homes are assessed at 40% of market value. There is a homeowner's property tax credit for property taxes that exceed a percentage of a homeowner's gross income. There is an exemption of all additions made to a home due to health reasons. There is also a homestead property tax credit available if an appraisal results in an increase of more than 10% on the state portion or 4% on the city portion of the assessed value from the prior year. Property tax includes garbage pickup.

Baltimore has no personal property tax for individuals.

★Total tax burdens in Baltimore are about average for the $24,281 income category and higher than average for the $34,275 and $68,098 income categories.

OCEAN CITY

Ocean City has a local income tax but does not levy an additional sales tax.

The local income tax is 30% of the state income tax due.

Most purchases are taxed at the state rate of 5%. Major consumer categories taxed at a different rate: None. Major consumer categories which are exempt from sales tax include: Drugs, medical services and groceries.

Within the city limits of Ocean City, the property tax rate is .0314. Homes are assessed at 40% of market value. There is a homeowner's property tax credit for property taxes that exceed a percentage of a homeowner's gross income. There is an exemption of all additions made to a home due to health reasons. There is also a homestead property tax credit available if an appraisal results in an increase of more than 10% on the state portion or 10% on the city portion of the assessed value from the prior year. Property tax includes garbage pickup.

Ocean City has no personal property tax for individuals.

★Total tax burdens in Ocean City are lower than average for the $24,281 and $34,275 income categories and about average for the $68,098 income category.

MASSACHUSETTS

Income	Home Value	Property Tax & Other Fees	Personal Property Tax & Auto Fees	Sales Tax	Local Income Tax	State Income Tax*	Total Tax	Rank From #1–#149
BOSTON								
$24,281	$50,000	$290	$186	$478	–	$415	$1,369	#23
	75,000	637	186	478	–	415	1,716	#31
	100,000	983	186	478	–	415	2,062	#33
$34,275	$75,000	$637	$186	$618	–	$1,087	$2,528	#63
	100,000	983	186	618	–	1,087	2,874	#69
	150,000	1,676	186	618	–	1,087	3,567	#62
$68,098	$150,000	$1,676	$186	$986	–	$2,905	$5,753	#73
	200,000	2,369	186	986	–	2,905	6,446	#70
	250,000	3,062	186	986	–	2,905	7,139	#71
CAPE COD								
$24,281	$50,000	$770	$186	$478	–	$415	$1,849	#80
	75,000	1,040	186	478	–	415	2,119	#70
	100,000	1,311	186	478	–	415	2,390	#65
$34,275	$75,000	$1,040	$186	$618	–	$1,087	$2,931	#101
	100,000	1,311	186	618	–	1,087	3,202	#90
	150,000	1,853	186	618	–	1,087	3,744	#76
$68,098	$150,000	$1,853	$186	$986	–	$2,905	$5,930	#79
	200,000	2,394	186	986	–	2,905	6,471	#73
	250,000	2,936	186	986	–	2,905	7,013	#68

Massachusetts has a state income tax and a state sales tax.

There are two state income tax rates depending upon type of income. For all filers with Part A income (interest not derived from a Massachusetts bank, dividends, net capital gains), the rate is 12%. For all filers with Part B income (earned income and interest earned from a Massachusetts bank), the rate is 5.95%.

In calculating the tax, there is no deduction for federal income tax paid. There is a deduction of up to $2,000 per person for amounts withheld from paychecks for Social Security and Medicare. People who work for the railroad or federal government are allowed a deduction of up to $2,000 per person for the amounts withheld for their retirement systems. There is also a 50% deduction for capital gain related property that is held for more than one year. Federal and state contributory pensions are exempt. Private pensions are not exempt. Social Security benefits are exempt. There is a $4,400 exemption for married couples filing jointly, which is applied first against Part B income. There is a $700 personal exemption per person for persons age 65 or older. There is a $200 exemption for married couples filing jointly from interest earned from Massachusetts banks.

Major tax credits or rebates include: Credit for income taxes paid to other states, child-care deduction and a limited-income credit. Some of our couples qualify for the limited income credit.

The state sales tax rate is 5%.

Our couples relocating to the cities listed below must pay a vehicle excise tax (personal property tax) based on the year and MSRP of each automobile. The vehicle excise tax is $188 for the Chrysler and $94 for the Oldsmobile. Our couples also pay a registration fee of $30 for two years per automobile and a title fee of $50 per automobile. Thereafter, our couples will pay a vehicle excise tax on an annual basis, and a registration fee every two years, per automobile.

BOSTON

Boston has no local income tax and does not levy an additional sales tax.

Most purchases are taxed at the state rate of 5%. Major consumer categories which are taxed at a different rate: None. Major consumer purchases which are exempt from sales tax include: Apparel and ser-

vices, drugs, groceries and medical services.

In the area of Beacon Hill, the property tax rate is .01386. Homes are assessed at 100% of market value. There is a residential exemption of up to 20% off assessed value for homeowners. There is an elderly exemption of up to $1,000 from property taxes due for homeowners age 70 or older who meet certain income, net worth and residency requirements. Property tax includes garbage pickup.

Boston has no personal property tax for individuals other than the vehicle excise tax discussed earlier.

★Total tax burdens in Boston are lower than average for the $24,281 income category and about average for the $34,275 and $68,098 income categories.

CAPE COD

Cape Cod has no local income tax and does not levy an additional sales tax.

Most purchases are taxed at the state rate of 5%. Major consumer categories which are taxed at a different rate: None. Major consumer purchases which are exempt from sales tax include: Apparel and services, drugs, groceries and medical services.

In the area of Barnstable Township, the property tax rate is .01083. Homes are assessed at 100% of market value. There is an elderly exemption for homeowners age 70 or older who meet certain income, net worth and residency requirements. Property tax does not cover garbage pickup; the additional fee is approximately $228 per year.

Cape Cod has a personal property tax rate of .01083 within Barnstable Township. Personal property is assessed at 7-10% of fair market value. Items subject to the tax include furnished properties other than legal domicile. The tax does not apply to automobiles. We've assumed our couples do not own any of the items subject to the personal property tax.

★Total tax burdens in Cape Cod are about average overall.

MICHIGAN

Income	Home Value	Property Tax & Other Fees	Personal Property Tax & Auto Fees	Sales Tax	Local Income Tax	State Income Tax*	Total Tax	Rank From #1–#149
DETROIT								
$24,281	$50,000	$1,383	$155	$565	$168	($514)	$1,757	#71
	75,000	2,075	155	565	168	(1,136)	1,827	#42
	100,000	2,766	155	565	168	(1,136)	2,518	#81
$34,275	$75,000	$2,075	$155	$760	$401	($521)	$2,870	#96
	100,000	2,766	155	760	401	(802)	3,280	#103
	150,000	4,150	155	760	401	(802)	4,664	#112
$68,098	$150,000	$4,150	$155	$1,175	$1,295	$487	$7,262	#120
	200,000	5,533	155	1,175	1,295	487	8,645	#125
	250,000	6,916	155	1,175	1,295	487	10,028	#128
LANSING								
$24,281	$50,000	$1,419	$135	$565	$56	($324)	$1,851	#82
	75,000	2,023	135	565	56	(928)	1,851	#45
	100,000	2,627	135	565	56	(1,121)	2,262	#53
$34,275	$75,000	$2,023	$135	$760	$134	($243)	$2,809	#94
	100,000	2,627	135	760	134	(787)	2,869	#68
	150,000	3,836	135	760	134	(787)	4,078	#95
$68,098	$150,000	$3,836	$135	$1,175	$432	$530	$6,108	#88
	200,000	5,044	135	1,175	432	530	7,316	#102
	250,000	6,252	135	1,175	432	530	8,524	#108

*Credits for local income tax paid and property tax paid are issued as a reduction of state income tax due or as a refund if the credits are greater than the tax liability.

Michigan has a state income tax and a state sales tax.

The state income tax rate is 4.47%. In calculating the tax, there is no deduction for federal income tax paid. Federal, state and local government pensions are exempt. Up to $22,500 of private pension income is excluded for married couples filing jointly. Social Security benefits are exempt. There is a $2,100 personal exemption per person from adjusted gross income and a $900 personal exemption per person from adjusted gross income for persons age 65 or older. There is an interest/dividends deduction of up to $250 per person for persons 65 and older who do not deduct retirement benefits.

Major tax credits or rebates include: Credit for income taxes paid to other states, which our couples do not qualify for; homestead credit, which our couples do qualify for; and city income tax credit, which our couples do qualify for.

The state sales tax rate changed from 4% to 6% during the period covered by this study.

Since car registration fees differ within the state, see city information for details.

DETROIT

Detroit has a local income tax but does not levy an additional sales tax.

The local income tax rate is 3% of taxable income for residents and 1.5% of taxable income for non-residents who work in the city limits. Federal, state and private pensions are exempt. Social Security benefits are exempt. There is a $600 exemption per person and a $600 exemption per person for people age 65 or older.

During the 12-month period covered by this study, the state sales tax rate changed from 4% to 6%. Our estimates for sales tax are based on a weighted average of these rates. Major consumer categories taxed at a different rate: None. Major consumer categories which are exempt from sales tax include: Drugs, groceries and medical services.

Within the city limits of Detroit, the homestead property tax rate is .055327. Homes are assessed at 50% of market value. Property tax includes garbage pickup.

Detroit has no personal property tax for individuals.

Our couples relocating to Detroit must pay a registration fee of $81 for the Chrysler and $62 for the Oldsmobile, an auto exhaust test fee of $10 per automobile and a title fee of $11 per automobile. Thereafter, on an annual basis, our couples will pay a registration fee and an auto exhaust test fee, per automobile.

★Total tax burdens in Detroit are about average for the $24,281 and $34,275 income categories and higher than average for the $68,098 income category.

LANSING

Lansing has a local income tax but does not levy an additional sales tax.

The local income tax rate is 1% of taxable income for residents and .5% of taxable income for non-residents who work in the city limits. Federal, state and private pensions are exempt. Social Security benefits are exempt. There is a $600 standard deduction per person and a $600 standard deduction per person for people age 65 or older.

During the 12-month period covered by this study, the state sales tax rate changed from 4% to 6%. Our estimates for sales tax are based on a weighted average of these rates. Major consumer categories taxed at a different rate: None. Major consumer categories which are exempt from sales tax include: Drugs, groceries and medical services.

In the Holt School District of Lansing, the homestead property tax rate is .0483288. Homes are assessed at 50% of market value. Property tax does not cover garbage pickup; the additional fee is approximately $156 per year. There is a recycling fee of $55 per year, and some residents may live within special assessment districts and be subject to additional charges for drains and street lighting.

Lansing has no personal property tax for individuals.

Our couples relocating to Lansing must pay a registration fee of $81 for the Chrysler and $62 for the Oldsmobile, and a title fee of $11 per automobile. Thereafter, on an annual basis, our couples will pay a registration fee per automobile.

★Total tax burdens in Lansing are lower than average for the $24,281 income category and about average for the $34,275 and $68,098 income categories.

MINNESOTA

Income	Home Value	Property Tax & Other Fees	Personal Property Tax & Auto Fees	Sales Tax	Local Income Tax	State Income Tax	Total Tax	Rank From #1–#149
MINNEAPOLIS								
$24,281	$50,000	$984	$407	$704	–	–	$2,095	#111 (tie)
	75,000	1,183	407	704	–	–	2,294	#95
	100,000	1,648	407	704	–	–	2,759	#102
$34,275	$75,000	$1,374	$407	$917	–	$736	$3,434	#129
	100,000	1,697	407	917	–	736	3,757	#119
	150,000	3,064	407	917	–	736	5,124	#125
$68,098	$150,000	$3,504	$407	$1,464	–	$3,548	$8,923	#140
	200,000	4,919	407	1,464	–	3,548	10,338	#141
	250,000	6,335	407	1,464	–	3,548	11,754	#140
ST. PAUL								
$24,281	$50,000	$1,083	$407	$670	–	–	$2,160	#120 (tie)
	75,000	1,272	407	670	–	–	2,349	#100
	100,000	1,794	407	670	–	–	2,871	#108
$34,275	$75,000	$1,463	$407	$866	–	$736	$3,472	#131
	100,000	1,802	407	866	–	736	3,811	#121
	150,000	3,269	407	866	–	736	5,278	#130
$68,098	$150,000	$3,709	$407	$1,381	–	$3,548	$9,045	#142
	200,000	5,184	407	1,381	–	3,548	10,520	#142
	250,000	6,658	407	1,381	–	3,548	11,994	#142

Minnesota has a state income tax and a state sales tax.

The state income tax is graduated from 6% to 8.5% depending upon income bracket. For married couples filing jointly the rate is 6% on the first $22,260 of taxable income; the rate is 8% on the next $66,200 of taxable income; and the rate is 8.5% on taxable income above $88,460.

In calculating the tax, there is no deduction for federal income tax paid. Federal, state and private pensions are not exempt. Social Security benefits subject to federal tax are not exempt. There is a $2,450 personal exemption per person from adjusted gross income. There is a $7,850 standard deduction from adjusted gross income for married couples filing jointly when both are age 65 or older. There are age 65 or older/disabled subtractions for singles or couples meeting certain income requirements.

Major tax credits or rebates include: Credit for income taxes paid to other states, child and dependent care credit, homeowner's and renter's property tax refund and targeted property tax refund for homeowners with an increase in net tax of greater than 12%. Several of our couples qualify for the homeowner's property tax refund, but do not qualify for the other programs.

The state sales tax rate is 6.5% but local governments can add to this amount.

Our couples relocating to the cities listed below must pay to register and annually renew their automobiles based on the base value of the car. The registration fee is $229 for the Chrysler and $184 for the Oldsmobile. Our couples must also pay a plate fee of $3 per automobile and a title fee of $6 per automobile at the time of registration. Thereafter, on an annual basis, our couples will pay a registration fee, a filing fee and an emissions test fee, per automobile.

MINNEAPOLIS

Minneapolis has no local income tax but does levy a sales tax.

Most purchases are taxed at a rate of 7%. Major consumer categories taxed at a different rate include: Food away from home, which is taxed at a rate of 10%. Major consumer categories exempt from sales tax include: Apparel and services, drugs, groceries and medical services.

For most residents within the city limits of Minneapolis, the property tax rate is 1.41568. Homes are as-sessed at 1% of the first $72,000 of market value of the home plus 2% of the market value in excess of $72,000. Property tax does not cover garbage pickup; the additional fee is approximately $276 per year.

Minneapolis has no personal property tax for individuals.

★Total tax burdens in Minneapolis are about average for the $24,281 income category and higher than average for the $34,275 and $68,098 income categories. Minneapolis is a tax hell in 3 of 9 income/home value categories.

ST. PAUL

St. Paul has no local income tax but does levy a sales tax.

Most purchases are taxed at a rate of 7%. Major consumer categories taxed at a different rate: None. Major consumer categories exempt from sales tax include: Apparel and services, drugs, groceries and medical services.

For most residents within the city limits of St. Paul, the property tax rate is 1.47486. Homes are assessed at 1% of the first $72,000 of market value of the home plus 2% of the market value in excess of $72,000. Property tax does not cover garbage pickup; the additional fee is approximately $164 per year. There is a waste management fee of approximately $15 per year, a city recycling fee of approximately $21 per year, a storm sewer separation fee of approximately $36 per year and a street maintenance fee which we have estimated to be approximately $110 per year for our couples.

St. Paul has no personal property tax for individuals.

★Total tax burdens in St. Paul are higher than average overall. St. Paul is a tax hell in 3 of 9 income/home value categories.

MISSISSIPPI

Income	Home Value	Property Tax & Other Fees	Personal Property Tax & Auto Fees	Sales Tax	Local Income Tax	State Income Tax	Total Tax	Rank From #1–#149
MERIDIAN								
$24,281	$50,000	$96	$541	$917	–	–	$1,554	#45
	75,000	317	541	917	–	–	1,775	#37
	100,000	685	541	917	–	–	2,143	#42
$34,275	$75,000	$317	$541	$1,210	–	–	$2,068	#25
	100,000	685	541	1,210	–	–	2,436	#29
	150,000	1,421	541	1,210	–	–	3,172	#36
$68,098	$150,000	$1,421	$541	$1,766	–	$1,334	$5,062	#41
	200,000	2,157	541	1,766	–	1,334	5,798	#49
	250,000	2,894	541	1,766	–	1,334	6,535	#50
OXFORD								
$24,281	$50,000	$192	$483	$939	–	–	$1,614	#54
	75,000	398	483	939	–	–	1,820	#40
	100,000	743	483	939	–	–	2,165	#45
$34,275	$75,000	$398	$483	$1,244	–	–	$2,125	#30
	100,000	743	483	1,244	–	–	2,470	#32
	150,000	1,431	483	1,244	–	–	3,158	#33
$68,098	$150,000	$1,431	$483	$1,821	–	$1,334	$5,069	#42
	200,000	2,119	483	1,821	–	1,334	5,757	#47
	250,000	2,807	483	1,821	–	1,334	6,445	#44

Mississippi has a state income tax and a state sales tax.

The state income tax rate is graduated from 3% to 5% depending upon income bracket. For all filers, the rate is 3% on the first $5,000 of taxable income; the rate is 4% on the next $5,000 of taxable income; and the rate is 5% on taxable income above $10,000.

In calculating the tax, there is no deduction for federal income tax paid. Federal, state and private pensions are exempt. Social Security benefits are exempt. There is a $3,400 standard deduction for married couples filing jointly. There is a $9,500 exemption for married couples filing jointly. There is a $1,500 exemption for each person age 65 or older.

Major tax credits or rebates include: Credit for income taxes paid to other states. Our couples do not qualify for this program.

The state sales tax rate is 7%.

Since car registration and renewal fees differ within the state, see city information for details.

MERIDIAN

Meridian has no local income tax and does not levy an additional sales tax.

Most purchases are taxed at the state rate of 7%. Major consumer categories taxed at a different rate: None. Major consumer categories which are exempt from sales tax include: Drugs and medical services.

Within the city limits of Meridian, the property tax rate is .14724. There is a homestead exemption in the form of a tax credit of up to $240 for all homeowners. There is also an elderly exemption of $60,000 off market value for residents age 65 or older. The homestead exemption cannot be taken if the elderly exemption is taken. Homes owned by residents taking the elderly exemption or homestead exemption are assessed at 10%. We've assumed our couples are taking the elderly exemption. Property tax does not cover garbage pickup; the additional fee is approximately $96 per year.

Meridian has no personal property tax for individuals.

Our couples relocating to Meridian must pay a tax based on the state's valuation of each car. Note: The Lauderdale County Tax Collector declined to verify our estimates of this tax. Based on the limited information we were able to obtain, we estimate the tax to be $426 for the Chrysler and

$274 for the Oldsmobile. Our couples also pay a title fee of $5 per automobile, a registration fee of $10 per automobile and a privilege tax of $15 per automobile, at the time of registration. Thereafter, on an annual basis, our couples will pay a renewal fee per automobile.

★Total tax burdens in Meridian are lower than average overall.

OXFORD

Oxford has no local income tax and does not levy an additional sales tax.

Most purchases are taxed at the state rate of 7%. Major consumer categories taxed at a different rate include: Food away from home, which is taxed at a rate of 9%. Major consumer categories which are exempt from sales tax include: Drugs and medical services.

In County District #4 in Oxford, the property tax rate is .13765. There is a homestead exemption in the form of a tax credit of up to $240 for all homeowners. There is also an elderly exemption of $60,000 off market value for residents age 65 or older. The homestead exemption cannot be taken if the elderly exemption is taken. Homes owned by residents taking the elderly exemption or homestead exemption are assessed at 10%. We've assumed our couples are taking the elderly exemption. Property tax does not cover garbage pickup; the additional fee is approximately $192 per year.

Oxford has no personal property tax for individuals.

Our couples relocating to Oxford must pay a tax based on the state's valuation of each car. Note: The Lafayette County Tax Collector declined to verify our estimates of this tax. Based on the limited information we were able to obtain, we estimate the tax to be $398 for the Chrysler and $256 for the Oldsmobile. Our couples also pay a plate fee of $5 per automobile, a tag fee of $10 per automobile and a privilege tax of $15 per automobile, at the time of registration. Thereafter, on an annual basis, our couples will pay a renewal fee per automobile.

★Total tax burdens in Oxford are lower than average overall.

MISSOURI

Income	Home Value	Property Tax & Other Fees	Personal Property Tax & Auto Fees	Sales Tax	Local Income Tax	State Income Tax	Total Tax	Rank From #1–#149
BRANSON								
$24,281	$50,000	$541	$436	$951	–	$141	$2,069	#108
	75,000	758	436	951	–	141	2,286	#93
	100,000	974	436	951	–	141	2,502	#78
$34,275	$75,000	$758	$436	$1,257	–	$551	$3,002	#108
	100,000	974	436	1,257	–	551	3,218	#91
	150,000	1,408	436	1,257	–	551	3,652	#71
$68,098	$150,000	$1,408	$436	$1,837	–	$2,545	$6,226	#91
	200,000	1,841	436	1,837	–	2,545	6,659	#80
	250,000	2,274	436	1,837	–	2,545	7,092	#69
KANSAS CITY								
$24,281	$50,000	$741	$652	$868	$44	$141	$2,446	#137
	75,000	1,112	652	868	44	141	2,817	#128
	100,000	1,483	652	868	44	141	3,188	#121
$34,275	$75,000	$1,112	$652	$1,148	$96	$551	$3,559	#135
	100,000	1,483	652	1,148	96	551	3,930	#130
	150,000	2,224	652	1,148	96	551	4,671	#113
$68,098	$150,000	$2,224	$652	$1,682	$302	$2,545	$7,405	#125
	200,000	2,965	652	1,682	302	2,545	8,146	#122
	250,000	3,706	652	1,682	302	2,545	8,887	#119

Missouri has a state income tax and a state sales tax.

The state income tax rate is graduated from 1.5% to 6% depending upon income bracket. For all filers the rate is 1.5% on the first $1,000 of taxable income; the rate is 2% on the next $1,000 of taxable income; the rate is 2.5% on the next $1,000 of taxable income; the rate is 3% on the next $1,000 of taxable income; the rate is 3.5% on the next $1,000 of taxable income; the rate is 4% on the next $1,000 of taxable income; the rate is 4.5% on the next $1,000 of taxable income; the rate is 5% on the next $1,000 of taxable income; the rate is 5.5% on the next $1,000 of taxable income; and the rate is 6% on taxable income above $9,000.

In calculating the tax, there is a deduction of up to $10,000 for married couples filing jointly for federal income tax paid. Federal, state and private pensions are not exempt. However, there is an exemption of up to $6,000 of federal or state pensions for married couples with modified Missouri adjusted gross income less than $32,000. Social Security benefits subject to federal tax are not exempt. There is a $1,200 personal exemption per person from adjusted gross income. There is a $7,850 standard deduction from adjusted gross income for married couples filing jointly when both are age 65 or older.

Major tax credits or rebates include: Credit for income taxes paid to other states and property tax credit. Our couples do not qualify for these programs.

The state sales tax rate is 4% but local governments can add to this amount.

Our couples relocating to the cities listed below must pay to register their automobiles based on horsepower. The registration fee is $51 for the Chrysler and $51 for the Oldsmobile. Our couples must also pay an inspection fee of $7 per automobile, a title fee of $9 per automobile, and a motor vehicle transaction fee of $2 per automobile. Thereafter, on an annual basis, our couples will pay a license renewal fee and an inspection fee, per automobile.

BRANSON

Branson has no local income tax but does levy a sales tax.

Most purchases are taxed at a rate of 7.225%. Major consumer categories taxed at a different rate include: Food away from home, which is taxed at a rate of 7.725%. Major consumer categories which are exempt from sales tax include: Drugs and medical services.

Within the city limits of Branson, the property tax rate is .0456. Homes are assessed at 19% of market value. There is a senior citizen tax rebate for residents age 65 or older who are married filing jointly with a household income of up to $17,000. Property tax does not cover garbage pickup; the additional fee is approximately $108 per year.

Branson has a personal property tax rate of .0456. Personal property is assessed at 33.3% of Blue Book value. Items subject to the personal property tax include airplanes, automobiles, boats, farm animals, farm equipment, motorcycles, motors, RVs, trailers and trucks.

★Total tax burdens in Branson are about average overall.

KANSAS CITY

Kansas City has a local income tax and a sales tax.

The local income tax rate is 1% of earned income, consisting of wages and salaries and self-employment income.

Most purchases are taxed at a rate

of 6.475%. Major consumer categories taxed at a different rate include: Food away from home, which is taxed at a rate of 8.225%. Major consumer categories which are exempt from sales tax include: Drugs and medical services.

In Jackson County, the property tax rate is .07653 for houses and .08403 for the land. Homes are assessed at 19% of market value. There is a senior citizen tax rebate for residents age 65 or older who are married filing jointly with a household income of up to $17,000. Property tax includes garbage pickup.

Kansas City has a personal property tax rate of .07653 within Jackson County. Personal property is assessed at 33.3% of market value. Items subject to the personal property tax include airplanes, automobiles, boats, farm animals, farm equipment, motorcycles, motors, RVs, trailers and trucks.

★Total tax burdens in Kansas City are higher than average overall.

MONTANA

Income	Home Value	Property Tax & Other Fees	Personal Property Tax & Auto Fees	Sales Tax	Local Income Tax	State Income Tax*	Total Tax	Rank From #1–#149
HELENA								
$24,281	$50,000	$1,070	$461	–	–	$16	$1,547	#42
	75,000	1,505	461	–	–	(327)	1,639	#25
	100,000	1,940	461	–	–	(327)	2,074	#36
$34,275	$75,000	$1,505	$461	–	–	$335	$2,301	#43
	100,000	1,940	461	–	–	(19)	2,382	#25
	150,000	2,810	461	–	–	(19)	3,252	#45
$68,098	$150,000	$2,810	$461	–	–	$4,207	$7,478	#126
	200,000	3,679	461	–	–	3,807	7,947	#118
	250,000	4,550	461	–	–	3,807	8,818	#118
MISSOULA								
$24,281	$50,000	$1,247	$461	–	–	($208)	$1,500	#38
	75,000	1,792	461	–	–	(327)	1,926	#51
	100,000	2,336	461	–	–	(327)	2,470	#72
$34,275	$75,000	$1,792	$461	–	–	($1)	$2,252	#40
	100,000	2,336	461	–	–	(19)	2,778	#56
	150,000	3,424	461	–	–	(19)	3,866	#85
$68,098	$150,000	$3,424	$461	–	–	$3,807	$7,692	#127
	200,000	4,513	461	–	–	3,807	8,781	#126
	250,000	5,601	461	–	–	3,807	9,869	#124

*Elderly Homeowner/Renter Credit is issued as a reduction of income tax due or as a refund if the credit is greater than the tax liability.

Montana has a state income tax but no state sales tax.

The state income tax rate is graduated from 2% to 11% depending upon income bracket. For all filers the rate is 2% on the first $1,800 of taxable income; the rate is 3% on the next $1,800 of taxable income; the rate is 4% on the next $3,600 of taxable income; the rate is 5% on the next $3,500 of taxable income; the rate is 6% on the next $3,600 of taxable income; the rate is 7% on the next $3,600 of taxable income; the rate is 8% on the next $7,200 of taxable income; the rate is 9% on the next $10,700 of taxable income; the rate is 10% on the next $26,900 of taxable income; and the rate is 11% on taxable income above $62,700.

In calculating the tax, there is no deduction for federal income tax paid. Federal, state and private pensions are exempt up to $3,600 per person for persons with an adjusted gross income of less than $30,000. Social Security benefits subject to federal tax are not exempt. There is a 20% standard deduction of up to $5,380 from adjusted gross income for married couples filing jointly.

There is a $1,430 personal exemption per person from adjusted gross income and a $1,430 personal exemption per person from adjusted gross income for persons age 65 or older.

Major tax credits or rebates include: Credit for income taxes paid to other states, which our couples do not qualify for; elderly care credit, which our couples do not qualify for; elderly homeowner/renter credit of up to $400 based on property taxes paid, which our couples do qualify for.

As noted, Montana has no general sales tax but does levy a one-time tax on new motor vehicles. The tax is 1.5% of the current market value of the car in the second year of ownership.

Our couples relocating to the cities listed below must pay a registration fee of $18 per automobile and a title fee of $7-9 per automobile. Thereafter, on an annual basis, our couples will pay a registration fee per automobile.

HELENA

Helena has no local income tax and no sales tax.

Within the city limits of Helena, the property tax rate is .44797. Homes are assessed at 3.86% of market value. There is a low-income credit for homeowners who meet certain income requirements. Property tax does not cover garbage pickup; the additional fee is approximately $116 per year. There is a street maintenance fee, based on the square footage of the lot, which we have estimated at $68 per year. There is a storm drain utility fee of approximately $11 per year, a water quality fee of approximately $5 per year and a cemetery fee that is .00277 of the assessed value of the home.

Helena has a personal property tax rate of .025. Personal property is assessed at 100% of the NADA trade in value. Items subject to the tax include automobiles and light trucks under one ton.

★Total tax burdens in Helena are lower than average for the $24,281 and $34,275 income categories and higher than average for the $68,098 income category.

MISSOULA

Missoula has no local income tax and no sales tax.

In the Missoula School District 1-

1, the property tax rate is .56395. Homes are assessed at 3.86% of market value. There is a low-income credit for homeowners who meet certain income requirements. Property tax does not cover garbage pickup; the additional fee is approximately $159 per year.

Missoula has a personal property tax rate of .025 on automobiles, which are assessed at 100% of the NADA trade in value. Missoula has a personal property tax rate of .0386 on mobile homes, which are assessed at 100% of market value.

★Total tax burdens in Missoula are lower than average for the $24,281 income category, about average for the $34,275 income category and higher than average for the $68,098 income category.

NEBRASKA

Income	Home Value	Property Tax & Other Fees	Personal Property Tax & Auto Fees	Sales Tax	Local Income Tax	State Income Tax	Total Tax	Rank From #1–#149
LINCOLN								
$24,281	$50,000	$1,377	$582	$681	–	$124	$2,764	#145
	75,000	1,993	582	681	–	124	3,380	#144
	100,000	2,609	582	681	–	124	3,996	#143
$34,275	$75,000	$1,993	$582	$919	–	$448	$3,942	#141
	100,000	2,609	582	919	–	448	4,558	#141
	150,000	3,842	582	919	–	448	5,791	#141
$68,098	$150,000	$3,842	$582	$1,424	–	$2,619	$8,467	#138
	200,000	5,074	582	1,424	–	2,619	9,699	#138
	250,000	6,307	582	1,424	–	2,619	10,932	#138
OMAHA								
$24,281	$50,000	$1,255	$557	$681	–	$124	$2,617	#141
	75,000	1,882	557	681	–	124	3,244	#140
	100,000	2,509	557	681	–	124	3,871	#141
$34,275	$75,000	$1,882	$557	$919	–	$448	$3,806	#139
	100,000	2,509	557	919	–	448	4,433	#139
	150,000	3,764	557	919	–	448	5,688	#139
$68,098	$150,000	$3,764	$557	$1,424	–	$2,619	$8,364	#137
	200,000	5,018	557	1,424	–	2,619	9,618	#137
	250,000	6,273	557	1,424	–	2,619	10,873	#137

Nebraska has a state income tax and a state sales tax.

The state income tax rate is graduated from 2.62% to 6.99% depending upon income bracket. For married couples filing jointly, the rate is 2.62% on the first $4,000 of taxable income; the rate is 3.65% on the next $26,000 of taxable income; the rate is 5.24% on the next $16,750 of taxable income; and the rate is 6.99% on income above $46,750.

In calculating the tax, there is no deduction for federal income tax paid. Federal, state and private pensions are not exempt. Social Security benefits subject to federal tax are not exempt. There is a $7,850 standard deduction from adjusted gross income for married couples filing jointly who are both age 65 or older. There is a personal exemption credit against tax of up to $69 per person.

Major tax credits or rebates include: Credit for income taxes paid to other states, credit for persons who qualify for the federal tax credit for the elderly and child care credit. Our couples do not qualify for these programs.

The state sales tax rate is 5% but local governments can add to this amount.

Since car registration and renewal fees differ within the state, see city information for details.

LINCOLN

Lincoln has no local income tax but does levy a sales tax.

Most purchases are taxed at a rate of 6.5%. Major consumer categories taxed at a different rate: None. Major consumer categories which are exempt from sales tax include: Drugs, groceries, medical services and medical supplies.

Within the city limits of Lincoln, the property tax rate is .02465185. Homes are assessed at 100% of market value. There is a homestead exemption of $45,300 off assessed value for homeowners age 65 or older with a federal adjusted gross income of less than $10,400. Property tax does not cover garbage pickup; the additional fee is approximately $144 per year.

Lincoln has no personal property tax for individuals.

Our couples relocating to Lincoln must pay a motor vehicle tax per automobile of .02954219 of the value of the automobile, which is determined by the state. The motor vehicle tax is $361.15 for the Chrysler and

$258.49 for the Oldsmobile. Our couples also pay a wheel tax and plate fees of $46 per automobile, an inspection fee of $10 per automobile and a title fee of $10 per automobile. Thereafter, on an annual basis, our couples will pay a motor vehicle tax, and a wheel tax and plate fee, per automobile.

★Total tax burdens in Lincoln are higher than average overall. Lincoln is a tax hell in 6 of 9 income/home value categories.

OMAHA

Omaha has no local income tax but does levy a sales tax.

Most purchases are taxed at a rate of 6.5%. Major consumer categories taxed at a different rate: None. Major consumer categories which are exempt from sales tax include: Drugs, groceries, medical services and medical supplies.

In the Omaha School District, the property tax rate is .0280608. Homes are assessed at 86% to 100% of market value with average assessment of 89.42% of market value. There is a homestead exemption of $42,600 off assessed value for homeowners age 65 or older with a household income of less than $10,400. Property tax includes garbage pickup.

Omaha has no personal property tax for individuals.

Our couples relocating to Omaha in the area of the Omaha School District must pay a motor vehicle tax per automobile of .0281991 of the value of the automobile, which is determined by the state. The motor vehicle tax is $296 for the Chrysler and $199 for the Oldsmobile. Our couples also pay a wheel tax and plate fees of $43 per automobile, an inspection fee of $10 per automobile and a title fee of $10 per automobile. Thereafter, on an annual basis, our couples will pay a motor vehicle tax, and a wheel tax and plate fee, per automobile.

★Total tax burdens in Omaha are higher than average overall. Omaha is a tax hell in 3 of 9 income/home value categories.

NEVADA

Income	Home Value	Property Tax & Other Fees	Personal Property Tax & Auto Fees	Sales Tax	Local Income Tax	State Income Tax	Total Tax	Rank From #1–#149
LAS VEGAS								
$24,281	$50,000	$789	$430	$804	–	–	$2,023	#102
	75,000	1,054	430	804	–	–	2,288	#94
	100,000	1,319	430	804	–	–	2,553	#87
$34,275	$75,000	$1,054	$430	$1,056	–	–	$2,540	#67
	100,000	1,319	430	1,056	–	–	2,805	#59
	150,000	1,850	430	1,056	–	–	3,336	#48
$68,098	$150,000	$1,850	$430	$1,610	–	–	$3,890	#10
	200,000	2,381	430	1,610	–	–	4,421	#10
	250,000	2,911	430	1,610	–	–	4,951	#12
RENO								
$24,281	$50,000	$752	$430	$804	–	–	$1,986	#98
	75,000	1,037	430	804	–	–	2,271	#90
	100,000	1,323	430	804	–	–	2,557	#88
$34,275	$75,000	$1,037	$430	$1,056	–	–	$2,523	#62
	100,000	1,323	430	1,056	–	–	2,809	#60
	150,000	1,893	430	1,056	–	–	3,379	#56
$68,098	$150,000	$1,893	$430	$1,610	–	–	$3,933	#11
	200,000	2,464	430	1,610	–	–	4,504	#13
	250,000	3,035	430	1,610	–	–	5,075	#14

Nevada has no state income tax but does have a state sales tax.

Major tax credits or rebates include: Senior citizens rebate. Our couples do not qualify for this program.

The state sales tax rate is 2% but local governments can add to this amount.

Our couples relocating to the cities listed below must pay a privilege tax based on the value of each automobile, a supplemental tax of one-fourth of the privilege tax per automobile and a registration fee of $33 per automobile. The privilege tax is $172 for the Chrysler and $116 for the Oldsmobile. The supplemental tax is $43 for the Chrysler and $29 for the Oldsmobile. Our couples also pay $20 per automobile for a title, $20 per automobile for an emissions check and $2 per automobile for inspection and plates at the time of registration. Thereafter, on an annual basis, our couples will pay a privilege tax, a supplemental tax, a registration fee and an emissions check fee, per automobile.

LAS VEGAS

Las Vegas has no local income tax but does levy a sales tax.

Most purchases are taxed at a rate of 7%. Major consumer categories taxed at a different rate: None. Major consumer categories which are exempt from the sales tax include: Drugs and groceries.

Within the city limits of Las Vegas, the property tax rate is .030322. Homes are assessed at 35% of taxable value. There is a senior citizens rebate of up to $500 for homeowners age 62 or older with a gross income of less than $19,100. Property tax does not cover garbage pickup; the additional fee is approximately $117 per year. There is a sewer usage charge of $141 per year.

Las Vegas has no personal property tax for individuals.

★Total tax burdens in Las Vegas are about average for the $24,281 and $34,275 income categories and lower than average for the $68,098 income category. Las Vegas is a tax heaven in 2 of 9 income/home value categories.

RENO

Reno has no local income tax but does levy a sales tax.

Most purchases are taxed at a rate of 7%. Major consumer categories taxed at a different rate: None. Major consumer categories which are exempt from the sales tax include: Drugs and groceries.

Within the city limits of Reno, the property tax rate is .032615. Homes are assessed at 35% of taxable value. There is a senior citizens rebate of up to $500 for homeowners age 62 or older with a gross income of less than $19,100. Property tax does not cover garbage pickup; the additional fee is approximately $76 per year. There is a sewer usage charge of $104 per year.

Reno has no personal property tax for individuals.

★Total tax burdens in Reno are about average for the $24,281 and $34,275 income categories and lower than average in the $68,098 income category.

NEW HAMPSHIRE

Income	Home Value	Property Tax & Other Fees	Personal Property Tax & Auto Fees	Sales Tax	Local Income Tax	State Income Tax	Total Tax	Rank From #1–#149
CONCORD								
$24,281	$50,000	$1,765	$330	–	–	–	$2,095	#111 (tie)
	75,000	2,648	330	–	–	–	2,978	#135
	100,000	3,530	330	–	–	–	3,860	#140
$34,275	$75,000	$2,648	$330	–	–	–	$2,978	#105
	100,000	3,530	330	–	–	–	3,860	#124
	150,000	5,295	330	–	–	–	5,625	#138
$68,098	$150,000	$5,295	$330	–	–	–	$5,625	#69
	200,000	7,060	330	–	–	–	7,390	#104
	250,000	8,825	330	–	–	–	9,155	#120
PORTSMOUTH								
$24,281	$50,000	$1,266	$324	–	–	–	$1,590	#51
	75,000	1,899	324	–	–	–	2,223	#86
	100,000	2,532	324	–	–	–	2,856	#106
$34,275	$75,000	$1,899	$324	–	–	–	$2,223	#38
	100,000	2,532	324	–	–	–	2,856	#63 (tie)
	150,000	3,798	324	–	–	–	4,122	#98
$68,098	$150,000	$3,798	$324	–	–	–	$4,122	#15
	200,000	5,063	324	–	–	–	5,387	#29
	250,000	6,329	324	–	–	–	6,653	#54

New Hampshire has no state income tax but does levy an interest and dividends tax. New Hampshire has no state sales tax.

The state interest and dividends tax rate is 5%. In calculating the tax, there is no deduction for federal income tax paid. Interest from New Hampshire and Vermont banks is exempt from tax. There is a $1,200 personal exemption per person for persons age 65 or older and a $2,400 exemption for married couples filing jointly. We've assumed our couples do not owe interest and dividends tax.

Major tax credits or rebates: None.

Since car registration and renewal fees differ within the state, see city information for details.

CONCORD

Concord has no local income tax and no sales tax.

Within the city limits of Concord, the property tax rate is .02824. Homes are assessed at 125% of market value. There is an elderly exemption of $25,000 to $80,000 off assessed value for persons age 65 or older with income of less than $12,000 (excluding Social Security) and assets of less than $50,000 (excluding home). Property tax includes garbage pickup.

Concord has no personal property tax for individuals.

Our couples relocating to Concord must pay a city permit fee based on year and list price of each automobile and a plate registration fee of $31.20 per automobile. The city permit fee is $226 for the Chrysler and $136 for the Oldsmobile. Our couples also pay $20 per automobile for a title and $9 per automobile in miscellaneous fees at the time of registration. Thereafter, on an annual basis, our couples will pay a city permit fee, a plate registration fee and miscellaneous fees, per automobile.

★Total tax burdens in Concord are higher than average for the $24,281 and $34,275 income categories and about average for the $68,098 income category. Concord is a tax hell in 1 of 9 income/home value categories.

PORTSMOUTH

Portsmouth has no local income tax and no sales tax.

Within the city limits of Portsmouth, the property tax rate is .02610. The equalized ratio is 97%, which means that individual homes may be assessed higher or lower than 97%, but the average is 97%. There is an elderly exemption of $50,000 to $100,000 off assessed value for persons age 65 or older with income of less than $12,000 (excluding Social Security) and assets of less than $30,000 (excluding home). Property tax includes garbage pickup.

Portsmouth has no personal property tax for individuals.

Our couples relocating to Portsmouth must pay a city permit fee based on year and list price of each automobile and a plate registration fee of $31.20 per automobile. The city permit fee is $226 for the Chrysler and $136 for the Oldsmobile. Our couples also pay $20 per automobile for a title and $6 per automobile in miscellaneous fees at the time of registration. Thereafter, on an annual basis, our couples will pay a city permit fee, a plate registration fee and miscellaneous fees, per automobile.

★Total tax burdens in Portsmouth are about average for the $24,281 and $34,275 income categories and lower than average for the $68,098 income category.

NEW JERSEY

Income	Home Value	Property Tax & Other Fees	Personal Property Tax & Auto Fees	Sales Tax	Local Income Tax	State Income Tax	Total Tax	Rank From #1–#149
CAPE MAY								
$24,281	$50,000	$665	$88	$636	–	$50	$1,439	#32
	75,000	887	88	636	–	50	1,661	#26
	100,000	1,262	88	636	–	50	2,036	#30
$34,275	$75,000	$1,052	$88	$855	–	$201	$2,196	#36
	100,000	1,262	88	855	–	201	2,406	#28
	150,000	2,010	88	855	–	201	3,154	#32
$68,098	$150,000	$2,360	$88	$1,321	–	$905	$4,674	#33
	200,000	2,759	88	1,321	–	905	5,073	#19
	250,000	3,508	88	1,321	–	905	5,822	#22
TOMS RIVER								
$24,281	$50,000	$630	$88	$636	–	$50	$1,404	#26
	75,000	1,195	88	636	–	50	1,969	#55
	100,000	1,759	88	636	–	50	2,533	#85 (tie)
$34,275	$75,000	$1,195	$88	$855	–	$201	$2,339	#47
	100,000	1,759	88	855	–	201	2,903	#71
	150,000	2,889	88	855	–	201	4,033	#93
$68,098	$150,000	$2,889	$88	$1,321	–	$905	$5,203	#50
	200,000	4,019	88	1,321	–	905	6,333	#63
	250,000	5,149	88	1,321	–	905	7,463	#79
TRENTON								
$24,281	$50,000	$1,145	$88	$636	–	$50	$1,919	#93
	75,000	1,968	88	636	–	50	2,742	#124
	100,000	2,790	88	636	–	50	3,564	#131
$34,275	$75,000	$1,968	$88	$855	–	$201	$3,112	#116
	100,000	2,790	88	855	–	201	3,934	#131
	150,000	4,435	88	855	–	201	5,579	#136
$68,098	$150,000	$4,435	$88	$1,321	–	$905	$6,749	#113
	200,000	6,080	88	1,321	–	905	8,394	#123
	250,000	7,725	88	1,321	–	905	10,039	#129

New Jersey has a state income tax and a state sales tax.

The state income tax rate is graduated from 1.9% to 6.65% depending upon income bracket. For married couples filing jointly the rate is 1.9% on the first $20,000 of taxable income; the rate is 2.375% on the next $30,000 of taxable income; the rate is 3.325% on the next $20,000 of taxable income; the rate is 4.75% on the next $10,000 of taxable income; the rate is 6.175% on the next $70,000 of taxable income; and the rate is 6.65% on taxable income above $150,000.

In calculating the tax, there is no deduction for federal income tax paid. There is an exclusion of up to $10,000 on federal, state and private pensions from adjusted gross income for married couples filing jointly who are both 62 or older. Social Security ben-

efits are exempt. There is a $1,000 personal exemption per person from New Jersey gross income and a $1,000 personal exemption per person from New Jersey gross income for persons age 65 or older.

Major tax credits or rebates include: Credit for income taxes paid to other states, homestead property tax rebate and lifeline utility credit program for senior citizens and disabled. Our couples qualify for the homestead property tax rebate but do not qualify for the other programs.

The state sales tax rate is 6%.

Our couples relocating to the cities listed below must pay a registration fee based on the weight and year of each automobile. The registration fee is $69 for the Chrysler and $44 for the Oldsmobile. Our couples also pay $20 per automobile for a title at the

time of registration. Thereafter, on an annual basis, our couples will pay a registration fee per automobile.

CAPE MAY

Cape May has no local income tax and does not levy an additional sales tax.

Most purchases are taxed at the state rate of 6%. Major consumer categories taxed at a different rate: None. Major consumer categories which are exempt from sales tax include: Drugs, groceries and medical services.

Within the city limits of Cape May, the property tax rate is .0156. Homes are assessed at 96% of market value. There is a homestead rebate program which ranges from $30 to $500 depending upon income, filing status and the amount of property tax or rent paid. There is also an elderly exemption of $250 credit on property taxes due for homeowners age 65 or older with an income of less than $10,000 (excluding Social Security). Property tax does not include garbage pickup; the additional fee is approximately $264 per year.

Cape May has no personal property tax for individuals.

★Total tax burdens in Cape May are lower than average overall.

TOMS RIVER

Toms River has no local income tax and does not levy an additional sales tax.

Most purchases are taxed at the state rate of 6%. Major consumer categories taxed at a different rate: None. Major consumer categories which are exempt from sales tax include: Drugs, groceries and medical services.

In Fire District #2 of Toms River, the property tax rate is .02332. Homes are assessed at 96.89% of market value. There is a homestead rebate program which ranges from $30 to $500 depending upon income, filing status, age and the amount of property tax or rent paid. There is also an elderly exemption of $250 credit on property taxes due for homeowners age 65 or older with an income of less than $10,000 (excluding Social Security). Property tax includes garbage pickup.

Toms River has no personal property tax for individuals.

★Total tax burdens in Toms River are about average overall.

TRENTON

Trenton has no local income tax and does not levy an additional sales tax.

Most purchases are taxed at the state rate of 6%. Major consumer categories taxed at a different rate: None. Major consumer categories which are exempt from sales tax include: Drugs, groceries and medical services.

Within the city limits of Trenton, the property tax rate is .0329. Homes are assessed at 100% of market value. There is a homestead rebate program which ranges from $30 to $500 depending upon income, filing status, age and the amount of property tax or rent paid. There is also an elderly exemption of $250 credit on property taxes due for homeowners age 65 or older with an income of less than $10,000 (excluding Social Security). Property tax includes garbage pickup.

Trenton has no personal property tax for individuals.

★Total tax burdens in Trenton are higher than average overall.

NEW MEXICO

Income	Home Value	Property Tax & Other Fees	Personal Property Tax & Auto Fees	Sales Tax	Local Income Tax	State Income Tax*	Total Tax	Rank From #1–#149
ALBUQUERQUE								
$24,281	$50,000	$666	$80	$843	–	($16)	$1,573	#49
	75,000	984	80	843	–	(16)	1,891	#49
	100,000	1,303	80	843	–	(16)	2,210	#48
$34,275	$75,000	$984	$80	$1,084	–	($16)	$2,132	#31
	100,000	1,303	80	1,084	–	(16)	2,451	#30
	150,000	1,940	80	1,084	–	(16)	3,088	#29
$68,098	$150,000	$1,940	$80	$1,557	–	$2,810	$6,387	#96
	200,000	2,577	80	1,557	–	2,810	7,024	#90
	250,000	3,214	80	1,557	–	2,810	7,661	#84
CARLSBAD								
$24,281	$50,000	$311	$80	$897	–	($16)	$1,272	#16
	75,000	441	80	897	–	(16)	1,402	#10
	100,000	572	80	897	–	(16)	1,533	#9
$34,275	$75,000	$441	$80	$1,154	–	($16)	$1,659	#8
	100,000	572	80	1,154	–	(16)	1,790	#7
	150,000	833	80	1,154	–	(16)	2,051	#6
$68,098	$150,000	$833	$80	$1,658	–	$2,810	$5,381	#57
	200,000	1,095	80	1,658	–	2,810	5,643	#41 (tie)
	250,000	1,356	80	1,658	–	2,810	5,904	#24
LAS CRUCES								
$24,281	$50,000	$476	$80	$915	–	($16)	$1,455	#33
	75,000	705	80	915	–	(16)	1,684	#29
	100,000	934	80	915	–	(16)	1,913	#22
$34,275	$75,000	$705	$80	$1,178	–	($16)	$1,947	#16
	100,000	934	80	1,178	–	(16)	2,176	#15
	150,000	1,391	80	1,178	–	(16)	2,633	#17
$68,098	$150,000	$1,391	$80	$1,691	–	$2,810	$5,972	#84
	200,000	1,848	80	1,691	–	2,810	6,429	#69
	250,000	2,306	80	1,691	–	2,810	6,887	#66
RIO RANCHO								
$24,281	$50,000	$495	$80	$897	–	($16)	$1,456	#34
	75,000	724	80	897	–	(16)	1,685	#30
	100,000	954	80	897	–	(16)	1,915	#23
$34,275	$75,000	$724	$80	$1154	–	($16)	$1,942	#15
	100,000	954	80	1154	–	(16)	2,172	#14
	150,000	1,414	80	1154	–	(16)	2,632	#16
$68,098	$150,000	$1,414	$80	$1,658	–	$2,810	$5,962	#83
	200,000	1,874	80	1,658	–	2,810	6,422	#67
	250,000	2,334	80	1,658	–	2,810	6,882	#65
ROSWELL								
$24,281	$50,000	$453	$80	$920	–	($16)	$1,437	#30 (tie)
	75,000	653	80	920	–	(16)	1,637	#24
	100,000	854	80	920	–	(16)	1,838	#17
$34,275	$75,000	$653	$80	$1,184	–	($16)	$1,901	#14
	100,000	854	80	1,184	–	(16)	2,102	#11
	150,000	1,255	80	1,184	–	(16)	2,503	#12
$68,098	$150,000	$1,255	$80	$1,700	–	$2,810	$5,845	#77
	200,000	1,656	80	1,700	–	2,810	6,246	#61
	250,000	2,057	80	1,700	–	2,810	6,647	#53

*Credit for prescription drugs is issued as a reduction of income tax due or as a refund if the credit is greater than the tax liability.

Income	Home Value	Property Tax & Other Fees	Personal Property Tax & Auto Fees	Sales Tax	Local Income Tax	State Income Tax*	Total Tax	Rank From #1–#149
SANTA FE								
$24,281	$50,000	$334	$80	$906	–	($16)	$1,304	#18
	75,000	468	80	906	–	(16)	1,438	#11
	100,000	602	80	906	–	(16)	1,572	#11
$34,275	$75,000	$468	$80	$1,166	–	($16)	$1,698	#9
	100,000	602	80	1,166	–	(16)	1,832	#9
	150,000	869	80	1,166	–	(16)	2,099	#7
$68,098	$150,000	$869	$80	$1,675	–	$2,810	$5,434	#61
	200,000	1,137	80	1,675	–	2,810	5,702	#44
	250,000	1,404	80	1,675	–	2,810	5,969	#26

*Credit for prescription drugs is issued as a reduction of income tax due or as a refund if the credit is greater than the tax liability.

New Mexico has a state income tax and a state gross receipts tax (sales tax).

The state income tax rate is graduated from 2.2% to 8.5% depending upon income bracket. For married couples filing jointly with taxable income up to $8,000, the rate is 2.2%; up to $16,000, the tax is $176 plus 3.2% of the amount above $8,000; up to $24,000, the tax is $432 plus 4.7% of the amount above $16,000; up to $36,000, the tax is $808 plus 6% of the amount above $24,000; up to $48,000, the tax is $1,528 plus 7.1% of the amount above $36,000; up to $64,000, the tax is $2,380 plus 7.9% of the amount above $48,000; above $64,000, the tax is $3,644 plus 8.5% of the amount above $64,000.

In calculating the tax, there is no deduction for federal income tax paid. Federal, state and private pensions are not exempt. Social Security benefits subject to federal tax are not exempt. There is a $2,450 personal exemption per person and a $7,850 standard deduction for married couples filing jointly when both are age 65 or older. There is a deduction of $1,000 to $8,000 per person for married couples filing jointly, both age 65 or older, with adjusted gross income of $51,000 or less.

Major tax credits or rebates include: Credit for income taxes paid to other states, child day-care credit, low-income comprehensive tax rebate, property tax rebate for persons 65 or older and credit for prescription drugs. Our couples qualify for the credit for prescription drugs but do not qualify for the other programs.

The state gross receipts tax rate is 5% but local governments can add to this amount. Although this tax is imposed on the seller (unlike a sales tax which is imposed on the buyer), businesses customarily pass the tax on to the buyer.

Our couples relocating to the cities listed below must pay to register and annually renew license plates based on year and weight of each automobile. The fees to register the Chrysler and the Oldsmobile are $43 and $35 respectively. Our couples also pay $4.50 per car in miscellaneous fees at the time of registration. Thereafter, on an annual basis, our couples will pay a registration fee and miscellaneous fees, per automobile.

ALBUQUERQUE

Albuquerque has no local income tax but does levy a gross receipts tax (sales tax).

Most purchases are taxed at a rate of 5.8125%. Major consumer categories taxed at a different rate: None. Major consumer categories which are exempt from gross receipts tax: None.

For most residents within the city limits of Albuquerque, the property tax rate is .038228. Homes are assessed at 100% of 1990 market value. Taxable value is one-third of assessed value. There is a head-of-household exemption for all homeowners of $2,000 off the taxable value. Property tax does not cover garbage pickup; the additional fee is approximately $105 per year.

Albuquerque has no personal property tax for individuals.

★Total tax burdens in Albuquerque are lower than average for the $24,281 and $34,275 income categories and about average for the $68,098 income category.

CARLSBAD

Carlsbad has no local income tax but does levy a gross receipts tax (sales tax).

Most purchases are taxed at a rate of 6.1875%. Major consumer categories taxed at a different rate: None. Major consumer categories which are exempt from gross receipts tax: None.

Within the city limits of Carlsbad, the property tax rate is .017426. Homes are assessed at 89% to 90% of market value. Taxable value is one-third of assessed value. There is a head-of-household exemption for all homeowners of $2,000 off the taxable value. Property tax does not cover garbage pickup; the additional fee is approximately $84 per year.

Carlsbad has no personal property tax for individuals.

★Total tax burdens in Carlsbad are lower than average overall. Carlsbad is a tax heaven in 5 of 9 income/home value categories.

LAS CRUCES

Las Cruces has no local income tax but does levy a gross receipts tax (sales tax).

Most purchases are taxed at a rate of 6.3125%. Major consumer categories taxed at a different rate: None. Major consumer categories which are exempt from gross receipts tax: None.

Within the city limits of Las Cruces, the property tax rate is .027438. Homes are assessed at 100% of market value. Taxable value is one-third of market value. There is a head-of-household exemption for all homeowners of $2,000 off the taxable value. Property tax does not cover garbage pickup; the additional fee is approximately $74 per year for homeowners age 60 or older.

Las Cruces has no personal property tax for individuals.

★Total tax burdens in Las Cruces are lower than average for the $24,281 and $34,275 income categories and about average for the $68,098 income category.

RIO RANCHO

Rio Rancho has no local income tax but does levy a gross receipts tax (sales tax).

Most purchases are taxed at a rate of 6.1875%. Major consumer categories taxed at a different rate: None. Major consumer categories which are exempt from gross receipts tax: None.

For residents within the 94-IN district within TVI in Rio Rancho, the property tax rate is .030658. Homes are assessed at 80% to 90% of market value. We have calculated the tax using a 90% assessment rate for a new home. Taxable value is one-third of assessed value. There is a head-of-household exemption for all homeowners of $2,000 off the taxable value. Property tax does not cov-

er garbage pickup; the additional fee is approximately $96 per year for homeowners age 62 or older.

Rio Rancho has no personal property tax for individuals.

★Total tax burdens in Rio Rancho are lower than average for the $24,281 and $34,275 income categories and about average for the $68,098 income category.

ROSWELL

Roswell has no local income tax but does levy a gross receipts tax (sales tax).

During the 12-month period covered by this study, the sales tax rate changed from 6.3125% to 6.375%. Our estimates for sales tax are based on a weighted average of these rates. Major consumer categories taxed at a different rate: None. Major consumer categories which are exempt from gross receipts tax: None.

Within the city limits of Roswell, the property tax rate is .024062. Homes are assessed at 100% of market value. Taxable value is one-third of market value. There is a head-of-household exemption for all homeowners of $2,000 off the taxable value. Property tax does not cover garbage pickup; the additional fee is

approximately $100 per year.

Roswell has no personal property tax for individuals.

★Total tax burdens in Roswell are lower than average for the $24,281 and $34,275 income categories and about average for the $68,098 income category.

SANTA FE

Santa Fe has no local income tax but does levy a gross receipts tax (sales tax).

Most purchases are taxed at a rate of 6.25%. Major consumer categories taxed at a different rate: None. Major consumer categories which are exempt from gross receipts tax: None.

Within the city limits of Santa Fe, the property tax rate is .016046. Homes are assessed at 100% of market value. Taxable value is one-third of assessed value. There is a head-of-household exemption for all homeowners of $2,000 off the taxable value. Property tax does not cover garbage pickup; the additional fee is approximately $99 per year.

Santa Fe has no personal property tax for individuals.

★Total tax burdens in Santa Fe are lower than average overall. Santa Fe is a tax heaven in 3 of 9 income/home value categories.

NEW YORK

Income	Home Value	Property Tax & Other Fees	Personal Property Tax & Auto Fees	Sales Tax	Local Income Tax	State Income Tax	Total Tax	Rank From #1–#149
BUFFALO								
$24,281	$50,000	$1,265	$57	$838	–	–	$2,160	#120 (tie)
	75,000	1,898	57	838	–	–	2,793	#126
	100,000	2,531	57	838	–	–	3,426	#129
$34,275	$75,000	$1,898	$57	$1,131	–	$251	$3,337	#124
	100,000	2,531	57	1,131	–	251	3,970	#133
	150,000	3,796	57	1,131	–	251	5,235	#128
$68,098	$150,000	$3,796	$57	$1,753	–	$2,123	$7,729	#128
	200,000	5,062	57	1,753	–	2,123	8,995	#130
	250,000	6,327	57	1,753	–	2,123	10,260	#131
ITHACA								
$24,281	$50,000	$1,732	$57	$838	–	–	$2,627	#142
	75,000	2,474	57	838	–	–	3,369	#143
	100,000	3,217	57	838	–	–	4,112	#146
$34,275	$75,000	$2,539	$57	$1,131	–	$251	$3,978	#143
	100,000	3,303	57	1,131	–	251	4,742	#144
	150,000	4,831	57	1,131	–	251	6,270	#145
$68,098	$150,000	$4,831	$57	$1,753	–	$2,123	$8,764	#139
	200,000	6,359	57	1,753	–	2,123	10,292	#139
	250,000	7,887	57	1,753	–	2,123	11,820	#141
LONG BEACH								
$24,281	$50,000	$1,211	$67	$891	–	–	$2,169	#122
	75,000	1,736	67	891	–	–	2,694	#121
	100,000	2,261	67	891	–	–	3,219	#122
$34,275	$75,000	$1,736	$67	$1,202	–	$251	$3,256	#121
	100,000	2,261	67	1,202	–	251	3,781	#120
	150,000	3,312	67	1,202	–	251	4,832	#119
$68,098	$150,000	$3,312	$67	$1,863	–	$2,123	$7,365	#124
	200,000	4,363	67	1,863	–	2,123	8,416	#124
	250,000	5,414	67	1,863	–	2,123	9,467	#123
NEW YORK CITY								
$24,281	$50,000	$428	$87	$865	–	–	$1,380	#24
	75,000	642	87	865	–	–	1,594	#21
	100,000	856	87	865	–	–	1,808	#15
$34,275	$75,000	$642	$87	$1,166	$157	$251	$2,303	#44 (tie)
	100,000	856	87	1,166	$157	251	2,517	#35
	150,000	1,283	87	1,166	$157	251	2,944	#24
$68,098	$150,000	$1,283	$87	$1,808	$1,204	$2,123	$6,505	#102 (tie)
	200,000	1,711	87	1,808	$1,204	2,123	6,933	#88
	250,000	2,139	87	1,808	1,204	2,123	7,361	#77
	$300,000	$2,567	$87	$1,808	$1,204	$2,123	$7,789	Not Ranked
	350,000	2,994	87	1,808	1,204	2,123	8,216	Not Ranked
	400,000	3,422	87	1,808	1,204	2,123	8,644	Not Ranked
SYRACUSE								
$24,281	$50,000	$1,541	$57	$734	–	–	$2,332	#132
	75,000	2,203	57	734	–	–	2,994	#136
	100,000	2,864	57	734	–	–	3,655	#133
$34,275	$75,000	$2,203	$57	$990	–	$251	$3,501	#133
	100,000	2,864	57	990	–	251	4,162	#134
	150,000	4,187	57	990	–	251	5,485	#134
$68,098	$150,000	$4,187	$57	$1,534	–	$2,123	$7,901	#131
	200,000	5,511	57	1,534	–	2,123	9,225	#132
	250,000	6,834	57	1,534	–	2,123	10,548	#135

New York has a state income tax and a state sales tax.

The state income tax rate is graduated from 4% to 7.875% depending upon income bracket. For married couples filing jointly with taxable income up to $11,000, the rate is 4%; for taxable income of $11,000 to $16,000, the tax is $440 plus 5% of the amount above $11,000; for taxable income of $16,000 to $22,000, the tax is $690 plus 6% of the amount above $16,000; for taxable income of $22,000 to $26,000, the tax is $1,050 plus 7% of the amount above $22,000; and for taxable income above $26,000, the tax is $1,330 plus 7.875% of the amount above $26,000.

In calculating the tax, there is no deduction for federal income tax paid. Federal and state pensions are exempt. Private pensions are not exempt, but there is an exclusion of up to $20,000 of private pension income per person. Social Security benefits are exempt. There is a $9,500 standard deduction from adjusted gross income for married couples filing jointly.

Major tax credits or rebates include: Credit for income taxes paid to other states and real property tax credit. Our couples do not qualify for these programs.

The state sales tax rate is 4% or 4.25% depending on location, but local governments can add to this amount.

Our couples relocating to the cities listed below must pay a registration fee of $57 per automobile every two years, a plate fee of $5.50 per automobile and a title fee of $5 per automobile at the time of registration. Some counties may also impose a $10 county use tax every two years, and New York City imposes a $30 city vehicle tax every two years. Thereafter, our couples will pay a renewal fee and, possibly, a county use tax or city vehicle tax per automobile, every two years.

BUFFALO

Buffalo has no local income tax but does levy a sales tax.

Most purchases are taxed at a rate of 8%. Major consumer categories taxed at a different rate: None. Major consumer categories exempt from sales tax include: Drugs, groceries, medical services and medical supplies.

Within the city limits of Buffalo, the property tax rate is .02531. Homes are assessed at 100% of market value. There is an elderly exemption of up to 50% off property tax due for homeowners age 65 or older with a gross income of less than $21,300. Property tax includes garbage pickup.

Buffalo has no personal property tax for individuals.

★Total tax burdens in Buffalo are higher than average overall.

ITHACA

Ithaca has no local income tax but does levy a sales tax.

Most purchases are taxed at a rate of 8%. Major consumer categories taxed at a different rate: None. Major consumer categories exempt from sales tax include: Drugs, groceries, medical services and medical supplies.

Within the city limits of Ithaca, the property tax rate is .03056. Homes are assessed at 100% of market value. There is an elderly exemption of up to 50% off property tax due for the school district portion for homeowners age 65 or older with a gross income of less than $25,000. Property tax does not cover garbage pickup; the additional fee is approximately $247 per year.

Ithaca has no personal property tax for individuals.

★Total tax burdens in Ithaca are higher than average overall. Ithaca is a tax hell in 7 of 9 income/home value categories.

LONG BEACH

Long Beach has no local income tax but does levy a sales tax.

Most purchases are taxed at a rate of 8.5%. Major consumer categories taxed at a different rate: None. Major consumer categories exempt from sales tax include: Drugs, groceries, medical services and medical supplies.

Within the city limits of Long Beach, the property tax rate is .41153 for the county plus .070225 for the city. Homes are assessed at 3.4% of market value for county tax and 10% of market value for city tax. There is

an elderly exemption of up to 50% off property tax due for homeowners age 65 or older with a gross income of less than $21,300. Property tax does not cover garbage pickup; the additional fee is approximately $160 per year.

Long Beach has no personal property tax for individuals.

★Total tax burdens in Long Beach are higher than average overall.

NEW YORK CITY

New York City has a local income tax and levies a sales tax.

The local income tax rate is graduated from 2.51% to 4.46% depending upon income bracket. For married couples filing jointly with New York taxable income of up to $14,400, the rate is 2.51%; for taxable income of $14,401 to $15,500, the tax is $361 plus 3.08% of the amount above $14,400; for taxable income of $15,501 to $27,000, the tax is $395 plus 3.66% of the amount above $15,500; for taxable income of $27,001 to $45,000, the tax is $816 plus 4.28% of the amount above $27,000; for taxable income of $45,001 to $108,000, the tax is $1,587 plus 4.4% of the amount above $45,000; and for taxable income above $108,000, the tax is $4,359 plus 4.46% of the amount above $108,000.

In calculating the tax, the same exemptions and deductions are available as those offered at the state level.

Most purchases are taxed at a rate of 8.25%. Major consumer categories taxed at a different rate: None. Major consumer categories exempt from sales tax include: Drugs, groceries, medical services and medical supplies.

In Manhattan, the property tax rate is .10694. Homes are assessed at a maximum of 8% of market value. There is an elderly exemption of up to 50% off property tax due for homeowners age 65 or older with a gross income of less than $21,300. Property tax includes garbage pickup.

New York City has no personal property tax for individuals.

★Total tax burdens in New York City are lower than average for the $24,281 and $34,275 income categories and about average for the $68,098 income category.

SYRACUSE

Syracuse has no local income tax but does levy a sales tax.

Most purchases are taxed at a rate of 7%. Major consumer categories taxed at a different rate: None. Major consumer categories exempt from sales tax include: Drugs, groceries, medical services and medical supplies.

Within the city limits of Syracuse, the property tax rate is .3295544. Homes are assessed at 8.03% of market value. There is an elderly exemption of up to 50% off property tax due for homeowners age 65 or older with a gross income of less than $21,300. Property tax includes garbage pickup.

There is a county sewer charge of approximately $218 per year. Some residents may live within special assessment districts and be subject to additional charges such as curbs, streets and sidewalks.

Syracuse has no personal property tax for individuals.

★Total tax burdens in Syracuse are higher than average overall.

NORTH CAROLINA

Income	Home Value	Property Tax & Other Fees	Personal Property Tax & Auto Fees	Sales Tax	Local Income Tax	State Income Tax	Total Tax	Rank From #1–#149
ASHEVILLE								
$24,281	$50,000	$755	$339	$600	–	$237	$1,931	#95
	75,000	1,133	339	600	–	237	2,309	#97
	100,000	1,510	339	600	–	237	2,686	#96
$34,275	$75,000	$1,133	$339	$798	–	$769	$3,039	#112
	100,000	1,510	339	798	–	769	3,416	#107
	150,000	2,265	339	798	–	769	4,171	#103
$68,098	$150,000	$2,265	$339	$1,108	–	$2,912	$6,624	#107
	200,000	3,020	339	1,108	–	2,912	7,379	#103
	250,000	3,775	339	1,108	–	2,912	8,134	#97
BREVARD								
$24,281	$50,000	$757	$298	$600	–	$237	$1,892	#90 (tie)
	75,000	1,064	298	600	–	237	2,199	#82
	100,000	1,371	298	600	–	237	2,506	#79
$34,275	$75,000	$1,064	$298	$798	–	$769	$2,929	#100
	100,000	1,371	298	798	–	769	3,236	#94
	150,000	1,985	298	798	–	769	3,850	#83
$68,098	$150,000	$1,985	$298	$1,108	–	$2,912	$6,303	#93 (tie)
	200,000	2,599	298	1,108	–	2,912	6,917	#87
	250,000	3,213	298	1,108	–	2,912	7,531	#80
CHAPEL HILL								
$24,281	$50,000	$767	$392	$600	–	$237	$1,996	#100
	75,000	1,150	392	600	–	237	2,379	#106
	100,000	1,534	392	600	–	237	2,763	#103
$34,275	$75,000	$1,150	$392	$798	–	$769	$3,109	#115
	100,000	1,534	392	798	–	769	3,493	#110
	150,000	2,301	392	798	–	769	4,260	#104
$68,098	$150,000	$2,301	$392	$1,108	–	$2,912	$6,713	#111
	200,000	3,067	392	1,108	–	2,912	7,479	#107
	250,000	3,834	392	1,108	–	2,912	8,246	#102
EDENTON								
$24,281	$50,000	$575	$281	$600	–	$237	$1,693	#59 (tie)
	75,000	863	281	600	–	237	1,981	#56
	100,000	1,150	281	600	–	237	2,268	#54
$34,275	$75,000	$863	$281	$798	–	$769	$2,711	#84
	100,000	1,150	281	798	–	769	2,998	#79
	150,000	1,725	281	798	–	769	3,573	#64
$68,098	$150,000	$1,725	$281	$1,108	–	$2,912	$6,026	#85
	200,000	2,300	281	1,108	–	2,912	6,601	#79
	250,000	2,875	281	1,108	–	2,912	7,176	#73
HENDERSONVILLE								
$24,281	$50,000	$749	$306	$600	–	$237	$1,892	#90 (tie)
	75,000	1,067	306	600	–	237	2,210	#85
	100,000	1,384	306	600	–	237	2,527	#83
$34,275	$75,000	$1,067	$306	$798	–	$769	$2,940	#103
	100,000	1,384	306	798	–	769	3,257	#98
	150,000	2,019	306	798	–	769	3,892	#86
$68,098	$150,000	$2,019	$306	$1,108	–	$2,912	$6,345	#95
	200,000	2,654	306	1,108	–	2,912	6,980	#89
	250,000	3,289	306	1,108	–	2,912	7,615	#83

Income	Home Value	Property Tax & Other Fees	Personal Property Tax & Auto Fees	Sales Tax	Local Income Tax	State Income Tax	Total Tax	Rank From #1–#149
PINEHURST								
$24,281	$50,000	$410	$212	$600	–	$237	$1,459	#35
	75,000	615	212	600	–	237	1,664	#27
	100,000	820	212	600	–	237	1,869	#18
$34,275	$75,000	$615	$212	$798	–	$769	$2,394	#54
	100,000	820	212	798	–	769	2,599	#40
	150,000	1,230	212	798	–	769	3,009	#26
$68,098	$150,000	$1,230	$212	$1,108	–	$2,912	$5,462	#62
	200,000	1,640	212	1,108	–	2,912	5,872	#51
	250,000	2,050	212	1,108	–	2,912	6,282	#39

North Carolina has a state income tax and a state sales tax.

The state income tax rate is graduated from 6% to 7.75% depending upon income bracket. For married couples filing jointly with taxable income of up to $21,250, the rate is 6%; up to $100,000, the tax is $1,275 plus 7% of the amount above $21,250; above $100,000, the tax is $6,787.50 plus 7.75% of the amount above $100,000.

In calculating the tax, there is no deduction for federal income tax paid. There is an exclusion of up to $4,000 in federal, state and local government pensions per person and an exclusion of up to $2,000 in private pensions per person, but no more than $4,000 in total retirement benefits (not counting Social Security) may be deducted per person. Social Security benefits are exempt. There is a $5,000 standard deduction from adjusted gross income for married couples filing jointly. There is a $2,000 personal exemption per person from adjusted gross income and a $600 personal exemption per person from adjusted gross income for persons age 65 or older.

Major tax credits or rebates include: Credit for income taxes paid to other states, child and dependent care credit, credit for North Carolina dividends and credit for the disabled taxpayer, dependent or spouse. Our couples do not qualify for these programs.

The state sales tax rate is 4% but local governments can add to this amount.

Since car registration and renewal fees differ within the state, see city information for details.

ASHEVILLE

Asheville has no local income tax but does levy a sales tax.

Most purchases are taxed at a rate of 6%. Major consumer categories taxed at a different rate: None. Major consumer categories which are exempt from the sales tax include: Drugs and transportation.

In the area of the City School District, the property tax rate is .0151. Homes are assessed at 100% of market value. There is a senior citizen exemption of $15,000 off assessed value for persons age 65 or older with a gross income of $11,000 or less. Property tax includes garbage pickup.

Asheville has a personal property tax rate of .0151 within the City School District. Personal property is assessed at 100% of market value. Items subject to the tax include tagged and untagged vehicles, boats, motorcycles and mobile homes.

Our couples relocating to Asheville must pay a highway use tax of $150 per automobile , a title fee of $35 per automobile and a plate fee of $20 per automobile at the time of registration. The highway use tax is 3% of the current fair market value of the automobile, with a minimum tax of $40 and a maximum tax of $150. Thereafter, on an annual basis, our couples will pay a plate fee per automobile.
★Total tax burdens in Asheville are about average for the $24,281 and $68,098 income categories and higher than average for the $34,275 income category.

BREVARD

Brevard has no local income tax but does levy a sales tax.

Most purchases are taxed at a rate of 6%. Major consumer categories taxed at a different rate: None. Major consumer categories which are exempt from the sales tax include: Drugs and transportation.

Within the city limits of Brevard the property tax rate is .01228. Homes are assessed at 100% of market value. There is a senior citizen exemption of $15,000 off assessed value for persons age 65 or older with a gross income of $11,000 or less. Property tax does not include garbage pickup; the additional fee is approximately $78 per year. There is a solid waste fee of $65 per year.

Brevard has a personal property tax rate of .01228. Personal property is assessed at 100% of market value. Items subject to the tax include boats, mobile homes and tagged and untagged vehicles.

Our couples relocating to Brevard must pay a highway use tax of $150 per automobile , a title fee of $35 per automobile and a plate fee of $20 per automobile at the time of registration. The highway use tax is 3% of the current computer value of the automobile, with a minimum tax of $40 and a maximum tax of $150. Thereafter, on an annual basis, our couples will pay a plate fee per automobile.
★Total tax burdens in Brevard are about average overall.

CHAPEL HILL

Chapel Hill has no local income tax but does levy a sales tax.

Most purchases are taxed at a rate of 6%. Major consumer categories taxed at a different rate: None. Major consumer categories which are exempt from the sales tax include: Drugs and transportation.

In Durham County, the property tax rate is .015337. Homes are assessed at 100% of market value. There is a senior citizen exemption of $15,000 off assessed value for persons age 65 or older with a gross income of $11,000 or less. Property tax includes garbage pickup.

Chapel Hill has a personal property tax rate of .015337 within Durham County. Personal property is assessed at 100% of NADA retail. Items subject to the tax include tagged and untagged vehicles. There is also a $10 vehicle fee per automobile.

Our couples relocating to Chapel Hill must pay a highway use tax of $150 per automobile, a title fee of $35 per automobile, a plate fee of $20 per automobile, and a transit tax of $5 per automobile at the time of registration. The highway use tax is 3% of the current wholesale value of the automobile, with a minimum tax of $40 and a maximum tax of $150. Thereafter, on an annual basis, our couples will pay a plate fee and a transit tax per automobile.

★Total tax burdens in Chapel Hill are higher than average overall.

EDENTON

Edenton has no local income tax but does levy a sales tax.

Most purchases are taxed at a rate of 6%. Major consumer categories taxed at a different rate: None. Major consumer categories which are exempt from the sales tax include: Drugs and transportation.

Within the city limits of Edenton, the property tax rate is .0115. Homes are assessed at 100% of market value. There is a senior citizen exemption of $15,000 off assessed value for persons age 65 or older with a gross income of $11,000 or less. Property tax includes garbage pickup.

Edenton has a personal property tax rate of .0115. Personal property is assessed at 100% of market value. Items subject to the tax include boats, mobile homes and tagged and untagged vehicles.

Our couples relocating to Edenton must pay a highway use tax of $150 per automobile, a title fee of $35 per automobile and a plate fee of $20 per automobile at the time of registration. The highway use tax is 3% of the current computer value of the automobile, with a minimum tax of $40 and a maximum tax of $150. Thereafter, on an annual basis, our couples will pay a plate fee per automobile.

★Total tax burdens in Edenton are about average overall.

HENDERSONVILLE

Hendersonville has no local income tax but does levy a sales tax.

Most purchases are taxed at a rate of 6%. Major consumer categories taxed at a different rate: None. Major consumer categories which are exempt from the sales tax include: Drugs and transportation.

Within the city limits of Hendersonville, the property tax rate is .0127. Homes are assessed at 100% of market value. There is a senior citizen exemption of $15,000 off assessed value for persons age 65 or older with a gross income of $11,000 or less. Property tax does not cover garbage pickup; the additional fee is approximately $114 per year.

Hendersonville has a personal property tax rate of .0127. Personal property is assessed at 100% of NADA retail. Items subject to the tax include boats, mobile homes and tagged and untagged vehicles.

Our couples relocating to Hendersonville must pay a highway use tax of $150 per automobile, a title fee of $35 per automobile and a plate fee of

$20 per automobile at the time of registration. The highway use tax is 3% of the current computer value of the automobile, with a minimum tax of $40 and a maximum tax of $150. Thereafter, on an annual basis, our couples will pay a plate fee per automobile.

★Total tax burdens in Hendersonville are about average overall.

PINEHURST

Pinehurst has no local income tax but does levy a sales tax.

Most purchases are taxed at a rate of 6%. Major consumer categories taxed at a different rate: None. Major consumer categories which are exempt from the sales tax include: Drugs and transportation.

Within the village limits of Pinehurst, the property tax rate is .0082. Homes are assessed at 100% of market value. There is a senior citizen exemption of $15,000 off assessed value for persons age 65 or older with a gross income of $11,000 or less. Property tax includes garbage pickup.

Pinehurst has a personal property tax rate of .0082. Personal property is assessed at 100% of NADA retail. Items subject to the tax include boats, mobile homes and tagged and untagged vehicles.

Our couples relocating to Pinehurst must pay a highway use tax of $150 per automobile, a title fee of $35 per automobile and a plate fee of $20 per automobile at the time of registration. The highway use tax is 3% of the current wholesale value of the automobile, with a minimum tax of $40 and a maximum tax of $150. Thereafter, on an annual basis, our couples will pay a plate fee per automobile.

★Total tax burdens in Pinehurst are lower than average overall.

NORTH DAKOTA

Income	Home Value	Property Tax & Other Fees	Personal Property Tax & Auto Fees	Sales Tax	Local Income Tax	State Income Tax	Total Tax	Rank From #1–#149
BISMARCK								
$24,281	$50,000	$1,248	$140	$647	–	$71	$2,106	#114
	75,000	1,812	140	647	–	71	2,670	#120
	100,000	2,376	140	647	–	71	3,234	#123
$34,275	$75,000	$1,812	$140	$871	–	$258	$3,081	#114
	100,000	2,376	140	871	–	258	3,645	#115
	150,000	3,504	140	871	–	258	4,773	#116
$68,098	$150,000	$3,504	$140	$1,349	–	$1,412	$6,405	#97 (tie)
	200,000	4,632	140	1,349	–	1,412	7,533	#110
	250,000	5,760	140	1,349	–	1,412	8,661	#112
FARGO								
$24,281	$50,000	$1,138	$140	$636	–	$71	$1,985	#97
	75,000	1,668	140	636	–	71	2,515	#117
	100,000	2,197	140	636	–	71	3,044	#117
$34,275	$75,000	$1,668	$140	$855	–	$258	$2,921	#99
	100,000	2,197	140	855	–	258	3,450	#108
	150,000	3,255	140	855	–	258	4,508	#107
$68,098	$150,000	$3,255	$140	$1,321	–	$1,412	$6,128	#89
	200,000	4,314	140	1,321	–	1,412	7,187	#98
	250,000	5,372	140	1,321	–	1,412	8,245	#101

North Dakota has a state income tax and a state sales tax.

The state income tax rate is 14% of federal income tax liability before subtracting any federal income tax credits.

Major tax credits or rebates include: Credit for income taxes paid to other states and senior citizens' or disabled property tax rebate. Our couples do not qualify for these programs.

The state sales tax rate is 5% but local governments can add to this amount.

Our couples relocating to the cities listed below must pay a registration fee of $70 per automobile and $5 per automobile for a title at the time of registration. Thereafter, on an annual basis, our couples will pay a registration fee per automobile.

BISMARCK

Bismarck has no local income tax but does levy a sales tax.

Most purchases are taxed at a rate of 6%. Major consumer categories taxed at a different rate include: Food away from home, which is taxed at a rate of 7%. Major consumer categories which are exempt from the sales tax include: Drugs, groceries and medical services.

For most residents within the city limits of Bismarck, the property tax rate is .50129. Homes are assessed at 50% of market value. Taxable value is 9% of assessed value. There is a homestead credit for homeowners age 65 or older or disabled with income of less than $13,000 after medical expenses and assets less than $50,000, excluding home. Property tax does not cover garbage pickup; the additional fee is approximately $120 per year.

Bismarck has no personal property tax for individuals.

★Total tax burdens in Bismarck are higher than average overall.

FARGO

Fargo has no local income tax but does levy a sales tax.

Most purchases are taxed at a rate of 6%. Major consumer categories taxed at a different rate: None. Major consumer categories which are exempt from the sales tax include: Drugs, groceries and medical services.

In Fargo School District #1, the property tax rate is .47044. Homes are assessed at 50% of market value. Taxable value is 9% of assessed value. There is a homestead credit for homeowners age 65 or older or disabled with income of less than $13,000 after medical expenses and assets less than $50,000, excluding home. There is a new home exemption of $75,000 off market value of the home, excluding land, for the first owners of a home for the first two years of ownership. Property tax does not cover garbage pickup; the additional fee is approximately $67 per year. Residents also pay approximately $13 per year in forestry fees.

Fargo has no personal property tax for individuals.

★Total tax burdens in Fargo are higher than average for the $24,281 and $34,275 income categories and about average for the $68,098 income category.

OHIO

Income	Home Value	Property Tax & Other Fees	Personal Property Tax & Auto Fees	Sales Tax	Local Income Tax	State Income Tax	Total Tax	Rank From #1–#149
CINCINNATI								
$24,281	$50,000	$930	$104	$583	$92	–	$1,709	#63 (tie)
	75,000	1,376	104	583	92	–	2,155	#79
	100,000	1,823	104	583	92	–	2,602	#90
$34,275	$75,000	$1,376	$104	$784	$202	$322	$2,788	#91
	100,000	1,823	104	784	202	322	3,235	#93
	150,000	2,716	104	784	202	322	4,128	#99
$68,098	$150,000	$2,716	$104	$1,211	$634	$1,855	$6,520	#104
	200,000	3,608	104	1,211	634	1,855	7,412	#105
	250,000	4,501	104	1,211	634	1,855	8,305	#105
CLEVELAND								
$24,281	$50,000	$767	$104	$742	$88	–	$1,701	#61 (tie)
	75,000	1,150	104	742	88	–	2,084	#67
	100,000	1,534	104	742	88	–	2,468	#71
$34,275	$75,000	$1,150	$104	$997	$193	$322	$2,766	#89
	100,000	1,534	104	997	193	322	3,150	#87
	150,000	2,301	104	997	193	322	3,917	#87
$68,098	$150,000	$2,301	$104	$1,541	$604	$1,855	$6,405	#97 (tie)
	200,000	3,067	104	1,541	604	1,855	7,171	#96
	250,000	3,834	104	1,541	604	1,855	7,938	#91
COLUMBUS								
$24,281	$50,000	$756	$85	$610	$88	–	$1,539	#40
	75,000	1,134	85	610	88	–	1,917	#50
	100,000	1,513	85	610	88	–	2,296	#56
$34,275	$75,000	$1,134	$85	$819	$193	$322	$2,553	#71
	100,000	1,513	85	819	193	322	2,932	#74
	150,000	2,269	85	819	193	322	3,688	#73
$68,098	$150,000	$2,269	$85	$1,266	$604	$1,855	$6,079	#87
	200,000	3,025	85	1,266	604	1,855	6,835	#85
	250,000	3,781	85	1,266	604	1,855	7,591	#82
DAYTON								
$24,281	$50,000	$981	$94	$689	$99	–	$1,863	#86
	75,000	1,496	94	689	99	–	2,378	#105
	100,000	2,012	94	689	99	–	2,894	#109
$34,275	$75,000	$1,496	$94	$926	$217	$322	$3,055	#113
	100,000	2,012	94	926	217	322	3,571	#113
	150,000	3,043	94	926	217	322	4,602	#110
$68,098	$150,000	$3,043	$94	$1,431	$679	$1,855	$7,102	#119
	200,000	4,073	94	1,431	679	1,855	8,132	#121
	250,000	5,104	94	1,431	679	1,855	9,163	#121

Ohio has a state income tax and a state sales tax.

The state income tax rate is graduated from .743% to 7.5% depending upon income bracket. For married couples filing jointly with taxable income up to $5,000, the rate is .743%; up to $10,000, the tax is $37.15 plus 1.486% of the amount above $5,000; up to $15,000, the tax is $111.45 plus 2.972% of the amount above $10,000; up to $20,000, the tax is $260.05 plus 3.715% of the amount above $15,000; up to $40,000, the tax is $445.80 plus 4.457% of the amount above $20,000; up to $80,000, the tax is $1,337.20 plus 5.201% of the amount above $40,000; up to $100,000, the tax is $3,417.60 plus 5.943% of the amount above $80,000; up to $200,000, the tax is $4,606.20 plus 6.9% of the amount above $100,000; above $200,000, the tax is $11,506.20 plus 7.5% of the amount above $200,000.

In calculating the tax, there is no deduction for federal income tax paid. There is a pension income credit of up to $200 for federal, state and private pensions of a married couple filing jointly. Social Security benefits are exempt. There is a $650 personal exemption per person from adjusted gross income. There is a $20 tax credit per person and a $50 tax credit for married couples filing jointly when one or both persons are age

65 or older. There is a joint filing credit of up to $650 for married couples filing jointly if both spouses are employed.

Major tax credits or rebates include: Credit for income taxes paid to other states and child-care credit. Our couples do not qualify for these programs.

The state sales tax rate is 5% but local governments can add to this amount.

Since car registration and renewal fees differ within the state, see city information for details.

CINCINNATI

Cincinnati has a local income tax and a sales tax.

The local income tax rate is 2.1%, which is applied to wages, salaries and self-employment income.

In calculating the tax, federal, state and private pensions are exempt. Social Security benefits are exempt. There is a 100% credit for income taxes paid to other cities.

Most purchases are taxed at a rate of 5.5%. Major consumer categories taxed at a different rate: None. Major consumer categories which are exempt from sales tax include: Drugs, groceries and medical services.

Within the Cincinnati School District, the property tax rate is .058307981. Homes are assessed at 35% of market value. There is a reduction of 10% of property taxes due for all homeowners. There is a reduction of 2.5% of property taxes due for all owner-occupied homes. There is also an elderly exemption of up to $5,000 off assessed home value for homeowners age 65 or older with income of less than $16,500. Property tax includes garbage pickup. There is a storm water utility fee of approximately $25 per year and a tree assessment which we have estimated at $12 per year for our couples.

Cincinnati has no personal property tax.

Our couples relocating to Cincinnati must pay a plate fee of $43 per automobile, a title fee of $6 per automobile, an emissions test fee of $19.50 per automobile and an inspection fee of $3 per automobile, at the time of registration. Thereafter, on an annual basis, our couples will pay a plate fee per automobile. Our couples will also pay an emissions test fee per automobile, every two years.

★Total tax burdens in Cincinnati are about average overall.

CLEVELAND

Cleveland has a local income tax and a sales tax.

The local income tax rate is 2%, which is applied to wages, salaries and self-employment income.

In calculating the tax, federal, state and private pensions are exempt. Social Security benefits are exempt. There is a 50% credit for income taxes paid to other cities.

Most purchases are taxed at a rate of 7%. Major consumer categories taxed at a different rate: None. Major consumer categories which are exempt from sales tax include: Drugs, groceries and medical services.

Within the Cleveland School District, the property tax rate is .05008. Homes are assessed at 35% of market value. There is a reduction of 10% of property taxes due for all homeowners. There is a reduction of 2.5% of property taxes due for all owner-occupied homes. There is also an elderly exemption of up to $5,000 off assessed home value for homeowners age 65 or older with income of less than $16,500. Property tax includes garbage pickup. Some residents may be subject to additional city fees, such as curb, lighting and sewer fees.

Cleveland has no personal property tax.

Our couples relocating to Cleveland must pay a plate fee of $43 per automobile, a title fee of $10 per automobile, an emissions test fee of $19.50 per automobile and an inspection fee of $3 per automobile. Thereafter, on an annual basis, our couples will pay a plate fee per automobile. Our couples will also pay an emissions test fee per automobile, every two years.

★Total tax burdens in Cleveland are about average overall.

COLUMBUS

Columbus has a local income tax and a sales tax.

The local income tax rate is 2%, which is applied to wages, salaries and self-employment income.

In calculating the tax, federal, state and private pensions are exempt. Social Security benefits are exempt. There is a 100% credit for income taxes paid to other cities.

Most purchases are taxed at a rate of 5.75%. Major consumer categories taxed at a different rate: None. Major consumer categories which are exempt from sales tax include: Drugs, groceries and medical services.

Within the Columbus city limits, the property tax rate is .04939. Homes are assessed at 35% of market value. There is a reduction of 10% of property taxes due for all homeowners. There is a reduction of 2.5% of property taxes due for all owner-occupied homes. There is also an elderly exemption of up to $5,000 off assessed home value for homeowners age 65 or older with income of less than $16,500. Property tax includes garbage pickup. Some residents may be subject to additional city fees, such as sidewalk, weed-cutting and sewer fees.

Columbus has no personal property tax.

Our couples relocating to Columbus must pay a plate fee of $43 per automobile, a title fee of $10 per automobile and an inspection fee of $3 per automobile. Thereafter, on an annual basis, our couples will pay a plate fee per automobile.

★Total tax burdens in Columbus are lower than average for the $24,281 income category and about average for the $34,275 and $68,098 income categories.

DAYTON

Dayton has a local income tax and a sales tax.

The local income tax rate is 2.25%, which is applied to wages, salaries and self-employment income.

In calculating the tax, federal, state and private pensions are exempt. Social Security benefits are exempt. There is a 100% credit for income taxes paid to other cities.

Most purchases are taxed at a rate of 6.5%. Major consumer categories taxed at a different rate: None. Major consumer categories which are exempt from sales tax include: Drugs, groceries and medical services.

Within the Dayton city limits, the property tax rate is .06732. Homes are assessed at 35% of market value. There is a reduction of 10% of property taxes due for all homeowners. There is a reduction of 2.5% of property taxes due for all owner-occupied homes. There is also an elderly exemption of up to $5,000 off assessed home value for homeowners age 65 or older with income of less than $16,500. There is a $50 credit against property taxes due for homeowners 60 years of age or older. Property tax includes garbage pickup. Some residents may be subject to additional city fees, such as curb, lighting, weed cutting, gutter and paving fees.

Dayton has no personal property tax.

Our couples relocating to Dayton must pay a plate fee of $38 per automobile, a title fee of $10 per automobile, an emissions test fee of $19.50 per automobile and an inspection fee of $3 per automobile. Thereafter, on an annual basis, our couples will pay a plate fee per automobile. Our couples will also pay an emissions test fee per automobile, every two years. ★Total tax burdens in Dayton are higher than average overall.

OKLAHOMA

Income	Home Value	Property Tax & Other Fees	Personal Property Tax & Auto Fees	Sales Tax	Local Income Tax	State Income Tax	Total Tax	Rank From #1–#149
OKLAHOMA CITY								
$24,281	$50,000	$586	$391	$1,086	–	$162	$2,225	#128
	75,000	875	422	1,086	–	162	2,545	#118
	100,000	1,164	454	1,086	–	162	2,866	#107
$34,275	$75,000	$875	$422	$1,438	–	$756	$3,491	#132
	100,000	1,164	454	1,438	–	756	3,812	#122
	150,000	1,742	517	1,438	–	756	4,453	#106
$68,098	$150,000	$1,742	$517	$2,104	–	$2,984	$7,347	#123
	200,000	2,319	580	2,104	–	2,984	7,987	#120
	250,000	2,897	643	2,104	–	2,984	8,628	#111
TULSA								
$24,281	$50,000	$608	$338	$1,005	–	$162	$2,113	#115
	75,000	885	338	1,005	–	162	2,390	#107
	100,000	1,163	338	1,005	–	162	2,668	#94
$34,275	$75,000	$885	$338	$1,331	–	$756	$3,310	#122
	100,000	1,163	338	1,331	–	756	3,588	#114
	150,000	1,719	338	1,331	–	756	4,144	#100
$68,098	$150,000	$1,719	$338	$1,947	–	$2,984	$6,988	#117
	200,000	2,274	338	1,947	–	2,984	7,543	#111
	250,000	2,830	338	1,947	–	2,984	8,099	#94

Oklahoma has a state income tax and a state sales tax.

There are two methods for determining the amount of state income tax due. Using Method I, the state income tax rate is graduated from .5% to 7% depending upon income bracket. For married couples filing jointly with taxable income of up to $2,000, the rate is .5%; up to $5,000, the tax is $10 plus 1% of the amount above $2,000; up to $7,500, the tax is $40 plus 2% of the amount above $5,000; up to $9,800, the tax is $90 plus 3% of the amount above $7,500; up to $12,200, the tax is $159 plus 4% of the amount above $9,800; up to $15,000, the tax is $255 plus 5% of the amount above $12,200; up to $21,000, the tax is $395 plus 6% of the amount above $15,000; above $21,000, the tax is $755 plus 7% of the amount above $21,000.

Using Method II, the income brackets and tax amounts stay the same as Method I for income of up to $7,500; up to $8,900, the tax is $90 plus 3% of the amount above $7,500; up to $10,400, the tax is $132 plus 4% of the amount above $8,900; up to $12,000, the tax is $192 plus 5% of the amount above $10,400; up to $13,250, the tax is $272 plus 6% of

the amount above $12,000; up to $15,000, the tax is $347 plus 7% of the amount above $13,250; up to $18,000, the tax is $469.50 plus 8% of the amount above $15,000; up to $24,000, the tax is $709.50 plus 9% of the amount above $18,000; above $24,000, the tax is $1,249.50 plus 10% of the amount above $24,000.

In calculating the tax, there is a deduction for federal income tax paid only if Method II is used. Federal and state pensions are exempt up to $5,500 per person. Private pensions are not exempt. Social Security benefits are exempt. There is a 15% standard deduction of Oklahoma adjusted gross income for married couples filing jointly. The deduction ranges from $1,000 to $2,000. There is a $1,000 personal exemption per person and an additional $1,000 personal exemption per person for married couples filing jointly age 65 or older whose federal adjusted gross income does not exceed $25,000.

Major tax credits or rebates include: Credit for income taxes paid to other states, child-care credit, credit or refund of property taxes and low-income sales tax credit. Our couples do not qualify for these programs.

The state sales tax rate is 4.5% but

local governments can add to this amount.

Our couples relocating to the cities listed below must pay a tag fee per automobile based on the year and MSRP of the automobile. The tag fee is $190 for the Chrysler and $137 for the Oldsmobile. Our couples also pay a title fee of $11 per automobile and $25 per automobile in road use and miscellaneous fees. Thereafter, on an annual basis, our couples will pay a tag fee and road use and miscellaneous fees, per automobile.

OKLAHOMA CITY

Oklahoma City has no local income tax but does levy a sales tax.

Most purchases are taxed at a rate of 8.375%. Major consumer categories taxed at a different rate: None. Major consumer categories which are exempt from the sales tax include: Drugs, medical services and medical supplies.

In the Oklahoma City School District, the property tax rate is .10507. Homes are assessed at 11% of market value. There is a homestead exemption of $1,000 off assessed value and an additional homestead exemption of $1,000 off assessed value available to homeowners with a gross income of less than $10,000. There is also an elderly exemption, which is a refund of real estate tax over 1% of income with a maximum refund of $200 available to homeowners who are age 65 or older or disabled with a gross income not exceeding $10,000. Property tax does not include garbage pickup; the additional fee is approximately $113 per year.

Oklahoma City has a personal property tax rate of .10507 within the Oklahoma City School District. Personal property is assessed at 15% of market value. Items subject to the tax include all items within a home, such as furnishings, clothing, jewelry, dishes, etc. The tax does not apply to automobiles. The market value of personal property is 10% of the market value of the house, excluding land value. Or, residents may itemize. In calculating the personal property tax, there is a standard exemption of $100 off assessed value available to all homeowners.

★Total tax burdens in Oklahoma City are higher than average overall.

TULSA

Tulsa has no local income tax but does levy a sales tax.

During the 12-month period covered by this study, the sales tax rate changed from 7.5% to 8%. Our estimates for sales tax are based on a weighted average of these rates. Major consumer categories taxed at a different rate: None. Major consumer categories which are exempt from the sales tax include: Drugs, medical services and medical supplies.

Within the Tulsa city limits, the property tax rate is .10100. Homes are assessed at 11% of market value. There is a homestead exemption of $1,000 off assessed value and an additional homestead exemption of $1,000 off assessed value available to homeowners with gross income of less than $10,000. There is also an elderly exemption, which is a refund of real estate tax over 1% of income with a maximum refund of $200 available to homeowners who are age 65 or older or disabled, with gross income less than $10,000. Property tax does not include garbage pickup; the additional fee is approximately $153 per year.

Tulsa has no personal property tax for individuals.

★Total tax burdens in Tulsa are higher than average overall.

OREGON

Income	Home Value	Property Tax & Other Fees	Personal Property Tax & Auto Fees	Sales Tax	Local Income Tax	State Income Tax	Total Tax	Rank From #1–#149
BEND								
$24,281	$50,000	$940	$30	–	–	–	$970	#7
	75,000	1,343	30	–	–	–	1,373	#9
	100,000	1,745	30	–	–	–	1,775	#13
$34,275	$75,000	$1,343	$30	–	–	$593	$1,966	#17
	100,000	1,745	30	–	–	593	2,368	#22
	150,000	2,551	30	–	–	593	3,174	#37
$68,098	$150,000	$2,551	$30	–	–	$3,869	$6,450	#101
	200,000	3,356	30	–	–	3,869	7,255	#100
	250,000	4,161	30	–	–	3,869	8,060	#93
EUGENE								
$24,281	$50,000	$1,000	$30	–	–	–	$1,030	#8
	75,000	1,430	30	–	–	–	1,460	#12
	100,000	1,861	30	–	–	–	1,891	#20
$34,275	$75,000	$1,430	$30	–	–	$593	$2,053	#24
	100,000	1,861	30	–	–	593	2,484	#33
	150,000	2,721	30	–	–	593	3,344	#49
$68,098	$150,000	$2,721	$30	–	–	$3,869	$6,620	#106
	200,000	3,581	30	–	–	3,869	7,480	#108
	250,000	4,442	30	–	–	3,869	8,341	#106
PORTLAND								
$24,281	$50,000	$1,108	$30	–	–	–	$1,138	#10
	75,000	1,558	30	–	–	–	1,588	#19
	100,000	2,009	30	–	–	–	2,039	#31
$34,275	$75,000	$1,558	$30	–	–	$593	$2,181	#35
	100,000	2,009	30	–	–	593	2,632	#42
	150,000	2,911	30	–	–	593	3,534	#61
$68,098	$150,000	$2,911	$30	–	–	$3,869	$6,810	#115
	200,000	3,813	30	–	–	3,869	7,712	#115
	250,000	4,714	30	–	–	3,869	8,613	#110

Oregon has a state income tax but no state sales tax.

The state income tax rate is graduated from 5% to 9% depending upon income bracket. For married couples filing jointly with taxable income up to $4,200, the rate is 5%; up to $10,500, the tax is $210 plus 7% of the amount above $4,200; above $10,500, the tax is $651 plus 9% of the amount above $10,500.

In calculating the tax, there is a deduction of up to $3,000 for federal income tax paid. Federal, state and private pensions are not exempt. Social Security benefits are exempt. There is a $5,000 standard deduction for married couples filing jointly when both are age 65 or older.

Major tax credits or rebates include: Credit for income taxes paid to other states, which our couples do not qualify for; $116 tax credit per person, which our couples qualify for; pension income credit, which some of our couples qualify for; child-and dependent-care credit, which our couples do not qualify for; and political contribution credit, which our couples do not qualify for.

Our couples relocating to the cities listed below must pay $47 to register each automobile. Thereafter, residents will pay a license renewal fee every two years, per automobile.

BEND

Bend has no local income tax and no sales tax.

Within the city limits of Bend, the property tax rate is .0161042. Homes are assessed at 100% of market value. There are no exemptions or deductions off the property tax. Property tax does not cover garbage pickup; the additional fee is approximately $135 per year.

Bend has no personal property tax for individuals.

★Total tax burdens in Bend are lower than average for the $24,281 and $34,275 income categories and about average for the $68,098 income category. Bend is a tax heaven in 2 of 9 income/home value categories.

EUGENE

Eugene has no local income tax and no sales tax.

Within the city limits of Eugene, the property tax rate is .0172064. Homes are assessed at 100% of market value. Property tax does not cover garbage pickup; the additional fee is approximately $140 per year.

Eugene has no personal property

tax for individuals.

★Total tax burdens in Eugene are lower than average in the $24,281 and $34,275 income categories and higher than average in the $68,098 income category. Eugene is a tax heaven in 1 of 9 income/home value categories.

PORTLAND

Portland has no local income tax and no sales tax.

Within the District 1 Portland Public Schools area of the city, the property tax rate is .0180331. Homes are assessed at 100% of market value. Property tax does not cover garbage pickup; the additional fee is approximately $206 per year.

Portland has a personal property tax rate of .0180331 within the District 1 Portland Public Schools area. Personal property is assessed at 100% of market value. Items subject to the

tax include mobile homes and houseboats. The tax does not apply to automobiles. We've assumed our couples do not own any of the items subject to the personal property tax.

★Total tax burdens in Portland are lower than average in the $24,281 and $34,275 income categories and higher than average in the $68,098 income category. Portland is a tax heaven in 1 of 9 income/home value categories.

PENNSYLVANIA

Income	Home Value	Property Tax & Other Fees	Personal Property Tax & Auto Fees	Sales Tax	Local Income Tax	State Income Tax	Total Tax	Rank From #1–#149
PHILADELPHIA								
$24,281	$50,000	$1,322	$48	$670	$387	$224	$2,651	#143
	75,000	1,983	48	670	387	224	3,312	#142
	100,000	2,644	48	670	387	224	3,973	#142
$34,275	$75,000	$1,983	$48	$866	$766	$441	$4,104	#145
	100,000	2,644	48	866	766	441	4,765	#145
	150,000	3,967	48	866	766	441	6,088	#143
$68,098	$150,000	$3,967	$48	$1,381	$2,334	$1,276	$9,006	#141
	200,000	5,289	48	1,381	2,334	1,276	10,328	#140
	250,000	6,611	48	1,381	2,334	1,276	11,650	#139
PITTSBURGH								
$24,281	$50,000	$1,984	$48	$670	$127	$224	$3,053	#148
	75,000	2,976	48	670	127	224	4,045	#149
	100,000	3,968	48	670	127	224	5,037	#149
$34,275	$75,000	$2,976	$48	$866	$258	$441	$4,589	#149
	100,000	3,968	48	866	258	441	5,581	#149
	150,000	5,951	48	866	258	441	7,564	#149
$68,098	$150,000	$5,951	$48	$1,381	$730	$1,276	$9,386	#145
	200,000	7,935	48	1,381	730	1,276	11,370	#147
	250,000	9,919	48	1,381	730	1,276	13,354	#148

Pennsylvania has a state income tax and a state sales tax.

The state income tax rate is 2.8%. In calculating the tax, there is no deduction for federal income tax paid. Federal, state and private pensions are exempt. Social Security benefits are exempt.

Major tax credits or rebates include: Credit for income taxes paid to other states and property tax rebates for people 65 or older. Our couples do not qualify for these programs.

The state sales tax rate is 6% but local governments can add to this amount.

Our couples relocating to the cities listed below must pay a registration fee of $24 per automobile and a title fee of $15 per automobile at the time of registration. Thereafter, on an annual basis, our couples will pay a renewal fee per automobile.

PHILADELPHIA

Philadelphia has a local income tax and a sales tax.

The local income tax rate is 4.96% of wages and salaries for residents and 4.3125% of wages and salaries for non-residents who work within the Philadelphia city limits. Self-employment income earned in Philadelphia is subject to a two-tier Business Privilege Tax, with a rate of .325% applied to taxable gross receipts plus a rate of 6.5% applied to taxable net income. In addition, there is a one-time Business Privilege License fee of $200. We've assumed our couples are residents of Philadelphia.

Philadelphia also has a school income tax which applies to unearned income including interest and dividends. The rate is 4.96%.

Most purchases are taxed at a rate of 7%. Major consumer categories taxed at a different rate: None. Major consumer categories which are exempt from sales tax include: Apparel and services, drugs, groceries and medical services.

Within the Philadelphia city limits, the property tax rate is .08264. Homes are assessed at 32% of market value. There is a property tax rebate of up to $500 for homeowners age 65 or older with a gross income of less than $15,000. Property tax includes garbage pickup.

Philadelphia refers to its tax on stocks, bonds and other investments as a personal property tax. This type of tax is sometimes called an intangibles tax in other states, and we do not include it in our calculations. (See Intangibles Tax in introduction.)

★Total tax burdens in Philadelphia are higher than average overall. Philadelphia is a tax hell in 8 of 9 income/home value categories.

PITTSBURGH

Pittsburgh has a local income tax and a sales tax.

The local income tax rate is 2.875% of wages and salaries for residents and 1% of wages and salaries for non-residents who work within the Pittsburgh city limits. There is an occupation tax of $10 per wage earner. Self-employment income earned in Pittsburgh is subject to a Business Privilege Tax, with a rate of .6% applied to gross receipts. We've assumed our couples are residents of Pittsburgh.

Most purchases are taxed at a rate of 7%. Major consumer categories taxed at a different rate: None. Major consumer categories which are exempt from sales tax include: Apparel and services, drugs, groceries and medical services.

Within the Pittsburgh city limits, the building property tax rate is .12870 and the land tax rate is .1845. Homes and land are assessed at 25% of market value. There is a property tax rebate of up to $500 for homeowners age 65 or older with a gross income of less than $15,000. Property tax includes garbage pickup.

Pittsburgh refers to its tax on stocks, bonds and other investments as a personal property tax. This type of tax is sometimes called an intangibles tax in other states, and we do not include it in our calculations. (See Intangibles Tax in introduction.)

★Total tax burdens in Pittsburgh are higher than average overall. Pittsburgh is a tax hell in all 9 income/home value categories.

RHODE ISLAND

Income	Home Value	Property Tax & Other Fees	Personal Property Tax & Auto Fees	Sales Tax	Local Income Tax	State Income Tax	Total Tax	Rank From #1–#149
NEWPORT								
$24,281	$50,000	$1,045	$499	$670	–	$139	$2,353	#133
	75,000	1,568	499	670	–	139	2,876	#130
	100,000	2,090	499	670	–	139	3,398	#128
$34,275	$75,000	$1,568	$499	$866	–	$506	$3,439	#130
	100,000	2,090	499	866	–	506	3,961	#132
	150,000	3,135	499	866	–	506	5,006	#122
$68,098	$150,000	$3,135	$499	$1,381	–	$2,774	$7,789	#130
	200,000	4,180	499	1,381	–	2,774	8,834	#129
	250,000	5,225	499	1,381	–	2,774	9,879	#125
PROVIDENCE								
$24,281	$50,000	$634	$1,481	$670	–	$139	$2,924	#147
	75,000	1,092	1,481	670	–	139	3,382	#145
	100,000	1,549	1,481	670	–	139	3,839	#139
$34,275	$75,000	$1,092	$1,481	$866	–	$506	$3,945	#142
	100,000	1,549	1,481	866	–	506	4,402	#138
	150,000	2,465	1,481	866	–	506	5,318	#131
$68,098	$150,000	$2,465	$1,481	$1,381	–	$2,774	$8,101	#133
	200,000	3,380	1,481	1,381	–	2,774	9,016	#131
	250,000	4,296	1,481	1,381	–	2,774	9,932	#127

Rhode Island has a state income tax and a state sales tax.

The state income tax rate is 27.5% of federal tax due.

Major tax credits or rebates include: Credit for income taxes paid to other states and property tax relief credit. Our couples do not qualify for these programs.

The state sales tax rate is 7%.

Our couples relocating to the cities listed below must pay a registration fee of $30 per automobile, $10 per automobile for a vehicle inspection and $25 per automobile for a title at the time of registration. Thereafter, on an annual basis, our couples will pay a registration fee per automobile.

NEWPORT

Newport has no local income tax and does not levy an additional sales tax.

Most purchases are taxed at the state rate of 7%. Major consumer categories taxed at a different rate: None. Major consumer categories which are exempt from the sales tax include: Apparel and services, drugs, groceries and medical services.

Within the city limits of Newport, the property tax rate is .0209. Homes are assessed at 100% of market value. There is an elderly exemption of $4,000 or 20% off assessed value available to homeowners age 65 or older with a gross income of less than $17,100 if they are married and have been residents of the city for at least five years. Property tax includes garbage pickup.

Newport has no personal property tax for individuals, however, it does have an excise tax on vehicles which is essentially the same as the personal property tax in several other states. The tax rate is .0209 and is assessed on the value of the vehicle as determined by the Rhode Island Vehicle Value Commission.

★Total tax burdens in Newport are higher than average overall.

PROVIDENCE

Providence has no local income tax and does not levy an additional sales tax.

Most purchases are taxed at the state rate of 7%. Major consumer categories taxed at a different rate: None. Major consumer categories which are exempt from the sales tax include: Apparel and services, drugs, groceries and medical services.

Within the city limits of Providence, the property tax rate is .02817. Homes are assessed at 100% of market value. There is a homestead deduction of 35% off assessed value available to all homeowners and an elderly exemption of $10,000 off assessed value available to homeowners age 62 or older if they are collecting Social Security and have been residents of the city for at least three years. Property tax includes garbage pickup.

Providence has no personal property tax for individuals, however, it does have an excise tax on vehicles which is essentially the same as the personal property tax in several other states. The tax rate is .06777 and is assessed on 100% of NADA average retail value.

NOTE: Repeated attempts to verify tax rates with Providence tax assessor's office were unsuccessful. Rates shown were supplied for an earlier edition of this publication and may no longer be valid.

★Total tax burdens in Providence are higher than average overall. Providence is a tax hell in 3 of 9 income/home value categories.

SOUTH CAROLINA

Income	Home Value	Property Tax & Other Fees	Personal Property Tax & Auto Fees	Sales Tax	Local Income Tax	State Income Tax	Total Tax	Rank From #1–#149
AIKEN								
$24,281	$50,000	$437	$681	$655	–	–	$1,773	#74
	75,000	724	681	655	–	–	2,060	#66
	100,000	1,010	681	655	–	–	2,346	#61
$34,275	$75,000	$724	$681	$864	–	$80	$2,349	#48
	100,000	1,010	681	864	–	80	2,635	#43
	150,000	1,584	681	864	–	80	3,209	#40
$68,098	$150,000	$1,584	$681	$1,261	–	$2,070	$5,596	#68
	200,000	2,157	681	1,261	–	2,070	6,169	#59
	250,000	2,731	681	1,261	–	2,070	6,743	#58
GREENVILLE								
$24,281	$50,000	$389	$681	$655	–	–	$1,725	#66
	75,000	678	681	655	–	–	2,014	#60
	100,000	966	681	655	–	–	2,302	#58
$34,275	$75,000	$678	$681	$864	–	$80	$2,303	#44 (tie)
	100,000	966	681	864	–	80	2,591	#39
	150,000	1,544	681	864	–	80	3,169	#35
$68,098	$150,000	$1,544	$681	$1,261	–	$2,070	$5,556	#64
	200,000	2,122	681	1,261	–	2,070	6,134	#58
	250,000	2,700	681	1,261	–	2,070	6,712	#55
HILTON HEAD								
$24,281	$50,000	$566	$547	$655	–	–	$1,768	#73
	75,000	796	547	655	–	–	1,998	#58
	100,000	1,027	547	655	–	–	2,229	#49
$34,275	$75,000	$796	$547	$864	–	$80	$2,287	#42
	100,000	1,027	547	864	–	80	2,518	#36
	150,000	1,487	547	864	–	80	2,978	#25
$68,098	$150,000	$1,487	$547	$1,261	–	$2,070	$5,365	#56
	200,000	1,947	547	1,261	–	2,070	5,825	#50
	250,000	2,408	547	1,261	–	2,070	6,286	#40
MYRTLE BEACH								
$24,281	$50,000	$335	$588	$655	–	–	$1,578	#50
	75,000	580	588	655	–	–	1,823	#41
	100,000	824	588	655	–	–	2,067	#34
$34,275	$75,000	$580	$588	$864	–	$80	$2,112	#29
	100,000	824	588	864	–	80	2,356	#20
	150,000	1,313	588	864	–	80	2,845	#22
$68,098	$150,000	$1,313	$588	$1,261	–	$2,070	$5,232	#51
	200,000	1,802	588	1,261	–	2,070	5,721	#46
	250,000	2,291	588	1,261	–	2,070	6,210	#34

South Carolina has a state income tax and a state sales tax.

The state income tax rate is graduated from 2.5% to 7% depending upon income bracket. For married couples filing jointly the rate is 2.5% on the first $2,190 of taxable income; the rate is 3% on the next $2,190 of taxable income; the rate is 4% on the next $2,190 of taxable income; the rate is 5% on the next $2,190 of taxable income; the rate is 6% on the next $2,190 of taxable income; and the rate is 7% on taxable income above $10,950.

In calculating the tax, there is no deduction for federal income tax paid. There is a deduction of up to $10,000 per person from federal taxable income for federal, state and private pensions received by residents age 65 or older. Social Security benefits are exempt. There is a $7,850 standard deduction from adjusted gross income for married couples filing jointly who are both 65 or older and a $2,450 personal exemption per person from adjusted gross income.

Major tax credits or rebates include: Credit for income taxes paid to other states, child-care credit, nursing home credit and two wage earner credit. Our couples do not qualify for these programs.

The state sales tax rate is 5%.

Our couples relocating to the cities

listed below must pay a $20 tag fee (which is the senior citizen rate) to register each automobile and $5 per automobile for a title. Thereafter, every two years, our couples will pay a renewal fee per automobile.

AIKEN

Aiken has no local income tax and does not levy an additional sales tax.

Most purchases are taxed at the state rate of 5%. However, persons age 85 or older qualify for a reduced rate of 4%. Major consumer categories taxed at a different rate: None. Major consumer categories which are exempt from sales tax include: Drugs and medical services.

Within the city limits of Aiken, the property tax rate is .2867. Homes are assessed at 4% of market value if owner occupied. There is a homestead exemption of $20,000 off market value for homeowners age 65 or older who have been residents for one year. We've assumed that our couples qualify for this exemption. Property tax does not cover garbage pickup; the additional fee is approximately $93 per year.

Aiken has a personal property tax rate of .2867. Personal property is assessed at 10.5% of market value. Items subject to the tax include aircraft, campers, motors, vehicles and water craft. There is a high mileage reduction of up to 40% off assessed value available to all vehicle owners. Our couples also pay a road maintenance fee of $15 per automobile.

★Total tax burdens in Aiken are about average for the $24,281 and $68,098 income categories and lower than average for the $34,275 income category.

GREENVILLE

Greenville has no local income tax and does not levy an additional sales tax.

Most purchases are taxed at the state rate of 5%. However, persons age 85 or older qualify for a reduced rate of 4%. Major consumer categories taxed at a different rate: None. Major consumer categories which are exempt from sales tax include: Drugs

and medical services.

Within the city limits of Greenville, the property tax rate is .2889. Homes are assessed at 4% of market value if owner occupied. There is a homestead exemption of $20,000 off market value for homeowners age 65 or older who have been residents for one year. We've assumed that our couples qualify for this exemption. Property tax does not cover garbage pickup; the additional fee is approximately $30 per year. There is a storm water fee of $12 per year.

Greenville has a personal property tax rate of .2863. Personal property is assessed at 10.5% of market value. Items subject to the tax at this rate include vehicles. There is a high mileage reduction of up to 40% off assessed value available to all vehicle owners.

★Total tax burdens in Greenville are about average for the $24,281 and $68,098 income categories and lower than average for the $34,275 income category.

HILTON HEAD

Hilton Head has no local income tax and does not levy an additional sales tax.

Most purchases are taxed at the state rate of 5%. However, persons age 85 or older qualify for a reduced rate of 4%. Major consumer categories taxed at a different rate: None. Major consumer categories which are exempt from sales tax include: Drugs and medical services.

Within the Sea Pines Public Service District of Hilton Head, the property tax rate is .2302. Homes are assessed at 4% of market value if owner occupied. There is a homestead exemption of $20,000 off market value for homeowners age 65 or older who have been residents for one year. We've assumed that our couples qualify for this exemption. Property tax does not cover garbage pickup; the additional fee is approximately $290 per year. Residents living within a Public Service District may be subject to additional charges ranging from $50 to $2,000.

Hilton Head has a personal proper-

ty tax rate of .2302 in the Sea Pines Public Service District. Personal property is assessed at 10.5% of market value. Items subject to the tax include aircraft, campers, motors, vehicles and water craft. There is a high mileage reduction of up to 40% off assessed value available to all vehicle owners. Our couples also pay a road maintenance fee of $10 per automobile.

★Total tax burdens in Hilton Head are about average for the $24,281 income category and lower than average for the $34,275 and $68,098 income categories.

MYRTLE BEACH

Myrtle Beach has no local income tax and does not levy an additional sales tax.

Most purchases are taxed at the state rate of 5%. However, persons age 85 or older qualify for a reduced rate of 4%. Major consumer categories taxed at a different rate: None. Major consumer categories which are exempt from sales tax include: Drugs and medical services.

Within the city limits of Myrtle Beach in District 88, the property tax rate is .2445. Homes are assessed at 4% of market value if owner occupied. There is a homestead exemption of $20,000 off market value for homeowners age 65 or older or persons totally and permanently disabled who have been residents for one year. We've assumed that our couples qualify for this exemption. Property tax does not cover garbage pickup; the additional fee is approximately $42 per year.

Myrtle Beach has a personal property tax rate of .2445 in District 88. Personal property is assessed at 10.5% of market value. Items subject to the tax include aircraft, campers, motors, vehicles and water craft. There is a high mileage reduction of up to 40% off assessed value available to all vehicle owners. Our couples also pay a road maintenance fee of $15 per automobile.

★Total tax burdens in Myrtle Beach are lower than average overall.

SOUTH DAKOTA

Income	Home Value	Property Tax & Other Fees	Personal Property Tax & Auto Fees	Sales Tax	Local Income Tax	State Income Tax	Total Tax	Rank From #1–#149
PIERRE								
$24,281	$50,000	$1,490	$78	$463	–	–	$2,031	#105
	75,000	2,215	78	463	–	–	2,756	#125
	100,000	2,940	78	463	–	–	3,481	#130
$34,275	$75,000	$2,215	$78	$639	–	–	$2,932	#102
	100,000	2,940	78	639	–	–	3,657	#117
	150,000	4,390	78	639	–	–	5,107	#124
$68,098	$150,000	$4,390	$78	$916	–	–	$5,384	#58
	200,000	5,840	78	916	–	–	6,834	#84
	250,000	7,290	78	916	–	–	8,284	#103
RAPID CITY								
$24,281	$50,000	$1,599	$62	$518	–	–	$2,179	#124
	75,000	2,345	62	518	–	–	2,925	#132
	100,000	3,092	62	518	–	–	3,672	#134
$34,275	$75,000	$2,345	$62	$717	–	–	$3,124	#117
	100,000	3,092	62	717	–	–	3,871	#129
	150,000	4,586	62	717	–	–	5,365	#132
$68,098	$150,000	$4,586	$62	$1,031	–	–	$5,679	#70
	200,000	6,079	62	1,031	–	–	7,172	#97
	250,000	7,573	62	1,031	–	–	8,666	#113

South Dakota has no state income tax but does have a state sales tax.

Major tax credits or rebates include: Sales or property tax refund for senior citizens. Our couples do not qualify for these programs.

The state sales tax rate is 4% but local governments can add to this amount.

Since car registration and renewal fees differ within the state, see city information for details.

PIERRE

Pierre has no local income tax but does levy a sales tax.

Most purchases are taxed at a rate of 5%. Major consumer categories which are taxed at a different rate include: Food away from home, which is taxed at a rate of 7%; and groceries, which are taxed at a rate of 4%. Major consumer categories which are exempt from sales tax include: Drugs, transportation and medical services.

Within the city limits of Pierre, the property tax rate is .029. Homes are assessed at 100% of market value. There is a senior citizen exemption available to homeowners age 65 or older with a gross income of less than $15,000 who have lived in the state for at least five years. There is also a

senior citizen refund available to homeowners age 65 or older with a gross income of less than $12,000. Property tax does not cover garbage pickup; the additional fee is approximately $40 per year.

Pierre has a personal property tax rate of .029. Personal property is assessed at 100% of market value. Items subject to the tax include mobile homes. We've assumed our couples do not own the items subject to the personal property tax. In calculating the personal property tax, there is a senior citizen exemption available to homeowners age 65 or older with a gross income of less than $15,000 who have lived in the state for at least five years. There is also a senior citizen refund available to homeowners age 65 or older with a gross income of less than $12,000.

Our couples relocating to Pierre are subject to an excise tax on automobiles which is 3% of the current market value and is paid when the vehicle is initially registered in the state. If a vehicle owner paid an excise or sales tax in another state when the automobile was purchased which is equal to or greater than the South Dakota excise tax, there is no additional charge. If a vehicle owner

paid an excise or sales tax to another state which is less than the South Dakota excise tax, they are required to pay the difference. We've assumed our couples have paid tax greater than or equal to the excise tax. Our couples will pay a registration fee of $30 per automobile, a wheel tax of $8 per automobile, a title transfer fee of $5 per automobile and a solid waste disposal fee of $1 per automobile at the time of registration. Thereafter, on an annual basis, our couples will pay a registration fee, wheel tax and solid waste disposal fee, per automobile.

★Total tax burdens in Pierre are higher than average for the $24,281 and $34,275 income categories and about average for the $68,098 income category.

RAPID CITY

Rapid City has no local income tax but does levy a sales tax.

Most purchases are taxed at a rate of 6%. Major consumer categories which are taxed at a different rate include: Food away from home, which is taxed at a rate of 7%; and groceries, which are taxed at a rate of 4%. Major consumer categories which are exempt from sales tax include: Drugs, transportation and medical services.

For most residents within the city limits of Rapid City, the property tax rate is .0298719. Homes are assessed at 100% of market value. There is a senior citizen exemption available to homeowners age 65 or older with a gross income of less than $15,000 who have lived in the state for at least five years. There is also a senior citizen refund available to homeowners age 65 or older with a gross income of less than $12,000. Property tax does not cover garbage pickup; the additional fee for residents age 65 or older is approximately $58 per year. There is also a disposal fee of approximately $46 per year for residents age 65 or older and an environmental charge, which is approximately $1 per year for residents age 65 or older.

Rapid City has a personal property tax rate of .0298719 for most residents within the city limits. Personal property tax is assessed at 100% of market value. Items subject to the tax include mobile homes. We've assumed our couples do not own the items subject to the personal property tax. In calculating the personal property tax, there is a senior citizen exemption available to homeowners age 65 or older with a gross income of less than $15,000 who have lived in the state for at least five years. There is also a senior citizen refund available to homeowners age 65 or older with a gross income of less than $12,000.

Our couples relocating to Rapid City are subject to an excise tax on automobiles which is 3% of the current market value and is paid when the vehicle is initially registered in the state. If a vehicle owner paid an excise or sales tax in another state when the automobile was purchased which is equal to or greater than the South Dakota excise tax, there is no additional charge. If a vehicle owner paid an excise or sales tax to another state which is less than the South Dakota excise tax, they are required to pay the difference. We've assumed our couples have paid tax greater than or equal to the excise tax. Our couples will pay a registration fee of $30 per automobile, a title transfer fee of $5 per automobile and a solid waste fee of $1 per automobile at the time of registration. Thereafter, on an annual basis, our couples will pay a registration fee and solid waste disposal fee, per automobile.

★Total tax burdens in Rapid City are higher than average for the $24,281 and $34,275 income categories and about average for the $68,098 income category.

TENNESSEE

Income	Home Value	Property Tax & Other Fees	Personal Property Tax & Auto Fees	Sales Tax	Local Income Tax	State Income Tax	Total Tax	Rank From #1–#149
NASHVILLE								
$24,281	$50,000	$563	$116	$1,080	–	–	$1,759	#72
	75,000	844	116	1,080	–	–	2,040	#63
	100,000	1,125	116	1,080	–	–	2,321	#59
$34,275	$75,000	$844	$116	$1,426	–	–	$2,386	#51
	100,000	1,125	116	1,426	–	–	2,667	#48
	150,000	1,688	116	1,426	–	–	3,230	#43
$68,098	$150,000	$1,688	$116	$2,081	–	–	$3,885	#9
	200,000	2,250	116	2,081	–	–	4,447	#11
	250,000	2,813	116	2,081	–	–	5,010	#13
PARIS								
$24,281	$50,000	$626	$77	$1,080	–	–	$1,783	#75
	75,000	879	77	1,080	–	–	2,036	#62
	100,000	1,133	77	1,080	–	–	2,290	#55
$34,275	$75,000	$879	$77	$1,426	–	–	$2,382	#50
	100,000	1,133	77	1,426	–	–	2,636	#44
	150,000	1,639	77	1,426	–	–	3,142	#30
$68,098	$150,000	$1,639	$77	$2,081	–	–	$3,797	#8
	200,000	2,145	77	2,081	–	–	4,303	#8
	250,000	2,651	77	2,081	–	–	4,809	#11

Tennessee has no state earned income tax but does levy an interest and dividends tax. Tennessee has a state sales tax.

The state interest and dividends tax rate is 6%, and applies to income from stocks, bonds, long-term notes and mortgages. In calculating the tax, there is no deduction for federal income tax paid. Interest from CDs and savings accounts is exempt from tax. Interest from government bonds issued by the federal government, Tennessee or a local government in Tennessee is exempt from tax. There is a $2,500 exemption for married couples filing jointly. Married couples filing jointly who are both age 65 or older with gross income of less than $15,000 are exempt from tax. We've assumed our couples do not owe interest and dividends tax.

Major tax credits or rebates include: Tennessee property tax relief. Our couples do not qualify for this program.

The state sales tax rate is 6% but local governments can add to this amount.

Since car registration and renewal fees differ within the state, see city information for details.

NASHVILLE

Nashville has no local income tax but does levy a sales tax.

Most purchases are taxed at a rate of 8.25%. Major consumer categories taxed at a different rate: None. Major consumer categories which are exempt from the sales tax include: Drugs and medical services.

In the Urban District of Nashville, the property tax rate is .0450. Homes are assessed at 25% of market value. There is a state tax relief credit of $338 for homeowners age 65 or older with a gross income of less than $10,000. Property tax includes garbage pickup.

Nashville has no personal property tax for individuals.

Our couples relocating to Nashville must pay a registration fee of $21 per automobile, a title fee of $5 per automobile, an emissions test fee of $6 per automobile, a county clerk fee of $6 per automobile and a privilege fee of $35 per automobile. Thereafter, on an annual basis, our couples will pay a renewal fee per automobile.

★Total tax burdens in Nashville are about average for the $24,281 income category and lower than average for the $34,281 and $68,098 income categories. Nashville is a tax heaven in 1 of 9 income/home value categories.

PARIS

Paris has no local income tax but does levy a sales tax.

Most purchases are taxed at a rate of 8.25%. Major consumer categories taxed at a different rate: None. Major consumer categories which are exempt from the sales tax include: Drugs and medical services.

In the Special School District of Paris, the property tax rate is .0405. Homes are assessed at 25% of market value. There is a state tax relief credit of $116 for homeowners age 65 or older with a gross income of less than $10,000. Property tax does not cover garbage pickup; the additional fee is approximately $120 per year.

Paris has no personal property tax for individuals.

Our couples relocating to Paris must pay a registration fee of $39 per automobile and a title fee of $8 per automobile. Thereafter, on an annual basis, our couples will pay a registration fee per automobile.

★Total tax burdens in Paris are about average for the $24,281 income category and lower than average for the $34,281 and $68,098 income categories. Paris is a tax heaven in 2 of 9 income/home value categories.

TEXAS

Income	Home Value	Property Tax & Other Fees	Personal Property Tax & Auto Fees	Sales Tax	Local Income Tax	State Income Tax	Total Tax	Rank From #1–#149
AUSTIN								
$24,281	$50,000	$286	$125	$848	–	–	$1,259	#15
	75,000	757	125	848	–	–	1,730	#34
	100,000	1,324	125	848	–	–	2,297	#57
$34,275	$75,000	$757	$125	$1,140	–	–	$2,022	#22
	100,000	1,324	125	1,140	–	–	2,589	#38
	150,000	2,521	125	1,140	–	–	3,786	#79
$68,098	$150,000	$2,521	$125	$1,762	–	–	$4,408	#23
	200,000	3,718	125	1,762	–	–	5,605	#37
	250,000	4,914	125	1,762	–	–	6,801	#62
BROWNSVILLE								
$24,281	$50,000	$1,076	$122	$875	–	–	$2,073	#109
	75,000	1,717	122	875	–	–	2,714	#123
	100,000	2,357	122	875	–	–	3,354	#126
$34,275	$75,000	$1,717	$122	$1,175	–	–	$3,014	#110
	100,000	2,357	122	1,175	–	–	3,654	#116
	150,000	3,638	122	1,175	–	–	4,935	#120
$68,098	$150,000	$3,638	$122	$1,817	–	–	$5,577	#65
	200,000	4,919	122	1,817	–	–	6,858	#86
	250,000	6,200	122	1,817	–	–	8,139	#99
DALLAS								
$24,281	$50,000	$128	$225	$875	–	–	$1,228	#14
	75,000	381	225	875	–	–	1,481	#13
	100,000	864	225	875	–	–	1,964	#27
$34,275	$75,000	$381	$225	$1,175	–	–	$1,781	#10
	100,000	864	225	1,175	–	–	2,264	#18
	150,000	1,956	225	1,175	–	–	3,356	#51
$68,098	$150,000	$1,956	$225	$1,817	–	–	$3,998	#12
	200,000	3,048	225	1,817	–	–	5,090	#20
	250,000	4,140	225	1,817	–	–	6,182	#31
FREDERICKSBURG								
$24,281	$50,000	$807	$335	$875	–	–	$2,017	#101
	75,000	1,249	335	875	–	–	2,459	#114
	100,000	1,690	335	875	–	–	2,900	#110
$34,275	$75,000	$1,249	$335	$1,175	–	–	$2,759	#88
	100,000	1,690	335	1,175	–	–	3,200	#89
	150,000	2,572	335	1,175	–	–	4,082	#96
$68,098	$150,000	$2,572	$335	$1,817	–	–	$4,724	#34
	200,000	3,455	335	1,817	–	–	5,607	#38
	250,000	4,337	335	1,817	–	–	6,489	#47 (tie)
HOUSTON								
$24,281	$50,000	$104	$122	$875	–	–	$1,101	#9
	75,000	593	122	875	–	–	1,590	#20
	100,000	1,082	122	875	–	–	2,079	#37
$34,275	$75,000	$593	$122	$1,175	–	–	$1,890	#13
	100,000	1,082	122	1,175	–	–	2,379	#24
	150,000	2,060	122	1,175	–	–	3,357	#52
$68,098	$150,000	$2,060	$122	$1,817	–	–	$3,999	#13
	200,000	3,062	122	1,817	–	–	5,001	#18
	250,000	4,290	122	1,817	–	–	6,229	#35

Income	Home Value	Property Tax & Other Fees	Personal Property Tax & Auto Fees	Sales Tax	Local Income Tax	State Income Tax	Total Tax	Rank From #1–#149
SAN ANTONIO								
$24,281	$50,000	$801	$125	$822	–	–	$1,748	#69
	75,000	1,449	125	822	–	–	2,396	#108
	100,000	2,158	125	822	–	–	3,105	#119
$34,275	$75,000	$1,449	$125	$1,104	–	–	$2,678	#81
	100,000	2,158	125	1,104	–	–	3,387	#105
	150,000	3,574	125	1,104	–	–	4,803	#118
$68,098	$150,000	$3,574	$125	$1,707	–	–	$5,406	#60
	200,000	4,991	125	1,707	–	–	6,823	#83
	250,000	6,408	125	1,707	–	–	8,240	#100
WIMBERLEY								
$24,281	$50,000	$847	$122	$716	–	–	$1,685	#58
	75,000	1,388	122	716	–	–	2,226	#87
	100,000	1,930	122	716	–	–	2,768	#104
$34,275	$75,000	$1,388	$122	$962	–	–	$2,472	#60
	100,000	1,930	122	962	–	–	3,014	#81
	150,000	3,012	122	962	–	–	4,096	#97
$68,098	$150,000	$3,012	$122	$1,486	–	–	$4,620	#30
	200,000	4,095	122	1,486	–	–	5,703	#45
	250,000	5,177	122	1,486	–	–	6,785	#61

Texas has no state income tax but does have a state sales tax.

Major tax credits or rebates: None.

The state sales tax rate is 6.25% but local governments can add to this amount.

Since car registration and renewal fees differ within the state, see city information for details.

AUSTIN

Austin has no local income tax but does levy a sales tax.

Most purchases are taxed at a rate of 8%. Major consumer categories taxed at a different rate: None. Major consumer categories which are exempt from sales tax include: Drugs, groceries and medical services.

Within the city limits of Austin, the property tax rate is .025093. Homes are assessed at 100% of market value. There are various exemptions off the city, community college, county and school district portions of the property tax. Property tax does not cover garbage pickup; the additional fee is approximately $151 per year. This amount also includes a solid waste fee, an anti-litter fee and taxes.

Austin has no personal property tax for individuals.

Our couples relocating to Austin must pay a registration fee of $59 for the Chrysler and $51 for the Oldsmobile, a county road and bridge fee of $12 per automobile, a new resident fee of $15 per automobile and an application fee of $13 per automobile at the time of registration. Thereafter, on an annual basis, our couples will pay a registration fee and county road and bridge fee, per automobile.

★Total tax burdens in Austin are lower than average overall.

BROWNSVILLE

Brownsville has no local income tax but does levy a sales tax.

Most purchases are taxed at a rate of 8.25%. Major consumer categories taxed at a different rate: None. Major consumer categories which are exempt from sales tax include: Drugs, groceries and medical services.

In the Brownsville School District, the property tax rate is .02561727. Homes are assessed at 100% of market value. There are various exemptions off the city, county and school district portions of the property tax. Property tax does not cover garbage pickup; the additional fee is approximately $135 per year.

Brownsville has no personal property tax for individuals.

Our couples relocating to Brownsville must pay a registration fee of $59 for the Chrysler and $51 for the Oldsmobile, a county road and bridge fee of $10 per automobile, a new resident fee of $15 per automobile and an application fee of $13 per automobile at the time of registration. Thereafter, on an annual basis, our couples will pay a registration fee and county road and bridge fee, per automobile.

★Total tax burdens in Brownsville are higher than average for the $24,281 and $34,275 income categories and about average for the $68,098 income category.

DALLAS

Dallas has no local income tax but does levy a sales tax.

Most purchases are taxed at a rate of 8.25%. Major consumer categories taxed at a different rate: None. Major consumer categories which are exempt from sales tax include: Drugs, groceries and medical services.

In the Dallas Independent School District, the property tax rate is .0255301. Homes are assessed at 100% of market value. There are various exemptions off the city, community college, county and school district portions of the property tax. Property tax does not cover garbage pickup; the additional fee is approximately $128 per year.

Dallas has a personal property tax

rate of .006744. Personal property is assessed at 100% of Jan. 1 NADA loan value. Items subject to the tax include vehicles eight years old or newer.

Our couples relocating to Dallas must pay a registration fee of $59 for the Chrysler and $51 for the Oldsmobile, a county road and bridge fee of $10 per automobile, a new resident fee of $15 per automobile and an application fee of $13 per automobile at the time of registration. Thereafter, on an annual basis, our couples will pay a registration fee and county road and bridge fee, per automobile.

★Total tax burdens in Dallas are lower than average overall. Dallas is a tax heaven in 1 of 9 income/home value categories.

FREDERICKSBURG

Fredericksburg has no local income tax but does levy a sales tax.

Most purchases are taxed at a rate of 8.25%. Major consumer categories taxed at a different rate: None. Major consumer categories which are exempt from sales tax include: Drugs, groceries and medical services.

In the Fredericksburg School District, the property tax rate is .017649. Homes are assessed at 100% of market value. There are exemptions off the school district portion of the property tax. Property tax does not cover garbage pickup; the additional fee is approximately $111 per year.

In the Fredericksburg School District, the personal property tax rate is .0124. Personal property is assessed at 100% of NADA trade-in value. Items subject to the tax include airplanes, boats, motorcycles, motor homes, travel trailers and vehicles. Items must be eight years old or newer to be subject to the tax.

Our couples relocating to Fredericksburg must pay a registration fee of $59 for the Chrysler and $51 for the Oldsmobile, a county road and bridge fee of $12 per automobile, a new resident fee of $15 per automobile and an application fee of $13 per automobile at the time of registration. Thereafter, on an annual basis, our couples will pay a registration fee and county road and bridge fee, per automobile.

★Total tax burdens in Fredericksburg are higher than average for the $24,281 income category, about average for the $34,275 income category and lower than average for the $68,098 income category.

HOUSTON

Houston has no local income tax but does levy a sales tax.

Most purchases are taxed at a rate of 8.25%. Major consumer categories taxed at a different rate: None. Major consumer categories which are exempt from sales tax include: Drugs, groceries and medical services.

In the Spring Branch Independent School District, the property tax rate is .0307165. Homes are assessed at 100% of market value. There are various exemptions off the city, county and school district portions of the property tax. Property tax includes garbage pickup.

Houston has no personal property tax for individuals.

Our couples relocating to Houston must pay a registration fee of $59 for the Chrysler and $51 for the Oldsmobile, a county road and bridge fee of $10 per automobile, a new resident fee of $15 per automobile and an application fee of $13 per automobile at the time of registration. Thereafter, on an annual basis, our couples will pay a registration fee and county road and bridge fee, per automobile.

★Total tax burdens in Houston are lower than average overall. Houston is a tax heaven in 1 of 9 income/home value categories.

SAN ANTONIO

San Antonio has no local income tax but does levy a sales tax.

Most purchases are taxed at a rate of 7.75%. Major consumer categories taxed at a different rate: None. Major consumer categories which are exempt from sales tax include: Drugs, groceries and medical services.

In the Alamo Heights School District, the property tax rate is .028334. Homes are assessed at 100% of market value. There are various exemptions off the city, community college, county, flood, water and school district portions of the property tax. Property tax does not cover garbage pick-

up; the additional fee is approximately $127 per year.

San Antonio has no personal property tax for individuals.

Our couples relocating to San Antonio must pay a registration fee of $59 for the Chrysler and $51 for the Oldsmobile, a county road and bridge fee of $12 per automobile, a new resident fee of $15 per automobile and an application fee of $13 per automobile at the time of registration. Thereafter, on an annual basis, our couples will pay a registration fee and county road and bridge fee, per automobile.

★Total tax burdens in San Antonio are higher than average for the $24,281 and $34,275 income categories and about average for the $68,098 income category.

WIMBERLEY

Wimberley has no local income tax but does levy a sales tax.

Most purchases are taxed at a rate of 6.75%. Major consumer categories taxed at a different rate: None. Major consumer categories which are exempt from sales tax include: Drugs, groceries and medical services.

Within the town limits of Wimberley, the property tax rate is .021652. Homes are assessed at 100% of market value. There are various exemptions off the county, road and school district portions of the property tax. Property tax does not cover garbage pickup; the additional fee is approximately $144 per year.

Wimberley has no personal property tax for individuals.

Our couples relocating to Wimberley must pay a registration fee of $59 for the Chrysler and $51 for the Oldsmobile, a county road and bridge fee of $10 per automobile, a new resident fee of $15 per automobile and an application fee of $13 per automobile at the time of registration. Thereafter, on an annual basis, our couples will pay a registration fee and county road and bridge fee, per automobile.

★Total tax burdens in Wimberley are about average for the $24,281 and $34,275 income categories and lower than average for the $68,098 income category.

UTAH

Income	Home Value	Property Tax & Other Fees	Personal Property Tax & Auto Fees	Sales Tax	Local Income Tax	State Income Tax	Total Tax	Rank From #1–#149
ST. GEORGE								
$24,281	$50,000	$568	$316	$781	–	–	$1,665	#57
	75,000	790	316	781	–	–	1,887	#48
	100,000	1,011	316	781	–	–.	2,108	#39
$34,275	$75,000	$790	$316	$1,032	–	–	$2,138	#32
	100,000	1,011	316	1,032	–	–	2,359	#21
	150,000	1,455	316	1,032	–	–	2,803	#19
$68,098	$150,000	$1,455	$316	$1,510	–	$3,379	$6,660	#110
	200,000	1,898	316	1,510	–	3,379	7,103	#94
	250,000	2,341	316	1,510	–	3,379	7,546	#81
SALT LAKE CITY								
$24,281	$50,000	$745	$316	$814	–	–	$1,875	#87
	75,000	1,070	316	814	–	–	2,200	#83
	100,000	1,394	316	814	–	–	2,524	#82
$34,275	$75,000	$1,070	$316	$1,076	–	–	$2,462	#58
	100,000	1,394	316	1,076	–	–	2,786	#57
	150,000	2,043	316	1,076	–	–	3,435	#58
$68,098	$150,000	$2,043	$316	$1,573	–	$3,379	$7,311	#121
	200,000	2,693	316	1,573	–	3,379	7,961	#119
	250,000	3,342	316	1,573	–	3,379	8,610	#109

Utah has a state income tax and a state sales tax.

The state income tax rate is graduated from 2.55% to 7.2% depending upon income bracket. For married couples filing jointly the rate is 2.55% on the first $1,500 of taxable income; the rate is 3.5% on the next $1,500 of taxable income; the rate is 4.4% on the next $1,500 of taxable income; the rate is 5.35% on the next $1,500 of taxable income; the rate is 6.25% on the next $1,500 of taxable income; and the rate is 7.2% on taxable income above $7,500.

In calculating the tax, there is a deduction of one-half of federal income tax paid. There is an exemption of up to $7,500 of federal, state and private pensions for each person age 65 or older. Taxpayers may qualify for this exemption based on their age and income even if they have no retirement income. Social Security benefits subject to federal tax are not exempt. There is a $7,850 standard deduction from adjusted gross income for married couples filing jointly who are both 65 or older and a $1,838 personal exemption per person from adjusted gross income.

Major tax credits or rebates include: Credit for income taxes paid to other states, disabled credit and credit for cash contributions to sheltered workshops. Our couples do not qualify for these programs.

The state sales tax rate is 4.875% but local governments can add to this amount.

Our couples relocating to the cities listed below must pay a registration fee of $24.50 per automobile at the time of registration. Thereafter, on an annual basis, our couples will pay a registration fee per automobile.

ST. GEORGE

St. George has no local income tax but does levy a sales tax.

Most purchases are taxed at a rate of 5.875%. Major consumer categories taxed at a different rate include: Food away from home, which is taxed at a rate of 6.875%. Major consumer categories which are exempt from sales tax include: Drugs and medical services.

Within the city limits of St. George, the property tax rate is .013235. Homes are assessed at 66.98% of market value. There is a state elderly exemption for homeowners age 65 or older with a gross income of up to $17,850. There is also a local elderly exemption for homeowners/rent- ers age 65 or older with a gross income of up to $17,850. Property tax does not cover garbage pickup; the additional fee is approximately $125 per year.

St. George has a personal property tax (which is called a fee in lieu of tax) rate of .017. Personal property is assessed at 100% of NADA wholesale value. Items subject to the tax include boats, motor homes, RVs and vehicles.

★Total tax burdens in St. George are lower than average for the $24,281 and $34,275 income categories and about average for the $68,098 income category.

SALT LAKE CITY

Salt Lake City has no local income tax but does levy a sales tax.

Most purchases are taxed at a rate of 6.125%. Major consumer categories taxed at a different rate include: Food away from home, which is taxed at a rate of 7.125%. Major consumer categories which are exempt from sales tax include: Drugs and medical services.

In Salt Lake City School Districts 1-13, the property tax rate is .0193830. Homes are assessed at 66.98% of market value. There is a state elderly exemption for homeowners age 65 or older with a gross income of up to $17,850. There is also a local elderly exemption for homeowners/renters age 65 or older with a gross income of up to $17,850. Property tax does not cover garbage pickup; the additional fee is approximately $96 per year.

Salt Lake City has a personal property tax (which is called a motor vehicle tax) rate of .017. Personal property is assessed at 100% of NADA wholesale value. Items subject to the tax include boats, motor homes, RVs and vehicles.

★Total tax burdens in Salt Lake City are about average for the $24,281 and $34,275 income categories and higher than average for the $68,098 income category.

VERMONT

Income	Home Value	Property Tax & Other Fees	Personal Property Tax & Auto Fees	Sales Tax	Local Income Tax	State Income Tax*	Total Tax	Rank From #1–#149
BURLINGTON								
$24,281	$50,000	$1,163	$86	$559	–	$127	$1,935	#96
	75,000	1,638	86	559	–	(100)	2,183	#81
	100,000	2,112	86	559	–	(574)	2,183	#46
$34,275	$75,000	$1,638	$86	$758	–	$460	$2,942	#104
	100,000	2,112	86	758	–	239	3,195	#88
	150,000	3,061	86	758	–	(710)	3,195	#39
$68,098	$150,000	$3,061	$86	$1,179	–	$2,522	$6,848	#116
	200,000	4,010	86	1,179	–	2,522	7,797	#116
	250,000	4,960	86	1,179	–	2,522	8,747	#117
MONTPELIER								
$24,281	$50,000	$1,906	$86	$547	–	($366)	$2,173	#123
	75,000	2,756	86	547	–	(1,211)	2,178	#80
	100,000	3,606	86	547	–	(1,223)	3,016	#113
$34,275	$75,000	$2,756	$86	$740	–	($398)	$3,184	#119
	100,000	3,606	86	740	–	(890)	3,542	#112
	150,000	5,306	86	740	–	(890)	5,242	#129
$68,098	$150,000	$5,306	$86	$1,151	–	$2,522	$9,065	#143
	200,000	7,006	86	1,151	–	2,522	10,765	#143
	250,000	8,706	86	1,151	–	2,522	12,465	#144

*Homeowner or Renter Rebate Claim is issued as a reduction of income tax due or as a refund if the credit is greater than the tax liability.

Vermont has a state income tax and a state sales tax.

The state income tax rate is 25% of federal tax due.

Major tax credits or rebates include: Credit for income taxes paid to other states, which our couples do not qualify for. There is also a homeowner or renter rebate claim and a property tax credit certificate. Both programs are offered to residents age 62 or older with an adjusted household income of up to $45,000. Several of our couples qualify for these programs, but Vermont homeowners may apply for only one of them. Our couples who qualify are taking the homeowner or renter rebate claim.

The state sales tax rate is 5%.

Our couples relocating to the cities listed may have to pay a use tax per automobile depending on the amount of tax paid in the state in which the vehicle was purchased. If a vehicle owner paid a sales tax in another state when the automobile was purchased which is equal to or greater than the 5% Vermont tax rate, no additional tax will be due. If a vehicle owner paid a sales tax to another state which is less than the Vermont sales tax, the owner is required to pay the difference. Our couples must also pay a registration and plate fee of $43 per automobile and a title fee of $10 per automobile at the time of registration. Thereafter, on an annual basis, our couples will pay a registration and plate fee per automobile.

BURLINGTON

Burlington has no local income tax and does not levy an additional sales tax on most purchases.

Most purchases are taxed at the state rate of 5%. Major consumer categories taxed at a different rate: Food away from home, which is taxed at a rate of 8%. Major consumer categories which are exempt from sales tax include: Drugs, groceries, medical services and medical supplies.

Within the city limits of Burlington, the property tax rate is .018982. Homes are assessed at 100% of market value. Property tax does not cover garbage pickup; the additional fee is approximately $214 per year.

Burlington has no personal property tax for individuals.

★Total tax burdens in Burlington are about average for the $24,281 and $34,275 income categories and above average for the $68,098 income category.

MONTPELIER

Montpelier has no local income tax and does not levy an additional sales tax.

Most purchases are taxed at the state rate of 5%. Major consumer categories taxed at a different rate: Food away from home, which is taxed at a rate of 7%. Major consumer categories which are exempt from sales tax include: Drugs, groceries, medical services and medical supplies.

Within the city limits of Montpelier, the property tax rate is .0338. Homes are assessed at 100% of market value. Property tax does not cover garbage pickup; the additional fee is approximately $206 per year. There is a sewer benefit charge of $.02 per $100 of home value per year.

Montpelier has no personal property tax for individuals.

★Total tax burdens in Montpelier are higher than average overall. Montpelier is a tax hell in 3 of 9 income/home value categories.

VIRGINIA

Income	Home Value	Property Tax & Other Fees	Personal Property Tax & Auto Fees	Sales Tax	Local Income Tax	State Income Tax	Total Tax	Rank From #1–#149
CHARLOTTESVILLE								
$24,281	$50,000	$597	$705	$624	–	–	$1,926	#94
	75,000	875	705	624	–	–	2,204	#84
	100,000	1,152	705	624	–	–	2,481	#74
$34,275	$75,000	$875	$705	$829	–	$4	$2,413	#55
	100,000	1,152	705	829	–	4	2,690	#49
	150,000	1,707	705	829	–	4	3,245	#44
$68,098	$150,000	$1,707	$705	$1,219	–	$1,698	$5,329	#55
	200,000	2,262	705	1,219	–	1,698	5,884	#52
	250,000	2,817	705	1,219	–	1,698	6,439	#43
RICHMOND								
$24,281	$50,000	$861	$680	$647	–	–	$2,188	#125
	75,000	1,222	680	647	–	–	2,549	#119
	100,000	1,583	680	647	–	–	2,910	#111
$34,275	$75,000	$1,222	$680	$863	–	$4	$2,769	#90
	100,000	1,583	680	863	–	4	3,130	#86
	150,000	2,306	680	863	–	4	3,853	#84
$68,098	$150,000	$2,306	$680	$1,274	–	$1,698	$5,958	#80
	200,000	3,028	680	1,274	–	1,698	6,680	#81
	250,000	3,751	680	1,274	–	1,698	7,403	#78
VIRGINIA BEACH								
$24,281	$50,000	$603	$618	$641	–	–	$1,862	#84 (tie)
	75,000	888	618	641	–	–	2,147	#74
	100,000	1,173	618	641	–	–	2,432	#68
$34,275	$75,000	$888	$618	$855	–	$4	$2,365	#49
	100,000	1,173	618	855	–	4	2,650	#46
	150,000	1,743	618	855	–	4	3,220	#41 (tie)
$68,098	$150,000	$1,743	$618	$1,260	–	$1,698	$5,319	#54
	200,000	2,313	618	1,260	–	1,698	5,889	#53
	250,000	2,883	618	1,260	–	1,698	6,459	#45

Virginia has a state income tax and a state sales tax.

The state income tax rate is graduated from 2% to 5.75% depending upon income bracket. For all filers the rate is 2% on the first $3,000 of taxable income; the rate is 3% on the next $2,000 of taxable income; the rate is 5% on the next $12,000 of taxable income; and the rate is 5.75% on taxable income above $17,000.

In calculating the tax, there is no deduction for federal income tax paid. Federal, state and private pensions are not exempt. Social Security benefits are exempt. There is a $5,000 standard deduction from adjusted gross income for married couples filing jointly. There is an $800 personal exemption from adjusted gross income per person and an $800 per-

sonal exemption from adjusted gross income per person for residents age 65 or older. There is a $6,472 deduction per person from adjusted gross income minus Social Security benefits for residents age 62-64, and a deduction of $12,944 per person from adjusted gross income minus Social Security benefits for residents age 65 or older.

Major tax credits or rebates include: Credit for income taxes paid to other states and neighborhood assistance act credit. Our couples do not qualify for these programs.

The state sales tax rate is 3.5% but local governments can add to this amount.

Our couples relocating to the cities listed below must pay a plate fee per automobile based on the weight of the vehicle. The plate fee is $26.50

for the Chrysler and $26.50 for the Oldsmobile. Our couples must also pay a title fee of $10 per automobile at the time of registration. Thereafter, on an annual basis, our couples will pay a plate fee per automobile.

CHARLOTTESVILLE

Charlottesville has no local income tax but does levy a sales tax.

Most purchases are taxed at a rate of 4.5%. Major consumer categories taxed at a different rate include: Food away from home, which is taxed at a rate of 7.5%. Major consumer categories which are exempt from sales tax include: Drugs and medical services.

Within the city limits of Charlottesville, the property tax rate is .0111. Homes are assessed at 100% of market value. There is a senior citizen exemption of a portion of property tax due for homeowners age 65 or older with a gross income of less than $22,000 and net worth of less than $75,000, excluding home value. Property tax does not cover garbage pickup; the additional fee is approximately $42 per year.

Charlottesville has a personal property tax rate of .0420. Personal property is assessed at 100% of NADA loan value for vehicles; 100% of trade-in value in motorcycle identification guide for motorcycles; and 100% of trade-in value in Abos Intertec guide for boats and trailers. We've assumed automobiles are the only items our couples own that are subject to the tax.

★Total tax burdens in Charlottesville are about average for the $24,281 income category and lower than average for the $34,275 and $68,098 income categories.

RICHMOND

Richmond has no local income tax but does levy a sales tax.

Most purchases are taxed at a rate of 4.5%. Major consumer categories taxed at a different rate include: Food away from home, which is taxed at a rate of 9.5%. Major consumer categories which are exempt from sales tax include: Drugs and medical services.

Within the city limits of Richmond, the property tax rate is .01445. Homes are assessed at 100% of market value. There is a senior citizen exemption of a portion of property tax due for homeowners age 65 or older with a gross income of less than $17,000 and assets of less than $75,000, excluding home value. Property tax includes garbage pickup. There is a landfill charge of approximately $120 per year and a recycling fee of approximately $18 per year.

Richmond has a personal property tax rate of .0370. Personal property is assessed at 90% of cost for new vehicles and 100% of NADA trade-in value for vehicles more than one year old. Items subject to the tax include automobiles, boats, mobile homes, motorcycles, RVs and trailers. We've assumed automobiles are the only items our couples own that are subject to the tax.

★Total tax burdens in Richmond are higher than average for the $24,281 income category and about average for the $34,075 and $68,098 income categories.

VIRGINIA BEACH

Virginia Beach has no local income tax but does levy a sales tax.

Most purchases are taxed at a rate of 4.5%. Major consumer categories taxed at a different rate include: Food away from home, which is taxed at a rate of 9%. Major consumer categories which are exempt from sales tax include: Drugs and medical services.

Within the city limits of Virginia Beach, the property tax rate is .0114. Homes are assessed at 100% of market value. There is a senior citizen exemption of a portion of property tax due for homeowners age 65 or older with a gross income of less than $22,000 and assets of less than $70,000, excluding home value. Property tax includes garbage pickup. There is a storm water management fee of approximately $33 per year.

Virginia Beach has a personal property tax rate of .0150 for boats, camping trailers and motor homes, which are assessed at 100% of wholesale value in NADA recreational vehicle guide. There is a personal property tax rate of .0370 for vehicles, which are assessed at 100% of NADA loan value. We've assumed automobiles are the only items our couples own that are subject to the tax.

★Total tax burdens in Virginia Beach are about average for the $24,281 income category and lower than average for the $34,275 and $68,098 income categories.

WASHINGTON

Income	Home Value	Property Tax & Other Fees	Personal Property Tax & Auto Fees	Sales Tax	Local Income Tax	State Income Tax	Total Tax	Rank From #1–#149
PORT TOWNSEND								
$24,281	$50,000	$599	$656	$838	–	–	$2,093	#110
	75,000	809	656	838	–	–	2,303	#96
	100,000	1,018	656	838	–	–	2,512	#80
$34,275	$75,000	$1,210	$656	$1,126	–	–	$2,992	#106 (tie)
	100,000	1,553	656	1,126	–	–	3,335	#104
	150,000	2,240	656	1,126	–	–	4,022	#92
$68,098	$150,000	$2,240	$656	$1,740	–	–	$4,636	#31
	200,000	2,928	656	1,740	–	–	5,324	#25
	250,000	3,615	656	1,740	–	–	6,011	#27
SEATTLE								
$24,281	$50,000	$596	$668	$869	–	–	$2,133	#117
	75,000	814	668	869	–	–	2,351	#101
	100,000	1,032	668	869	–	–	2,569	#89
$34,275	$75,000	$980	$668	$1,168	–	–	$2,816	#95
	100,000	1,253	668	1,168	–	–	3,089	#84
	150,000	1,799	668	1,168	–	–	3,635	#68
$68,098	$150,000	$1,799	$668	$1,806	–	–	$4,273	#19
	200,000	2,345	668	1,806	–	–	4,819	#15
	250,000	2,892	668	1,806	–	–	5,366	#16
SPOKANE								
$24,281	$50,000	$544	$668	$848	–	–	$2,060	#107
	75,000	764	668	848	–	–	2,280	#91 (tie)
	100,000	985	668	848	–	–	2,501	#77
$34,275	$75,000	$1,222	$668	$1,140	–	–	$3,030	#111
	100,000	1,596	668	1,140	–	–	3,404	#106
	150,000	2,342	668	1,140	–	–	4,150	#101 (tie)
$68,098	$150,000	$2,342	$668	$1,762	–	–	$4,772	#35
	200,000	3,088	668	1,762	–	–	5,518	#34
	250,000	3,834	668	1,762	–	–	6,264	#37
TACOMA								
$24,281	$50,000	$700	$698	$838	–	–	$2,236	#129
	75,000	948	698	838	–	–	2,484	#115
	100,000	1,196	698	838	–	–	2,732	#98
$34,275	$75,000	$1,582	$698	$1,126	–	–	$3,406	#126
	100,000	2,042	698	1,126	–	–	3,866	#127
	150,000	2,961	698	1,126	–	–	4,785	#117
$68,098	$150,000	$2,961	$698	$1,740	–	–	$5,399	#59
	200,000	3,879	698	1,740	–	–	6,317	#62
	250,000	4,798	698	1,740	–	–	7,236	#74 (tie)
WENATCHEE								
$24,281	$50,000	$532	$656	$838	–	–	$2,026	#103
	75,000	760	656	838	–	–	2,254	#89
	100,000	988	656	838	–	–	2,482	#75
$34,275	$75,000	$1,120	$656	$1,126	–	–	$2,902	#97
	100,000	1,467	656	1,126	–	–	3,249	#95
	150,000	2,162	656	1,126	–	–	3,944	#88
$68,098	$150,000	$2,162	$656	$1,740	–	–	$4,558	#27
	200,000	2,857	656	1,740	–	–	5,253	#23
	250,000	3,552	656	1,740	–	–	5,948	#25

Washington has no state income tax but does have a state sales tax.

Major tax credits or rebates: None.

The state sales tax rate is 6.5% but local governments can add to this amount.

Since car registration and renewal fees differ within the state, see city information for details.

PORT TOWNSEND

Port Townsend has no local income tax but does levy a sales tax.

Most purchases are taxed at a rate of 7.9%. Major consumer categories taxed at a different rate: None. Major consumer categories which are exempt from sales tax include: Drugs, groceries and medical services.

Within the city limits of Port Townsend, the property tax rate is .01374312. Homes are assessed at 100% of fair market value. There is a homeowner's exemption available to homeowners age 61 or older with a gross income of $28,000 or less. Property tax does not cover garbage pickup; the additional fee is approximately $120 per year. Homeowners also pay a storm water utilities fee, which averages $60 per year.

Port Townsend has a personal property tax rate of .01374312 that applies to mobile homes located on rented or leased land.

Our couples relocating to Port Townsend must pay an excise tax based on year and MSRP of each automobile and a license fee of $28 per automobile. The excise tax is $378 for the Chrysler and $276 for the Oldsmobile. Our couples also pay $15 per automobile for inspection and $12 per automobile in miscellaneous fees at the time of registration. Thereafter, on an annual basis, our couples will pay an excise tax, license fee and miscellaneous fees, per automobile.

★Total tax burdens in Port Townsend are about average for the $24,281 and $34,275 income categories and lower than average for the $68,098 income category.

SEATTLE

Seattle has no local income tax but does levy a sales tax.

Most purchases are taxed at a rate of 8.2%. Major consumer categories taxed at a different rate: None. Major consumer categories which are exempt from sales tax include: Drugs, groceries and medical services.

Within the city limits of Seattle, the property tax rate is .01092247. Homes are assessed at 100% of market value. There is a homeowner's exemption available to homeowners age 61 or older with a gross income of $28,000 or less. Property tax does not cover garbage pickup; the additional fee is approximately $121 per year. Homeowners also pay a surface water management fee, which averages $40 per year.

Seattle has no personal property tax for individuals.

Our couples relocating to Seattle must pay an excise tax based on year and MSRP of each automobile and a license fee of $28 per automobile. The excise tax is $378 for the Chrysler and $276 for the Oldsmobile. Our couples also pay $15 per automobile for inspection, a $12 emissions test fee for the Chrysler and $12 per automobile in miscellaneous fees at the time of registration. Thereafter, on an annual basis, our couples will pay an excise tax, license fee and miscellaneous fees, per automobile, and an emissions test fee for one car.

★Total tax burdens in Seattle are about average for the $24,281 and $34,275 income categories and lower than average for the $68,098 income category.

SPOKANE

Spokane has no local income tax but does levy a sales tax.

Most purchases are taxed at a rate of 8%. Major consumer categories taxed at a different rate: None. Major consumer categories which are exempt from sales tax include: Drugs, groceries and medical services.

Within the city limits of Spokane, the property tax rate is .0149252. Homes are assessed at 100% of market value. There is a homeowner's exemption available to homeowners age 61 or older with a gross income of $28,000 or less. Property tax does not cover garbage pickup; the additional fee is approximately $103 per year.

Spokane has no personal property tax for individuals.

Our couples relocating to Spokane must pay an excise tax based on year and MSRP of each automobile and a license fee of $28 per automobile. The excise tax is $378 for the Chrysler and $276 for the Oldsmobile. Our couples also pay $15 per automobile for inspection, a $12 emissions test fee for the Chrysler and $12 per automobile in miscellaneous fees at the time of registration. Thereafter, on an annual basis, our couples will pay an excise tax, license fee and miscellaneous fees, per automobile, and an emissions test fee for one car.

★Total tax burdens in Spokane are about average for the $24,281 income category, higher than average for the $34,275 income category and lower than average for the $68,098 income category.

TACOMA

Tacoma has no local income tax but does levy a sales tax.

Most purchases are taxed at a rate of 7.9%. Major consumer categories taxed at a different rate: None. Major consumer categories which are exempt from sales tax include: Drugs, groceries and medical services.

Within the city limits of Tacoma, the property tax rate is .018377. Homes are assessed at 100% of market value. There is a homeowner's exemption available to homeowners age 61 or older with a gross income of $28,000 or less. Property tax does not cover garbage pickup; the additional fee is approximately $204 per year.

Tacoma has no personal property tax for individuals.

Our couples relocating to Tacoma must pay an excise tax based on year and MSRP of each automobile, a license fee of $28 and a transportation tax of $15 per automobile. The excise tax is $378 for the Chrysler and $276 for the Oldsmobile. Our couples also pay $15 per automobile for inspection, a $12 emissions test fee for the Chrysler and $12 per automobile in miscellaneous fees at the time of registration. Thereafter, on an annual basis, our couples will pay an excise tax, license fee, transportation tax and miscellaneous fees, per automobile, and an emissions test fee for one car.

★Total tax burdens in Tacoma are

higher than average for the $24,281 and $34,275 income categories and about average for the $68,098 income category.

WENATCHEE

Wenatchee has no local income tax but does levy a sales tax.

Most purchases are taxed at a rate of 7.9%. Major consumer categories taxed at a different rate: None. Major consumer categories which are exempt from sales tax include: Drugs, groceries and medical services.

In School District #246 in Wenatchee, the property tax rate is .01389986. Homes are assessed at 100% of market value. There is a homeowner's exemption available to homeowners age 61 or older with a gross income of $28,000 or less. Property tax does not cover garbage pickup; the additional fee is approximately $77 per year.

Wenatchee has no personal property tax for individuals.

Our couples relocating to Wenatchee must pay an excise tax based on year and MSRP of each automobile and a license fee of $28 per automobile. The excise tax is $378 for the Chrysler and $276 for the Oldsmobile. Our couples also pay $15 per automobile for inspection and $12 per automobile in miscellaneous fees at the time of registration. Thereafter, on an annual basis, our couples will pay an excise tax, license fee and miscellaneous fees, per automobile.

★Total tax burdens in Wenatchee are about average for the $24,281 and $34,275 income categories and lower than average for the $68,098 income category.

WEST VIRGINIA

Income	Home Value	Property Tax & Other Fees	Personal Property Tax & Auto Fees	Sales Tax	Local Income Tax	State Income Tax	Total Tax	Rank From #1–#149
CHARLESTON								
$24,281	$50,000	$219	$345	$786	–	–	$1,350	#22
	75,000	450	345	786	–	–	1,581	#18
	100,000	681	345	786	–	–	1,812	#16
$34,275	$75,000	$450	$345	$1,037	–	$206	$2,038	#23
	100,000	681	345	1,037	–	206	2,269	#19
	150,000	1,144	345	1,037	–	206	2,732	#18
$68,098	$150,000	$1,144	$345	$1,514	–	$1,960	$4,963	#38
	200,000	1,606	345	1,514	–	1,960	5,425	#31
	250,000	2,068	345	1,514	–	1,960	5,887	#23
CLARKSBURG								
$24,281	$50,000	$275	$370	$786	–	–	$1,431	#29
	75,000	526	370	786	–	–	1,682	#28
	100,000	778	370	786	–	–	1,934	#26
$34,275	$75,000	$526	$370	$1,037	–	$206	$2,139	#33
	100,000	778	370	1,037	–	206	2,391	#27
	150,000	1,281	370	1,037	–	206	2,894	#23
$68,098	$150,000	$1,281	$370	$1,514	–	$1,960	$5,125	#46
	200,000	1,784	370	1,514	–	1,960	5,628	#40
	250,000	2,287	370	1,514	–	1,960	6,131	#29

West Virginia has a state income tax and a state sales tax.

The state income tax rate is graduated from 3% to 6.5% depending upon income bracket. For married couples filing jointly with taxable income up to $10,000, the rate is 3%; for taxable income of $10,000 to $25,000, the tax is $300 plus 4% of the amount above $10,000; for taxable income of $25,000 to $40,000, the tax is $900 plus 4.5% of the amount above $25,000; for taxable income of $40,000 to $60,000, the tax is $1,575 plus 6% of the amount above $40,000; and for taxable income above $60,000, the tax is $2,775 plus 6.5% of the amount above $60,000.

In calculating the tax, there is no deduction for federal income tax paid. Federal, state and private pensions are not exempt, although there is a deduction of up to $2,000 from certain federal and state pensions. Social Security benefits subject to federal tax are not exempt. Interest and dividends from West Virginia and federal obligations are exempt. There is a $2,000 standard deduction per person from adjusted gross income. There is an exclusion of up to $8,000 of any source of income from adjusted gross income per person for persons age 65 or older.

Major tax credits or rebates include: Credit for income taxes paid to other states. Our couples do not qualify for this program.

The state sales tax rate is 6%.

Our couples relocating to the cities listed below must pay a 5% privilege tax per automobile based on the NADA loan value of the car. The privilege tax is $450 for the Chrysler and $314 for the Oldsmobile. Our couples must also pay a plate fee of $32 per automobile and a title fee of $5 per automobile at the time of registration. Thereafter, on an annual basis, our couples will pay a plate fee per automobile.

CHARLESTON

Charleston has no local income tax and does not levy an additional sales tax.

Most purchases are taxed at the state rate of 6%. Major consumer categories taxed at a different rate: None. Major consumer categories which are exempt from sales tax include: Drugs and medical services.

Within the city limits of Charleston, the property tax rate is .015408. Homes are assessed at 60% of market value. There is a homestead exemp-

tion of $20,000 off assessed value available to homeowners if at least one is age 65 or older. Property tax does not cover garbage pickup; the additional fee is approximately $65 per year.

Charleston has a personal property tax rate of .007704 for Class I items; a rate of .015408 for Class II items; and a rate of .030816 for Class IV items. Personal property is assessed at 60% of face value for Class I; 60% of replacement cost for Class II; and 60% of loan value for Class IV.

Items subject to the personal property tax include: Class I-notes, stocks, bonds, farm animals and farm equipment; Class II-mobile homes; and Class IV-vehicles, satellite dishes, pets, watercraft, aircraft, trailers, campers and motorcycles. There is a homestead exemption of $20,000 off assessed value available to homeowners age 65 or older for Class II items only. The Class I personal property tax is sometimes referred to as an intangibles tax in other states, and we do not include it in our calculations. (See Intangibles Tax in Introduction.) We've assumed that automobiles are the only items owned by our couples that are subject to personal property tax.

★Total tax burdens in Charleston are lower than average overall.

CLARKSBURG

Clarksburg has no local income tax and does not levy an additional sales tax.

Most purchases are taxed at the state rate of 6%. Major consumer categories taxed at a different rate: None. Major consumer categories which are exempt from sales tax include: Drugs and medical services.

Within the city limits of Clarksburg, the property tax rate is .016770. Homes are assessed at 60% of market value. There is a homestead exemption of $20,000 off assessed value available to homeowners age 65 or older. Property tax does not cover garbage pickup; the additional fee is approximately $107 per year.

Clarksburg has a personal property tax rate of .008385 for Class I items; a rate of .016770 for Class II items; and a rate of .033540 for Class IV items. Personal property is assessed at 60% of actual value for Class I; 60% of value in state guide for Class II; and 60% of NADA loan value for Class IV.

Items subject to the personal property tax include: Class I-notes, stocks, bonds; Class II-mobile homes; and Class IV-vehicles, satellite dishes, pets, watercraft, aircraft, trailers, campers and motorcycles. There is a homestead exemption of $20,000 off assessed value available to homeowners age 65 or older for Class II items only. The Class I personal property tax is sometimes referred to as an intangibles tax in other states, and we do not include it in our calculations. (See Intangibles Tax in Introduction.) We've assumed that automobiles are the only items owned by our couples that are subject to personal property tax.

★Total tax burdens in Clarksburg are lower than average overall.

WISCONSIN

Income	Home Value	Property Tax & Other Fees	Personal Property Tax & Auto Fees	Sales Tax	Local Income Tax	State Income Tax*	Total Tax	Rank From #1–#1499
EAGLE RIVER								
$24,281	$50,000	$1,479	$80	$583	–	$229	$2,371	#134
	75,000	2,229	80	583	–	165	3,057	#138
	100,000	2,978	80	583	–	165	3,806	#137
$34,275	$75,000	$2,229	$80	$784	–	$838	$3,931	#140
	100,000	2,978	80	784	–	838	4,680	#143
	150,000	4,478	80	784	–	838	6,180	#144
$68,098	$150,000	$4,478	$80	$1,211	–	$3,865	$9,634	#147
	200,000	5,978	80	1,211	–	3,865	11,134	#146
	250,000	7,477	80	1,211	–	3,865	12,633	#146
GREEN BAY								
$24,281	$50,000	$1,406	$80	$530	–	$224	$2,240	#130
	75,000	2,165	80	530	–	165	2,940	#133
	100,000	2,923	80	530	–	165	3,698	#135
$34,275	$75,000	$2,165	$80	$712	–	$838	$3,795	#138
	100,000	2,923	80	712	–	838	4,553	#140
	150,000	4,440	80	712	–	838	6,070	#142
$68,098	$150,000	$4,440	$80	$1,101	–	$3,865	$9,486	#146
	200,000	5,957	80	1,101	–	3,865	11,003	#145
	250,000	7,474	80	1,101	–	3,865	12,520	#145
MADISON								
$24,281	$50,000	$1,521	$80	$583	–	$214	$2,398	#135
	75,000	2,345	80	583	–	165	3,173	#139
	100,000	3,169	80	583	–	165	3,997	#144
$34,275	$75,000	$2,345	$80	$784	–	$838	$4,047	#144
	100,000	3,169	80	784	–	838	4,871	#146
	150,000	4,818	80	784	–	838	6,520	#147
$68,098	$150,000	$4,818	$80	$1,211	–	$3,865	$9,974	#148
	200,000	6,467	80	1,211	–	3,865	11,623	#148
	250,000	8,116	80	1,211	–	3,865	13,272	#147
MILWAUKEE								
$24,281	$50,000	$1,687	$80	$583	–	$196	$2,546	#140
	75,000	2,588	80	583	–	165	3,416	#146
	100,000	3,488	80	583	–	165	4,316	#148
$34,275	$75,000	$2,588	$80	$784	–	$838	$4,290	#148
	100,000	3,488	80	784	–	838	5,190	#148
	150,000	5,289	80	784	–	838	6,991	#148
$68,098	$150,000	$5,289	$80	$1,211	–	$3,865	$10,445	#149
	200,000	7,090	80	1,211	–	3,865	12,246	#149
	250,000	8,891	80	1,211	–	3,865	14,047	#149

*School property tax credit is issued as a reduction of income tax due.

Wisconsin has a state income tax and a state sales tax.

The state income tax is graduated from 4.9% to 6.93% depending upon income bracket. For married couples filing jointly with taxable income up to $10,000, the rate is 4.9%; up to $20,000, the tax is $490 plus 6.55% of the amount above $10,000; above $20,000, the tax is $1,145 plus 6.93% of the amount above $20,000.

In calculating the tax, there is no deduction for federal income tax paid. Federal and state pensions are not generally exempt, although Wisconsin does exempt pensions received by persons who were members of, or retired from, the federal retirement system, the Wisconsin state teachers retirement system, and certain Mil-waukee city and county retirement systems, prior to January 1, 1964. Private pensions are not exempt. Some Social Security benefits subject to federal tax are not exempt. There is a sliding-scale standard deduction for married couples filing jointly that starts at $8,900 and decreases until it is completely phased out at $55,000 of income. There is an itemized deductions credit. We've assumed our couples do not itemize. There is a school property tax credit, which our couples do qualify for. There is a $25 tax credit per person for persons age 65 or older.

Major tax credits or rebates include: Credit for income taxes paid to other states and married couple credit. Our couples do not qualify for these programs.

The state also collects a temporary recycling surcharge based on type and amount of income, and some of our couples pay a surcharge of $28.

The state sales tax rate is 5% but local governments can add to this amount.

Our couples relocating to the cities listed below must pay a plate fee of $40 per automobile and a title fee of $13 per automobile at the time of registration. Thereafter, on an annual basis, our couples will pay a plate fee per automobile.

EAGLE RIVER

Eagle River has no local income tax but does levy a sales tax.

Most purchases are taxed at a rate of 5.5%. Major consumer categories taxed at a different rate: None. Major consumer categories which are exempt from sales tax include: Drugs, groceries and medical services.

Within the city limits of Eagle River, the property tax rate is .03322. Homes are assessed at 90.28% of market value. There is a lottery property tax credit available to all homeowners that is based on the amount of funds in the program. The credit was approximately $126. There is also a homestead credit of $10 to $1,160 based on income and property taxes paid that is available to homeowners with gross income less than $19,154. Property tax does not cover garbage pickup; the additional fee is approximately $105 per year.

Eagle River has no personal property tax for individuals.

★Total tax burdens in Eagle River are higher than average overall. Eagle River ranks as a tax hell in 6 of 9 income/home value categories.

GREEN BAY

Green Bay has no local income tax and does not levy an additional sales tax.

Most purchases are taxed at the state rate of 5%. Major consumer categories taxed at a different rate: None. Major consumer categories which are exempt from sales tax include: Drugs, groceries and medical services.

Within the city limits of Green Bay, the property tax rate is .03985. Homes are assessed at 76.13% of market value. There is a lottery property tax credit available to all homeowners that is based on the amount of funds in the program. The credit was approximately $110. There is also a homestead credit of $10 to $1,160 based on income and property taxes paid that is available to homeowners with gross income less than $19,154. Property tax includes garbage pickup. Some residents may live within special assessment districts and be subject to additional charges for items such as sidewalks, streets, paving and sewer.

Green Bay has no personal property tax for individuals.

★Total tax burdens in Green Bay are higher than average overall. Green Bay ranks as a tax hell in 5 of 9 income/home value categories.

MADISON

Madison has no local income tax but does levy a sales tax.

Most purchases are taxed at a rate of 5.5%. Major consumer categories taxed at a different rate: None. Major consumer categories which are exempt from sales tax include: Drugs, groceries and medical services.

In the Madison Metropolitan School District, the property tax rate is .0329764. Homes are assessed at 100% of market value. There is a lottery property tax credit available to all homeowners that is based on the amount of funds in the program. The credit was approximately $128. There is also a homestead credit of $10 to $1,160 based on income and property taxes paid that is available to homeowners with gross income less than $19,154. Property tax includes garbage pickup.

Madison has no personal property tax for individuals.

★Total tax burdens in Madison are higher than average overall. Madison ranks as a tax hell in 7 of 9 income/home value categories.

MILWAUKEE

Milwaukee has no local income tax but does levy a sales tax.

Most purchases are taxed at a rate of 5.5%. Major consumer categories taxed at a different rate: None. Major consumer categories which are exempt from sales tax include: Drugs, groceries and medical services.

Within the city limits of Milwaukee, the property tax rate is .036667. Homes are assessed at 98.23% of market value. There is a lottery property tax credit available to all homeowners that is based on the amount of funds in the program. The credit was approximately $114. There is also a homestead credit of $10 to $1,160 based on income and property taxes paid that is available to homeowners with gross income less than $19,154. Property tax includes garbage pickup. Some residents may be subject to additional charges for items such as sidewalks, streets and sewer replacement/reconstruction.

Milwaukee has no personal property tax for individuals.

★Total tax burdens in Milwaukee are higher than average overall. Milwaukee ranks as a tax hell in all 9 income/home value categories.

WYOMING

Income	Home Value	Property Tax & Other Fees	Personal Property Tax & Auto Fees	Sales Tax	Local Income Tax	State Income Tax	Total Tax	Rank From #1–#149
CHEYENNE								
$24,281	$50,000	$501	$264	$786	–	–	$1,551	#43 (tie)
	75,000	691	264	786	–	–	1,741	#35
	100,000	881	264	786	–	–	1,931	#25
$34,275	$75,000	$691	$264	$1,037	–	–	$1,992	#21
	100,000	881	264	1,037	–	–	2,182	#17
	150,000	1,262	264	1,037	–	–	2,563	#14
$68,098	$150,000	$1,262	$264	$1,514	–	–	$3,040	#4
	200,000	1,643	264	1,514	–	–	3,421	#4
	250,000	2,023	264	1,514	–	–	3,801	#4
JACKSON								
$24,281	$50,000	$483	$290	$786	–	–	$1,559	#46
	75,000	641	290	786	–	–	1,717	#32
	100,000	799	290	786	–	–	1,875	#19
$34,275	$75,000	$641	$290	$1,037	–	–	$1,968	#18
	100,000	799	290	1,037	–	–	2,126	#12
	150,000	1,114	290	1,037	–	–	2,441	#11
$68,098	$150,000	$1,114	$290	$1,514	–	–	$2,918	#3
	200,000	1,430	290	1,514	–	–	3,234	#3
	250,000	1,745	290	1,514	–	–	3,549	#3

Wyoming has no state income tax but does have a state sales tax.

Major tax credits or rebates include: Wyoming tax refund to the elderly and disabled. Our couples do not qualify for this program.

The state sales tax rate is 4% but local governments can add to this amount.

Since car registration and renewal fees differ within the state, see city information for details.

CHEYENNE

Cheyenne has no local income tax but does levy a sales tax.

Most purchases are taxed at a rate of 6%. Major consumer categories taxed at a different rate: None. Major consumer categories which are exempt from sales tax include: Drugs and medical services.

Within the city limits of Cheyenne, the property tax rate is .08014. Homes are assessed at 9.5% of market value. Property tax does not cover garbage pickup; the additional fee is approximately $120 per year.

Cheyenne has no personal property tax for individuals.

Our couples relocating to Cheyenne must pay a county fee per automobile based on the year and factory price of the vehicle. The county fee is $204 for the Chrysler and $122 for the Oldsmobile. Our couples must also pay a title fee of $7 per automobile, a Vehicle Identification Number (VIN) inspection of $5 per automobile and a state fee of $15 per automobile, at the time of registration. Thereafter, on an annual basis, our couples will pay a county fee and a state fee, per automobile.

★Total tax burdens in Cheyenne are lower than average overall. Cheyenne ranks as a tax heaven in 3 of 9 income/home values categories.

JACKSON

Jackson has no local income tax but does levy a sales tax.

Most purchases are taxed at a rate of 6%. Major consumer categories taxed at a different rate: None. Major consumer categories which are exempt from sales tax include: Drugs and medical services.

Within the city limits of Jackson, the property tax rate is .0664. Homes are assessed at 9.5% of market value. Property tax does not cover garbage pickup; the additional fee is approximately $168 per year.

Jackson has no personal property tax for individuals.

Our couples relocating to Jackson must pay a plate fee per automobile based on the year and factory price of the vehicle. The plate fee is $226 for the Chrysler and $136 for the Oldsmobile. Our couples must also pay a title fee of $6 per automobile, a Vehicle Identification Number (VIN) inspection of $5 per automobile and a state fee of $15 per automobile, at the time of registration. Thereafter, on an annual basis, our couples will pay a plate fee and a state fee, per automobile.

★Total tax burdens in Jackson are lower than average overall. Jackson ranks as a tax heaven in 3 of 9 income/home value categories.

WASHINGTON, DC

Income	Home Value	Property Tax & Other Fees	Personal Property Tax & Auto Fees	Sales Tax	Local Income Tax	State Income Tax	Total Tax	Rank From #1–#149
WASHINGTON, DC								
$24,281	$50,000	$96	$130	$670	$520	–	$1,416	#28
	75,000	216	130	670	520	–	1,536	#14
	100,000	336	130	670	520	–	1,656	#12
$34,275	$75,000	$216	$130	$906	$1,203	–	$2,455	#57
	100,000	336	130	906	1,203	–	2,575	#37
	150,000	576	130	906	1,203	–	2,815	#20
$68,098	$150,000	$576	$130	$1,404	$4,189	–	$6,299	#92
	200,000	816	130	1,404	4,189	–	6,539	#76
	250,000	1,056	130	1,404	4,189	–	6,779	#60

Washington, DC, has an income tax and a sales tax.

The income tax rate is graduated from 6% to 9.5% depending upon income bracket. For married couples filing jointly with taxable income of up to $10,000, the rate is 6%; for taxable income of $10,001 to $20,000, the tax is $600 plus 8% of the amount above $10,000; and for taxable income above $20,000, the tax is $1,400 plus 9.5% of the amount above $20,000.

In calculating the tax, there is no deduction for federal income tax paid. Federal, District of Columbia and private pensions are not exempt, though there is a $3,000 exemption per person from federal and District of Columbia pensions. Social Security benefits are exempt. There is a $2,000 standard deduction from adjusted gross income for married couples filing jointly. There is a $2,740 personal exemption from adjusted gross income for married couples filing jointly and there is a $1,370 personal exemption per person from adjusted gross income for persons age 65 or older.

Major tax credits or rebates include: Credit for income taxes paid to other states, low income credit and property tax credit. Our couples do not qualify for these programs.

During the 12-month period covered by this study, base sales tax rate was changed twice, from 6% to 7% and from 7% to 5.75%. Our estimates are based on 6%, which was the rate in effect for the longest period. The only major consumer category taxed at a different rate was food away from home, which was taxed at 9% or 10% during the year. We based our estimates on 9%, since that rate was in effect the longest. Major consumer categories which are exempt from sales tax include: Drugs, groceries and medical services.

Within the city limits of Washington, DC, the property tax rate is .0096. Homes are assessed at 100% of market value. There is a homestead exemption of $30,000 off assessed value available to all homeowners. There is a reduction of 50% of property taxes due available to homeowners age 65 or older with a gross income of less than $100,000. Property tax includes garbage pickup.

Washington, DC, has no personal property tax for individuals.

Our couples relocating to Washington, DC, must pay an excise tax of 6% per automobile based on the vehicle's current market value in NADA. The excise tax is $733.50 for the Chrysler and $525 for the Oldsmobile. Our couples must also pay a tags, registration and inspection fee per automobile based on the weight of the vehicle. The fee is $65 for the Chrysler and $65 for the Oldsmobile. And, our couples must pay a title fee of $20 per automobile at the time of registration. Thereafter, on an annual basis, our couples will pay a tags, registration and inspection fee per automobile.

★Total tax burdens in Washington, DC, are lower than average for the $24,281 and $34,275 income categories and about average for the $68,098 income category.

Ranking of Total Tax Burdens for Retirees
Earning $24,281 and Owning a Home Valued at $50,000

Rank	City, State	Total Tax
1	ANCHORAGE, AK	$ 182
2	JUNEAU, AK	299
3	WILMINGTON, DE	468
4	KAHULUI, HI	588
5	HONOLULU, HI	611
6	DOVER, DE	619
7	BEND, OR	970
8	EUGENE, OR	1,030
9	HOUSTON, TX	1,101
10	PORTLAND, OR	1,138
11	FAIRHOPE, AL	1,146
12	BATON ROUGE, LA	1,170
13	NAPLES, FL	1,219
14	DALLAS, TX	1,228
15	AUSTIN, TX	1,259
16	CARLSBAD, NM	1,272
17	OCEAN CITY, MD	1,297
18	SANTE FE, NM	1,304
19	JACKSONVILLE, FL	1,313
20	LAKELAND, FL	1,337
21	HARTFORD, CT	1,344
22	CHARLESTON, WV	1,350
23	BOSTON, MA	1,369
24	NEW YORK CITY, NY	1,380
25	COLORADO SPRINGS, CO	1,385
26	TOMS RIVER, NJ	1,404
27	ORLANDO, FL	1,408
28	WASHINGTON, DC	1,416
29	CLARKSBURG, WV	1,431
(TIE) 30	BOCA RATON, FL	1,437
(TIE) 30	ROSWELL, NM	1,437
32	CAPE MAY, NJ	1,439
33	LAS CRUCES, NM	1,455
34	RIO RANCHO, NM	1,456
35	PINEHURST, NC	1,459
36	OCALA, FL	1,476
37	BOISE, ID	1,499
38	MISSOULA, MT	1,500
39	COEUR D'ALENE, ID	1,525
40	COLUMBUS, OH	1,539
41	GULF SHORES, AL	1,545
42	HELENA, MT	1,547
(TIE) 43	CHEYENNE, WY	1,551
(TIE) 43	NEW ORLEANS, LA	1,551
45	MERIDIAN, MS	1,554
46	JACKSON, WY	1,559
47	FORT COLLINS, CO	1,564
48	SAVANNAH, GA	1,571
49	ALBUQUERQUE, NM	1,573
50	MYRTLE BEACH, SC	1,578
51	PORTSMOUTH, NH	1,590
52	GAINESVILLE, FL	1,595
53	SARASOTA, FL	1,606
54	OXFORD, MS	1,614
55	TAMPA, FL	1,631
56	MOUNTAIN HOME, AR	1,635
57	ST. GEORGE, UT	1,665
58	WIMBERLEY, TX	1,685
(TIE) 59	ST. PETERSBURG, FL	1,693
(TIE) 59	EDENTON, NC	1,693
(TIE) 61	FORT LAUDERDALE, FL	1,701
(TIE) 61	CLEVELAND, OH	1,701
(TIE) 63	MIAMI, FL	1,709
(TIE) 63	CINCINNATI, OH	1,709
65	ATLANTA, GA	1,721
66	GREENVILLE, SC	1,725
67	FLAGSTAFF, AZ	1,745
68	HOT SPRINGS, AR	1,746
69	SAN ANTONIO, TX	1,748
70	LEXINGTON, KY	1,756
71	DETROIT, MI	1,757
72	NASHVILLE, TN	1,759
73	HILTON HEAD, SC	1,768
74	AIKEN, SC	1,773
75	PARIS, TN	1,783

Rank	City, State	Total Tax
	AVERAGE	**$1,790**
76	SCOTTSDALE, AZ	1,817
77	CAMDEN, ME	1,826
78	BLOOMINGTON, IN	1,830
79	PRESCOTT, AZ	1,833
80	CAPE COD, MA	1,849
81	MONTEREY, CA	1,850
82	LANSING, MI	1,851
83	SAN DIEGO, CA	1,854
(TIE) 84	VIRGINIA BEACH, VA	1,862
(TIE) 84	YUMA, AZ	1,862
86	DAYTON, OH	1,863
87	SALT LAKE CITY, UT	1,875
88	MURRAY, KY	1,882
89	PHOENIX, AZ	1,883
(TIE) 90	BALTIMORE, MD	1,892
(TIE) 90	BREVARD, NC	1,892
(TIE) 90	HENDERSONVILLE, NC	1,892
93	TRENTON, NJ	1,919
94	CHARLOTTESVILLE, VA	1,926
95	ASHEVILLE, NC	1,931
96	BURLINGTON, VT	1,935
97	FARGO, ND	1,985
98	RENO, NV	1,986
99	TUCSON, AZ	1,992
100	CHAPEL HILL, NC	1,996
101	FREDERICKSBURG, TX	2,017
102	LAS VEGAS, NV	2,023
103	WENATCHEE, WA	2,026
104	ONTARIO, CA	2,027
105	PIERRE, SD	2,031
106	DECATUR, IL	2,052
107	SPOKANE, WA	2,060
108	BRANSON, MO	2,069
109	BROWNSVILLE, TX	2,073
110	PORT TOWNSEND, WA	2,093
(TIE) 111	MINNEAPOLIS, MN	2,095
(TIE) 111	CONCORD, NH	2,095
113	LITTLE ROCK, AR	2,104
114	BISMARCK, ND	2,106
115	TULSA, OK	2,113
116	PALM SPRINGS, CA	2,122
117	SEATTLE, WA	2,133
118	BARSTOW, CA	2,147
119	SAN FRANCISCO, CA	2,156
(TIE) 120	ST. PAUL, MN	2,160
(TIE) 120	BUFFALO, NY	2,160
122	LONG BEACH, NY	2,169
123	MONTPELIER, VT	2,173
124	RAPID CITY, SD	2,179
125	RICHMOND, VA	2,188
126	LOS ANGELES, CA	2,194
127	CHICAGO, IL	2,207
128	OKLAHOMA CITY, OK·	2,225
129	TACOMA, WA	2,236
130	GREEN BAY, WI	2,240
131	AUGUSTA, ME	2,263
132	SYRACUSE, NY	2,332
133	NEWPORT, RI	2,353
134	EAGLE RIVER, WI	2,371
135	MADISON, WI	2,398
136	CEDAR RAPIDS, IA	2,443
137	KANSAS CITY, MO	2,446
138	INDIANAPOLIS, IN	2,454
139	WICHITA, KS	2,507
140	MILWAUKEE, WI	2,546
141	OMAHA, NE	2,617
142	ITHACA, NY	2,627
143	PHILADELPHIA, PA	2,651
144	NEW HAVEN, CT	2,702
145	LINCOLN, NE	2,764
146	DES MOINES, IA	2,772
147	PROVIDENCE, RI	2,924
148	PITTSBURGH, PA	3,053
149	TOPEKA, KS	3,095

Ranking of Total Tax Burdens for Retirees
Earning $24,281 and Owning a Home Valued at $75,000

Rank	City, State	Total Tax		Rank	City, State	Total Tax
1	ANCHORAGE, AK	$ 182		76	CAMDEN, ME	$2,150
2	JUNEAU, AK	299		77	SAN DIEGO, CA	2,151
3	KAHULUI, HI	588		78	YUMA, AZ	2,154
4	HONOLULU, HI	611		79	CINCINNATI, OH	2,155
5	WILMINGTON, DE	672			**AVERAGE**	**2,158**
6	DOVER, DE	909		80	MONTPELIER, VT	2,178
7	FAIRHOPE, AL	1,146		81	BURLINGTON, VT	2,183
8	BATON ROUGE, LA	1,192		82	BREVARD, NC	2,199
9	BEND, OR	1,373		83	SALT LAKE CITY, UT	2,200
10	CARLSBAD, NM	1,402		84	CHARLOTTESVILLE, VA	2,204
11	SANTE FE, NM	1,438		85	HENDERSONVILLE, NC	2,210
12	EUGENE, OR	1,460		86	PORTSMOUTH, NH	2,223
13	DALLAS, TX	1,481		87	WIMBERLEY, TX	2,226
14	WASHINGTON, DC	1,536		88	ATLANTA, GA	2,229
15	GULF SHORES, AL	1,545		89	WENATCHEE, WA	2,254
16	NAPLES, FL	1,563		90	RENO, NV	2,271
17	NEW ORLEANS, LA	1,578	(TIE)	91	SPOKANE, WA	2,280
18	CHARLESTON, WV	1,581	(TIE)	91	ONTARIO, CA	2,280
19	PORTLAND, OR	1,588		93	BRANSON, MO	2,286
20	HOUSTON, TX	1,590		94	LAS VEGAS, NV	2,288
21	NEW YORK CITY, NY	1,594		95	MINNEAPOLIS, MN	2,294
22	COLORADO SPRINGS, CO	1,595		96	PORT TOWNSEND, WA	2,303
23	OCEAN CITY, MD	1,611		97	ASHEVILLE, NC	2,309
24	ROSWELL, NM	1,637		98	TAMPA, FL	2,311
25	HELENA, MT	1,639		99	GAINESVILLE, FL	2,314
26	CAPE MAY, NJ	1,661		100	ST. PAUL, MN	2,349
27	PINEHURST, NC	1,664		101	SEATTLE, WA	2,351
28	CLARKSBURG, WV	1,682		102	ST. PETERSBURG, FL	2,355
29	LAS CRUCES, NM	1,684		103	TUCSON, AZ	2,363
30	RIO RANCHO, NM	1,685		104	FORT LAUDERDALE, FL	2,375
31	BOSTON, MA	1,716		105	DAYTON, OH	2,378
32	JACKSON, WY	1,717		106	CHAPEL HILL, NC	2,379
33	HARTFORD, CT	1,718		107	TULSA, OK	2,390
34	AUSTIN, TX	1,730		108	SAN ANTONIO, TX	2,396
35	CHEYENNE, WY	1,741		109	PALM SPRINGS, CA	2,401
36	SAVANNAH, GA	1,774		110	BARSTOW, CA	2,403
37	MERIDIAN, MS	1,775		111	LITTLE ROCK, AR	2,439
38	BOISE, ID	1,796		112	SAN FRANCISCO, CA	2,447
39	MOUNTAIN HOME, AR	1,812		113	LOS ANGELES, CA	2,452
40	OXFORD, MS	1,820		114	FREDERICKSBURG, TX	2,459
41	MYRTLE BEACH, SC	1,823		115	TACOMA, WA	2,484
42	DETROIT, MI	1,827		116	MIAMI, FL	2,486
43	COEUR D'ALENE, ID	1,843		117	FARGO, ND	2,515
44	FORT COLLINS, CO	1,849		118	OKLAHOMA CITY, OK	2,545
45	LANSING, MI	1,851		119	RICHMOND, VA	2,549
46	LAKELAND, FL	1,860		120	BISMARCK, ND	2,670
47	JACKSONVILLE, FL	1,867		121	LONG BEACH, NY	2,694
48	ST. GEORGE, UT	1,887		122	DECATUR, IL	2,705
49	ALBUQUERQUE, NM	1,891		123	BROWNSVILLE, TX	2,714
50	COLUMBUS, OH	1,917		124	TRENTON, NJ	2,742
51	MISSOULA, MT	1,926		125	PIERRE, SD	2,756
52	HOT SPRINGS, AR	1,940		126	BUFFALO, NY	2,793
53	ORLANDO, FL	1,949		127	AUGUSTA, ME	2,806
54	FLAGSTAFF, AZ	1,965		128	KANSAS CITY, MO	2,817
55	TOMS RIVER, NJ	1,969		129	WICHITA, KS	2,829
56	EDENTON, NC	1,981		130	NEWPORT, RI	2,876
57	BOCA RATON, FL	1,984		131	INDIANAPOLIS, IN	2,879
58	HILTON HEAD, SC	1,998		132	RAPID CITY, SD	2,925
59	LEXINGTON, KY	2,004		133	GREEN BAY, WI	2,940
60	GREENVILLE, SC	2,014		134	CHICAGO, IL	2,951
61	SCOTTSDALE, AZ	2,032		135	CONCORD, NH	2,978
62	PARIS, TN	2,036		136	SYRACUSE, NY	2,994
63	NASHVILLE, TN	2,040		137	CEDAR RAPIDS, IA	3,005
64	BALTIMORE, MD	2,045		138	EAGLE RIVER, WI	3,057
65	OCALA, FL	2,057		139	MADISON, WI	3,173
66	AIKEN, SC	2,060		140	OMAHA, NE	3,244
67	CLEVELAND, OH	2,084		141	NEW HAVEN, CT	3,267
68	PRESCOTT, AZ	2,086		142	PHILADELPHIA, PA	3,312
69	MONTEREY, CA	2,103		143	ITHACA, NY	3,369
70	CAPE COD, MA	2,119		144	LINCOLN, NE	3,380
71	BLOOMINGTON, IN	2,131		145	PROVIDENCE, RI	3,382
72	SARASOTA, FL	2,133		146	MILWAUKEE, WI	3,416
73	PHOENIX, AZ	2,134		147	DES MOINES, IA	3,523
74	VIRGINIA BEACH, VA	2,147		148	TOPEKA, KS	3,582
75	MURRAY, KY	2,149		149	PITTSBURGH, PA	4,045

Ranking of Total Tax Burdens for Retirees
Earning $24,281 and Owning a Home Valued at $100,000

Rank	City, State	Total Tax	Rank	City, State	Total Tax
1	ANCHORAGE, AK	$ 182	76	ORLANDO, FL	$2,489
2	JUNEAU, AK	299	77	SPOKANE, WA	2,501
3	KAHULUI, HI	598	78	BRANSON, MO	2,502
4	HONOLULU, HI	611	79	BREVARD, NC	2,506
5	WILMINGTON, DE	877	80	PORT TOWNSEND, WA	2,512
6	FAIRHOPE, AL	1,146	81	DETROIT, MI	2,518
7	DOVER, DE	1,198	82	SALT LAKE CITY, UT	2,524
8	BATON ROUGE, LA	1,442	83	HENDERSONVILLE, NC	2,527
9	CARLSBAD, NM	1,533	84	BOCA RATON, FL	2,532
10	GULF SHORES, AL	1,545	(TIE) 85	ONTARIO, CA	2,533
11	SANTE FE, NM	1,572	(TIE) 85	TOMS RIVER, NJ	2,533
12	WASHINGTON, DC	1,656		**AVERAGE**	**2,551**
13	BEND, OR	1,775	87	LAS VEGAS, NV	2,553
14	COLORADO SPRINGS, CO	1,804	88	RENO, NV	2,557
15	NEW YORK CITY, NY	1,808	89	SEATTLE, WA	2,569
16	CHARLESTON, WV	1,812	90	CINCINNATI, OH	2,602
17	ROSWELL, NM	1,838	91	OCALA, FL	2,637
18	PINEHURST, NC	1,869	(TIE) 92	SARASOTA, FL	2,660
19	JACKSON, WY	1,875	(TIE) 92	BARSTOW, CA	2,660
20	EUGENE, OR	1,891	94	TULSA, OK	2,668
21	NAPLES, FL	1,908	95	PALM SPRINGS, CA	2,679
22	LAS CRUCES, NM	1,913	96	ASHEVILLE, NC	2,686
23	RIO RANCHO, NM	1,915	97	LOS ANGELES, CA	2,710
24	OCEAN CITY, MD	1,925	98	TACOMA, WA	2,732
25	CHEYENNE, WY	1,931	99	TUCSON, AZ	2,733
26	CLARKSBURG, WV	1,934	100	ATLANTA, GA	2,736
27	DALLAS, TX	1,964	101	SAN FRANCISCO, CA	2,738
28	NEW ORLEANS, LA	1,979	102	MINNEAPOLIS, MN	2,759
29	MOUNTAIN HOME, AR	1,988	103	CHAPEL HILL, NC	2,763
30	CAPE MAY, NJ	2,036	104	WIMBERLEY, TX	2,768
31	PORTLAND, OR	2,039	105	LITTLE ROCK, AR	2,773
32	BALTIMORE, MD	2,045	106	PORTSMOUTH, NH	2,856
33	BOSTON, MA	2,062	107	OKLAHOMA CITY, OK	2,866
34	MYRTLE BEACH, SC	2,067	108	ST. PAUL, MN	2,871
35	HARTFORD, CT	2,070	109	DAYTON, OH	2,894
36	HELENA, MT	2,074	110	FREDERICKSBURG, TX	2,900
37	HOUSTON, TX	2,079	111	RICHMOND, VA	2,910
38	BOISE, ID	2,093	112	TAMPA, FL	2,991
39	ST. GEORGE, UT	2,108	113	MONTPELIER, VT	3,016
(TIE) 40	HOT SPRINGS, AR	2,134	114	ST. PETERSBURG, FL	3,018
(TIE) 40	FORT COLLINS, CO	2,134	115	AUGUSTA, ME	3,019
42	MERIDIAN, MS	2,143	116	GAINESVILLE, FL	3,033
43	SAVANNAH, GA	2,151	117	FARGO, ND	3,044
44	COEUR D'ALENE, ID	2,160	118	FORT LAUDERDALE, FL	3,048
45	OXFORD, MS	2,165	119	SAN ANTONIO, TX	3,105
46	BURLINGTON, VT	2,183	120	WICHITA, KS	3,152
47	FLAGSTAFF, AZ	2,184	121	KANSAS CITY, MO	3,188
48	ALBUQUERQUE, NM	2,210	122	LONG BEACH, NY	3,219
49	HILTON HEAD, SC	2,229	123	BISMARCK, ND	3,234
50	BLOOMINGTON, IN	2,238	124	MIAMI, FL	3,264
51	SCOTTSDALE, AZ	2,248	125	INDIANAPOLIS, IN	3,304
52	LEXINGTON, KY	2,252	126	BROWNSVILLE, TX	3,354
53	LANSING, MI	2,262	127	DECATUR, IL	3,360
54	EDENTON, NC	2,268	128	NEWPORT, RI	3,398
55	PARIS, TN	2,290	129	BUFFALO, NY	3,426
56	COLUMBUS, OH	2,296	130	PIERRE, SD	3,481
57	AUSTIN, TX	2,297	131	TRENTON, NJ	3,564
58	GREENVILLE, SC	2,302	132	CEDAR RAPIDS, IA	3,568
59	NASHVILLE, TN	2,321	133	SYRACUSE, NY	3,655
60	PRESCOTT, AZ	2,340	134	RAPID CITY, SD	3,672
61	AIKEN, SC	2,346	135	GREEN BAY, WI	3,698
62	MONTEREY, CA	2,355	136	CHICAGO, IL	3,699
63	LAKELAND, FL	2,383	137	EAGLE RIVER, WI	3,806
64	PHOENIX, AZ	2,385	138	NEW HAVEN, CT	3,833
65	CAPE COD, MA	2,390	139	PROVIDENCE, RI	3,839
66	MURRAY, KY	2,416	140	CONCORD, NH	3,860
67	JACKSONVILLE, FL	2,422	141	OMAHA, NE	3,871
68	VIRGINIA BEACH, VA	2,432	142	PHILADELPHIA, PA	3,973
69	YUMA, AZ	2,446	143	LINCOLN, NE	3,996
70	SAN DIEGO, CA	2,447	144	MADISON, WI	3,997
71	CLEVELAND, OH	2,468	145	TOPEKA, KS	4,069
72	MISSOULA, MT	2,470	146	ITHACA, NY	4,112
73	CAMDEN, ME	2,473	147	DES MOINES, IA	4,273
74	CHARLOTTESVILLE, VA	2,481	148	MILWAUKEE, WI	4,316
75	WENATCHEE, WA	2,482	149	PITTSBURGH, PA	5,037

Ranking of Total Tax Burdens for Retirees
Earning $34,275 and Owning a Home Valued at $75,000

Rank	City, State	Total Tax		Rank	City, State	Total Tax
1	ANCHORAGE, AK	$ 182		76	ST. PETERSBURG, FL	$2,610
2	JUNEAU, AK	299		77	ONTARIO, CA	2,612
3	KAHULUI, HI	1,253			**AVERAGE**	**2,667**
4	HONOLULU, HI	1,276		78	CAMDEN, ME	2,669
5	WILMINGTON, DE	1,324		79	PHOENIX, AZ	2,671
6	DOVER, DE	1,460		80	HOT SPRINGS, AR	2,674
7	BATON ROUGE, LA	1,580		81	SAN ANTONIO, TX	2,678
8	CARLSBAD, NM	1,659		82	YUMA, AZ	2,703
9	SANTE FE, NM	1,698		83	BLOOMINGTON, IN	2,704
10	DALLAS, TX	1,781		84	EDENTON, NC	2,711
11	NAPLES, FL	1,782		85	MIAMI, FL	2,728
12	FAIRHOPE, AL	1,862		86	PALM SPRINGS, CA	2,733
13	HOUSTON, TX	1,890		87	BARSTOW, CA	2,735
14	ROSWELL, NM	1,901		88	FREDERICKSBURG, TX	2,759
15	RIO RANCHO, NM	1,942		89	CLEVELAND, OH	2,766
16	LAS CRUCES, NM	1,947		90	RICHMOND, VA	2,769
17	BEND, OR	1,966		91	CINCINNATI, OH	2,788
18	JACKSON, WY	1,968		92	LOS ANGELES, CA	2,802
19	COLORADO SPRINGS, CO	1,972		93	SAN FRANCISCO, CA	2,807
20	NEW ORLEANS, LA	1,989		94	LANSING, MI	2,809
21	CHEYENNE, WY	1,992		95	SEATTLE, WA	2,816
22	AUSTIN, TX	2,022		96	DETROIT, MI	2,870
23	CHARLESTON, WV	2,038		97	WENATCHEE, WA	2,902
24	EUGENE, OR	2,053		98	TUCSON, AZ	2,907
25	MERIDIAN, MS	2,068		99	FARGO, ND	2,921
26	LAKELAND, FL	2,079		100	BREVARD, NC	2,929
27	SAVANNAH, GA	2,092		101	CAPE COD, MA	2,931
28	JACKSONVILLE, FL	2,104		102	PIERRE, SD	2,932
29	MYRTLE BEACH, SC	2,112		103	HENDERSONVILLE, NC	2,940
30	OXFORD, MS	2,125		104	BURLINGTON, VT	2,942
31	ALBUQUERQUE, NM	2,132		105	CONCORD, NH	2,978
32	ST. GEORGE, UT	2,138	(TIE)	106	PORT TOWNSEND, WA	2,992
33	CLARKSBURG, WV	2,139	(TIE)	106	MURRAY, KY	2,992
34	ORLANDO, FL	2,168		108	BRANSON, MO	3,002
35	PORTLAND, OR	2,181		109	LEXINGTON, KY	3,004
36	CAPE MAY, NJ	2,196		110	BROWNSVILLE, TX	3,014
37	BOCA RATON, FL	2,203		111	SPOKANE, WA	3,030
38	PORTSMOUTH, NH	2,223		112	ASHEVILLE, NC	3,039
39	FORT COLLINS, CO	2,231		113	DAYTON, OH	3,055
40	MISSOULA, MT	2,252		114	BISMARCK, ND	3,081
41	OCALA, FL	2,276		115	CHAPEL HILL, NC	3,109
42	HILTON HEAD, SC	2,287		116	TRENTON, NJ	3,112
43	HELENA, MT	2,301		117	RAPID CITY, SD	3,124
(TIE) 44	GREENVILLE, SC	2,303		118	LITTLE ROCK, AR	3,148
(TIE) 44	NEW YORK CITY, NY	2,303		119	MONTPELIER, VT	3,184
46	GULF SHORES, AL	2,312		120	DECATUR, IL	3,208
47	TOMS RIVER, NJ	2,339		121	LONG BEACH, NY	3,256
48	AIKEN, SC	2,349		122	TULSA, OK	3,310
49	VIRGINIA BEACH, VA	2,365		123	AUGUSTA, ME	3,325
50	PARIS, TN	2,382		124	BUFFALO, NY	3,337
51	NASHVILLE, TN	2,386		125	WICHITA, KS	3,385
52	SARASOTA, FL	2,388		126	TACOMA, WA	3,406
53	MONTEREY, CA	2,390		127	BALTIMORE, MD	3,416
54	PINEHURST, NC	2,394		128	INDIANAPOLIS, IN	3,430
55	CHARLOTTESVILLE, VA	2,413		129	MINNEAPOLIS, MN	3,434
56	OCEAN CITY, MD	2,431		130	NEWPORT, RI	3,439
57	WASHINGTON, DC	2,455		131	ST. PAUL, MN	3,472
58	SALT LAKE CITY, UT	2,462		132	OKLAHOMA CITY, OK	3,491
59	SAN DIEGO, CA	2,463		133	SYRACUSE, NY	3,501
60	WIMBERLEY, TX	2,472		134	CHICAGO, IL	3,519
61	FLAGSTAFF, AZ	2,502		135	KANSAS CITY, MO	3,559
62	RENO, NV	2,523		136	NEW HAVEN, CT	3,667
63	BOSTON, MA	2,528		137	CEDAR RAPIDS, IA	3,715
64	BOISE, ID	2,529		138	GREEN BAY, WI	3,795
65	MOUNTAIN HOME, AR	2,530		139	OMAHA, NE	3,806
66	GAINESVILLE, FL	2,533		140	EAGLE RIVER, WI	3,931
67	LAS VEGAS, NV	2,540		141	LINCOLN, NE	3,942
68	HARTFORD, CT	2,546		142	PROVIDENCE, RI	3,945
69	ATLANTA, GA	2,547		143	ITHACA, NY	3,978
70	TAMPA, FL	2,548		144	MADISON, WI	4,047
71	COLUMBUS, OH	2,553		145	PHILADELPHIA, PA	4,104
72	SCOTTSDALE, AZ	2,572		146	TOPEKA, KS	4,148
73	COEUR D'ALENE, ID	2,576		147	DES MOINES, IA	4,233
74	FORT LAUDERDALE, FL	2,594		148	MILWAUKEE, WI	4,290
75	PRESCOTT, AZ	2,607		149	PITTSBURGH, PA	4,589

Ranking of Total Tax Burdens for Retirees
Earning $34,275 and Owning a Home Valued at $100,000

Rank	City, State	Total Tax		Rank	City, State	Total Tax
1	ANCHORAGE, AK	$ 182	(TIE)	76	BARSTOW, CA	$2,992
2	JUNEAU, AK	299	(TIE)	76	CAMDEN, ME	2,992
3	KAHULUI, HI	1,263		78	YUMA, AZ	2,995
4	HONOLULU, HI	1,276		79	EDENTON, NC	2,998
5	WILMINGTON, DE	1,528		80	PALM SPRINGS, CA	3,011
6	DOVER, DE	1,749		81	WIMBERLEY, TX	3,014
7	CARLSBAD, NM	1,790		82	ATLANTA, GA	3,054
8	BATON ROUGE, LA	1,830		83	LOS ANGELES, CA	3,060
9	SANTE FE, NM	1,832			**AVERAGE**	**3,060**
10	FAIRHOPE, AL	1,952		84	SEATTLE, WA	3,089
11	ROSWELL, NM	2,102		85	SAN FRANCISCO, CA	3,098
12	JACKSON, WY	2,126		86	RICHMOND, VA	3,130
13	NAPLES, FL	2,127		87	CLEVELAND, OH	3,150
14	RIO RANCHO, NM	2,172		88	BURLINGTON, VT	3,195
15	LAS CRUCES, NM	2,176		89	FREDERICKSBURG, TX	3,200
16	COLORADO SPRINGS, CO	2,181		90	CAPE COD, MA	3,202
17	CHEYENNE, WY	2,182		91	BRANSON, MO	3,218
18	DALLAS, TX	2,264		92	TAMPA, FL	3,228
19	CHARLESTON, WV	2,269		93	CINCINNATI, OH	3,235
20	MYRTLE BEACH, SC	2,356		94	BREVARD, NC	3,236
21	ST. GEORGE, UT	2,359		95	WENATCHEE, WA	3,249
22	BEND, OR	2,368	(TIE)	96	GAINESVILLE, FL	3,252
23	GULF SHORES, AL	2,377	(TIE)	96	LEXINGTON, KY	3,252
24	HOUSTON, TX	2,379		98	HENDERSONVILLE, NC	3,257
25	HELENA, MT	2,382		99	MURRAY, KY	3,259
26	NEW ORLEANS, LA	2,390		100	FORT LAUDERDALE, FL	3,267
27	CLARKSBURG, WV	2,391		101	ST. PETERSBURG, FL	3,273
28	CAPE MAY, NJ	2,406		102	TUCSON, AZ	3,277
29	MERIDIAN, MS	2,436		103	DETROIT, MI	3,280
30	ALBUQUERQUE, NM	2,451		104	PORT TOWNSEND, WA	3,335
31	SAVANNAH, GA	2,469		105	SAN ANTONIO, TX	3,387
32	OXFORD, MS	2,470		106	SPOKANE, WA	3,404
33	EUGENE, OR	2,484		107	ASHEVILLE, NC	3,416
34	FORT COLLINS, CO	2,516		108	FARGO, ND	3,450
35	NEW YORK CITY, NY	2,517		109	LITTLE ROCK, AR	3,482
36	HILTON HEAD, SC	2,518		110	CHAPEL HILL, NC	3,493
37	WASHINGTON, DC	2,575		111	MIAMI, FL	3,506
38	AUSTIN, TX	2,589		112	MONTPELIER, VT	3,542
39	GREENVILLE, SC	2,591		113	DAYTON, OH	3,571
40	PINEHURST, NC	2,599		114	TULSA, OK	3,588
41	LAKELAND, FL	2,602		115	BISMARCK, ND	3,645
42	PORTLAND, OR	2,632		116	BROWNSVILLE, TX	3,654
43	AIKEN, SC	2,635		117	PIERRE, SD	3,657
44	PARIS, TN	2,636		118	WICHITA, KS	3,708
45	MONTEREY, CA	2,642		119	MINNEAPOLIS, MN	3,757
46	VIRGINIA BEACH, VA	2,650		120	LONG BEACH, NY	3,781
47	JACKSONVILLE, FL	2,659		121	ST. PAUL, MN	3,811
48	NASHVILLE, TN	2,667		122	OKLAHOMA CITY, OK	3,812
49	CHARLOTTESVILLE, VA	2,690		123	INDIANAPOLIS, IN	3,855
50	MOUNTAIN HOME, AR	2,706		124	CONCORD, NH	3,860
51	ORLANDO, FL	2,708	(TIE)	125	DECATUR, IL	3,863
52	FLAGSTAFF, AZ	2,721	(TIE)	125	BALTIMORE, MD	3,863
53	OCEAN CITY, MD	2,745		127	TACOMA, WA	3,866
54	BOCA RATON, FL	2,751		128	AUGUSTA, ME	3,867
55	SAN DIEGO, CA	2,759		129	RAPID CITY, SD	3,871
56	MISSOULA, MT	2,778		130	KANSAS CITY, MO	3,930
57	SALT LAKE CITY, UT	2,786		131	TRENTON, NJ	3,934
58	SCOTTSDALE, AZ	2,788		132	NEWPORT, RI	3,961
59	LAS VEGAS, NV	2,805		133	BUFFALO, NY	3,970
60	RENO, NV	2,809		134	SYRACUSE, NY	4,162
61	BLOOMINGTON, IN	2,811		135	CHICAGO, IL	4,263
62	BOISE, ID	2,826		136	CEDAR RAPIDS, IA	4,278
(TIE) 63	OCALA, FL	2,856		137	NEW HAVEN, CT	4,295
(TIE) 63	PORTSMOUTH, NH	2,856		138	PROVIDENCE, RI	4,402
65	PRESCOTT, AZ	2,861		139	OMAHA, NE	4,433
66	ONTARIO, CA	2,865		140	GREEN BAY, WI	4,553
67	HOT SPRINGS, AR	2,868		141	LINCOLN, NE	4,558
68	LANSING, MI	2,869		142	TOPEKA, KS	4,635
69	BOSTON, MA	2,874		143	EAGLE RIVER, WI	4,680
70	COEUR D'ALENE, ID	2,893		144	ITHACA, NY	4,742
71	TOMS RIVER, NJ	2,903		145	PHILADELPHIA, PA	4,765
72	SARASOTA, FL	2,915		146	MADISON, WI	4,871
73	PHOENIX, AZ	2,922		147	DES MOINES, IA	4,983
74	COLUMBUS, OH	2,932		148	MILWAUKEE, WI	5,190
75	HARTFORD, CT	2,937		149	PITTSBURGH, PA	5,581

Ranking of Total Tax Burdens for Retirees
Earning $34,275 and Owning a Home Valued at $150,000

Rank	City, State	Total Tax	Rank	City, State	Total Tax
1	ANCHORAGE, AK	$ 182	76	CAPE COD, MA	$3,744
2	JUNEAU, AK	299	77	LEXINGTON, KY	3,747
3	HONOLULU, HI	1,348	78	JACKSONVILLE, FL	3,767
4	KAHULUI, HI	1,438	79	AUSTIN, TX	3,786
5	WILMINGTON, DE	1,936	80	ORLANDO, FL	3,789
6	CARLSBAD, NM	2,051	81	MURRAY, KY	3,793
7	SANTE FE, NM	2,099	82	BOCA RATON, FL	3,845
8	FAIRHOPE, AL	2,132	83	BREVARD, NC	3,850
9	DOVER, DE	2,328	84	RICHMOND, VA	3,853
10	BATON ROUGE, LA	2,330	85	MISSOULA, MT	3,866
11	JACKSON, WY	2,441		**AVERAGE**	**3,891**
12	ROSWELL, NM	2,503	86	HENDERSONVILLE, NC	3,892
13	GULF SHORES, AL	2,507	87	CLEVELAND, OH	3,917
14	CHEYENNE, WY	2,563	88	WENATCHEE, WA	3,944
15	COLORADO SPRINGS, CO	2,601	89	SARASOTA, FL	3,969
16	RIO RANCHO, NM	2,632	(TIE) 90	OCALA, FL	4,017
17	LAS CRUCES, NM	2,633	(TIE) 90	TUCSON, AZ	4,017
18	CHARLESTON, WV	2,732	92	PORT TOWNSEND, WA	4,022
19	ST. GEORGE, UT	2,803	93	TOMS RIVER, NJ	4,033
20	WASHINGTON, DC	2,815	94	ATLANTA, GA	4,069
21	NAPLES, FL	2,816	95	LANSING, MI	4,078
22	MYRTLE BEACH, SC	2,845	96	FREDERICKSBURG, TX	4,082
23	CLARKSBURG, WV	2,894	97	WIMBERLEY, TX	4,096
24	NEW YORK CITY, NY	2,944	98	PORTSMOUTH, NH	4,122
25	HILTON HEAD, SC	2,978	99	CINCINNATI, OH	4,128
26	PINEHURST, NC	3,009	100	TULSA, OK	4,144
27	MOUNTAIN HOME, AR	3,059	(TIE) 101	SPOKANE, WA	4,150
28	FORT COLLINS, CO	3,086	(TIE) 101	LITTLE ROCK, AR	4,150
29	ALBUQUERQUE, NM	3,088	103	ASHEVILLE, NC	4,171
30	PARIS, TN	3,142	104	CHAPEL HILL, NC	4,260
31	MONTEREY, CA	3,147	105	WICHITA, KS	4,354
32	CAPE MAY, NJ	3,154	106	OKLAHOMA CITY, OK	4,453
33	OXFORD, MS	3,158	107	FARGO, ND	4,508
34	FLAGSTAFF, AZ	3,161	108	TAMPA, FL	4,588
35	GREENVILLE, SC	3,169	109	ST. PETERSBURG, FL	4,598
36	MERIDIAN, MS	3,172	110	DAYTON, OH	4,602
37	BEND, OR	3,174	111	FORT LAUDERDALE, FL	4,614
38	NEW ORLEANS, LA	3,193	112	DETROIT, MI	4,664
39	BURLINGTON, VT	3,195	113	KANSAS CITY, MO	4,671
40	AIKEN, SC	3,209	114	GAINESVILLE, FL	4,691
(TIE) 41	VIRGINIA BEACH, VA	3,220	115	INDIANAPOLIS, IN	4,705
(TIE) 41	SCOTTSDALE, AZ	3,220	116	BISMARCK, ND	4,773
43	NASHVILLE, TN	3,230	117	TACOMA, WA	4,785
44	CHARLOTTESVILLE, VA	3,245	118	SAN ANTONIO, TX	4,803
45	HELENA, MT	3,252	119	LONG BEACH, NY	4,832
46	HOT SPRINGS, AR	3,257	120	BROWNSVILLE, TX	4,935
47	BLOOMINGTON, IN	3,296	121	AUGUSTA, ME	4,952
48	LAS VEGAS, NV	3,336	122	NEWPORT, RI	5,006
49	EUGENE, OR	3,344	123	MIAMI, FL	5,062
50	SAN DIEGO, CA	3,352	124	PIERRE, SD	5,107
51	DALLAS, TX	3,356	125	MINNEAPOLIS, MN	5,124
52	HOUSTON, TX	3,357	126	DECATUR, IL	5,171
53	PRESCOTT, AZ	3,369	127	BALTIMORE, MD	5,234
54	ONTARIO, CA	3,372	128	BUFFALO, NY	5,235
55	OCEAN CITY, MD	3,373	129	MONTPELIER, VT	5,242
56	RENO, NV	3,379	130	ST. PAUL, MN	5,278
57	PHOENIX, AZ	3,424	131	PROVIDENCE, RI	5,318
58	SALT LAKE CITY, UT	3,435	132	RAPID CITY, SD	5,365
59	SAVANNAH, GA	3,472	133	CEDAR RAPIDS, IA	5,402
60	BARSTOW, CA	3,505	134	SYRACUSE, NY	5,485
61	PORTLAND, OR	3,534	135	NEW HAVEN, CT	5,551
62	BOSTON, MA	3,567	136	TRENTON, NJ	5,579
63	PALM SPRINGS, CA	3,568	137	TOPEKA, KS	5,610
64	EDENTON, NC	3,573	138	CONCORD, NH	5,625
65	LOS ANGELES, CA	3,576	139	OMAHA, NE	5,688
66	YUMA, AZ	3,579	140	CHICAGO, IL	5,751
67	BOISE, ID	3,618	141	LINCOLN, NE	5,791
68	SEATTLE, WA	3,635	142	GREEN BAY, WI	6,070
69	CAMDEN, ME	3,639	143	PHILADELPHIA, PA	6,088
70	LAKELAND, FL	3,649	144	EAGLE RIVER, WI	6,180
71	BRANSON, MO	3,652	145	ITHACA, NY	6,270
72	SAN FRANCISCO, CA	3,679	146	DES MOINES, IA	6,485
73	COLUMBUS, OH	3,688	147	MADISON, WI	6,520
74	HARTFORD, CT	3,718	148	MILWAUKEE, WI	6,991
75	COEUR D'ALENE, ID	3,739	149	PITTSBURGH, PA	7,564

Ranking of Total Tax Burdens for Retirees
Earning $68,098 and Owning a Home Valued at $150,000

Rank	City, State	Total Tax		Rank	City, State	Total Tax
1	ANCHORAGE, AK	$ 182		76	LOS ANGELES, CA	$5,837
2	JUNEAU, AK	299		77	ROSWELL, NM	5,845
3	JACKSON, WY	2,918		78	OCEAN CITY, MD	5,894
4	CHEYENNE, WY	3,040		79	CAPE COD, MA	5,930
5	NAPLES, FL	3,282			**AVERAGE**	**5,935**
6	FAIRHOPE, AL	3,644		80	RICHMOND, VA	5,958
7	BATON ROUGE, LA	3,707	(TIE)	81	SAN FRANCISCO, CA	5,959
8	PARIS, TN	3,797	(TIE)	81	HOT SPRINGS, AR	5,959
9	NASHVILLE, TN	3,885		83	RIO RANCHO, NM	5,962
10	LAS VEGAS, NV	3,890		84	LAS CRUCES, NM	5,972
11	RENO, NV	3,933		85	EDENTON, NC	6,026
12	DALLAS, TX	3,998		86	ATLANTA, GA	6,072
13	HOUSTON, TX	3,999		87	COLUMBUS, OH	6,079
14	LAKELAND, FL	4,115		88	LANSING, MI	6,108
15	PORTSMOUTH, NH	4,122		89	FARGO, ND	6,128
16	ORLANDO, FL	4,255		90	MURRAY, KY	6,168
17	GULF SHORES, AL	4,258		91	BRANSON, MO	6,226
18	JACKSONVILLE, FL	4,272		92	WASHINGTON, DC	6,299
19	SEATTLE, WA	4,273	(TIE)	93	BREVARD, NC	6,303
20	HONOLULU, HI	4,303	(TIE)	93	HARTFORD, CT	6,303
21	BOCA RATON, FL	4,311		95	HENDERSONVILLE, NC	6,345
22	KAHULUI, HI	4,393		96	ALBUQUERQUE, NM	6,387
23	AUSTIN, TX	4,408	(TIE)	97	CLEVELAND, OH	6,405
24	WILMINGTON, DE	4,431	(TIE)	97	BISMARCK, ND	6,405
25	OCALA, FL	4,483		99	INDIANAPOLIS, IN	6,408
26	SARASOTA, FL	4,513		100	CAMDEN, ME	6,433
27	WENATCHEE, WA	4,558		101	BEND, OR	6,450
28	DOVER, DE	4,566	(TIE)	102	BOISE, ID	6,505
29	COLORADO SPRINGS, CO	4,573	(TIE)	102	NEW YORK CITY, NY	6,505
30	WIMBERLEY, TX	4,620		104	CINCINNATI, OH	6,520
31	PORT TOWNSEND, WA	4,636		105	SAVANNAH, GA	6,607
32	NEW ORLEANS, LA	4,644		106	EUGENE, OR	6,620
33	CAPE MAY, NJ	4,674		107	ASHEVILLE, NC	6,624
34	FREDERICKSBURG, TX	4,724		108	COEUR D'ALENE, ID	6,626
35	SPOKANE, WA	4,772		109	DECATUR, IL	6,631
36	FLAGSTAFF, AZ	4,882		110	ST. GEORGE, UT	6,660
37	SCOTTSDALE, AZ	4,937		111	CHAPEL HILL, NC	6,713
38	CHARLESTON, WV	4,963		112	LEXINGTON, KY	6,738
39	FORT COLLINS, CO	5,046		113	TRENTON, NJ	6,749
40	PRESCOTT, AZ	5,047		114	LITTLE ROCK, AR	6,800
41	MERIDIAN, MS	5,062		115	PORTLAND, OR	6,810
42	OXFORD, MS	5,069		116	BURLINGTON, VT	6,848
43	FORT LAUDERDALE, FL	5,080		117	TULSA, OK	6,988
44	BLOOMINGTON, IN	5,084		118	WICHITA, KS	7,000
45	TAMPA, FL	5,093		119	DAYTON, OH	7,102
46	CLARKSBURG, WV	5,125		120	DETROIT, MI	7,262
47	ST. PETERSBURG, FL	5,142		121	SALT LAKE CITY, UT	7,311
48	PHOENIX, AZ	5,146		122	CHICAGO, IL	7,341
49	GAINESVILLE, FL	5,157		123	OKLAHOMA CITY, OK	7,347
50	TOMS RIVER, NJ	5,203		124	LONG BEACH, NY	7,365
51	MYRTLE BEACH, SC	5,232		125	KANSAS CITY, MO	7,405
52	MONTEREY, CA	5,271		126	HELENA, MT	7,478
53	YUMA, AZ	5,314		127	MISSOULA, MT	7,692
54	VIRGINIA BEACH, VA	5,319		128	BUFFALO, NY	7,729
55	CHARLOTTESVILLE, VA	5,329		129	AUGUSTA, ME	7,746
56	HILTON HEAD, SC	5,365		130	NEWPORT, RI	7,789
57	CARLSBAD, NM	5,381		131	SYRACUSE, NY	7,901
58	PIERRE, SD	5,384		132	BALTIMORE, MD	8,083
59	TACOMA, WA	5,399		133	PROVIDENCE, RI	8,101
60	SAN ANTONIO, TX	5,406		134	NEW HAVEN, CT	8,136
61	SANTE FE, NM	5,434		135	CEDAR RAPIDS, IA	8,230
62	PINEHURST, NC	5,462		136	TOPEKA, KS	8,277
63	SAN DIEGO, CA	5,530		137	OMAHA, NE	8,364
64	GREENVILLE, SC	5,556		138	LINCOLN, NE	8,467
65	BROWNSVILLE, TX	5,577		139	ITHACA, NY	8,764
66	MIAMI, FL	5,578		140	MINNEAPOLIS, MN	8,923
67	ONTARIO, CA	5,594		141	PHILADELPHIA, PA	9,006
68	AIKEN, SC	5,596		142	ST. PAUL, MN	9,045
69	CONCORD, NH	5,625		143	MONTPELIER, VT	9,065
70	RAPID CITY, SD	5,679		144	DES MOINES, IA	9,313
71	BARSTOW, CA	5,727		145	PITTSBURGH, PA	9,386
72	MOUNTAIN HOME, AR	5,729		146	GREEN BAY, WI	9,486
73	BOSTON, MA	5,753		147	EAGLE RIVER, WI	9,634
74	TUCSON, AZ	5,755		148	MADISON, WI	9,974
75	PALM SPRINGS, CA	5,790		149	MILWAUKEE, WI	10,445

Ranking of Total Tax Burdens for Retirees
Earning $68,098 and Owning a Home Valued at $200,000

Rank	City, State	Total Tax	Rank	City, State	Total Tax
1	ANCHORAGE, AK	$ 756	76	WASHINGTON, DC	$6,539
2	JUNEAU, AK	1,000	77	SAN FRANCISCO, CA	6,541
3	JACKSON, WY	3,234	78	GAINESVILLE, FL	6,596
4	CHEYENNE, WY	3,421	79	EDENTON, NC	6,601
5	FAIRHOPE, AL	3,824	80	BRANSON, MO	6,659
6	NAPLES, FL	3,972	81	RICHMOND, VA	6,680
7	BATON ROUGE, LA	4,207	82	MURRAY, KY	6,702
8	PARIS, TN	4,303		**AVERAGE**	**6,778**
9	GULF SHORES, AL	4,388	83	SAN ANTONIO, TX	6,823
10	LAS VEGAS, NV	4,421	84	PIERRE, SD	6,834
11	NASHVILLE, TN	4,447	85	COLUMBUS, OH	6,835
12	HONOLULU, HI	4,491	86	BROWNSVILLE, TX	6,858
13	RENO, NV	4,504	87	BREVARD, NC	6,917
14	KAHULUI, HI	4,568	88	NEW YORK CITY, NY	6,933
15	SEATTLE, WA	4,819	89	HENDERSONVILLE, NC	6,980
16	WILMINGTON, DE	4,840	90	ALBUQUERQUE, NM	7,024
17	COLORADO SPRINGS, CO	4,992	91	CAMDEN, ME	7,080
18	HOUSTON, TX	5,001	92	HARTFORD, CT	7,085
19	CAPE MAY, NJ	5,073	93	ATLANTA, GA	7,086
20	DALLAS, TX	5,090	94	ST. GEORGE, UT	7,103
21	DOVER, DE	5,145	95	MIAMI, FL	7,133
22	LAKELAND, FL	5,161	96	CLEVELAND, OH	7,171
23	WENATCHEE, WA	5,253	97	RAPID CITY, SD	7,172
24	FLAGSTAFF, AZ	5,322	98	FARGO, ND	7,187
25	PORT TOWNSEND, WA	5,324	99	LEXINGTON, KY	7,233
26	ORLANDO, FL	5,336	100	BEND, OR	7,255
27	SCOTTSDALE, AZ	5,369	101	INDIANAPOLIS, IN	7,258
28	JACKSONVILLE, FL	5,380	102	LANSING, MI	7,316
29	PORTSMOUTH, NH	5,387	103	ASHEVILLE, NC	7,379
30	BOCA RATON, FL	5,406	104	CONCORD, NH	7,390
31	CHARLESTON, WV	5,425	105	CINCINNATI, OH	7,412
32	NEW ORLEANS, LA	5,447	106	LITTLE ROCK, AR	7,468
33	BLOOMINGTON, IN	5,473	107	CHAPEL HILL, NC	7,479
34	SPOKANE, WA	5,518	108	EUGENE, OR	7,480
35	PRESCOTT, AZ	5,554	109	BOISE, ID	7,494
36	SARASOTA, FL	5,567	110	BISMARCK, ND	7,533
37	AUSTIN, TX	5,605	111	TULSA, OK	7,543
38	FREDERICKSBURG, TX	5,607	112	SAVANNAH, GA	7,639
39	FORT COLLINS, CO	5,616	113	WICHITA, KS	7,645
40	CLARKSBURG, WV	5,628	114	COEUR D'ALENE, ID	7,683
(TIE) 41	OCALA, FL	5,643	115	PORTLAND, OR	7,712
(TIE) 41	CARLSBAD, NM	5,643	116	BURLINGTON, VT	7,797
43	PHOENIX, AZ	5,649	117	DECATUR, IL	7,939
44	SANTE FE, NM	5,702	118	HELENA, MT	7,947
45	WIMBERLEY, TX	5,703	119	SALT LAKE CITY, UT	7,961
46	MYRTLE BEACH, SC	5,721	120	OKLAHOMA CITY, OK	7,987
47	OXFORD, MS	5,757	121	DAYTON, OH	8,132
48	MONTEREY, CA	5,776	122	KANSAS CITY, MO	8,146
49	MERIDIAN, MS	5,798	123	TRENTON, NJ	8,394
50	HILTON HEAD, SC	5,825	124	LONG BEACH, NY	8,416
51	PINEHURST, NC	5,872	125	DETROIT, MI	8,645
52	CHARLOTTESVILLE, VA	5,884	126	MISSOULA, MT	8,781
53	VIRGINIA BEACH, VA	5,889	127	CHICAGO, IL	8,829
54	YUMA, AZ	5,898	128	AUGUSTA, ME	8,831
55	MOUNTAIN HOME, AR	6,082	129	NEWPORT, RI	8,834
56	ONTARIO, CA	6,100	130	BUFFALO, NY	8,995
57	SAN DIEGO, CA	6,123	131	PROVIDENCE, RI	9,016
58	GREENVILLE, SC	6,134	132	SYRACUSE, NY	9,225
59	AIKEN, SC	6,169	133	TOPEKA, KS	9,251
60	BARSTOW, CA	6,240	134	BALTIMORE, MD	9,295
61	ROSWELL, NM	6,246	135	CEDAR RAPIDS, IA	9,354
62	TACOMA, WA	6,317	136	NEW HAVEN, CT	9,393
63	TOMS RIVER, NJ	6,333	137	OMAHA, NE	9,618
64	PALM SPRINGS, CA	6,347	138	LINCOLN, NE	9,699
65	HOT SPRINGS, AR	6,348	139	ITHACA, NY	10,292
66	LOS ANGELES, CA	6,353	140	PHILADELPHIA, PA	10,328
67	RIO RANCHO, NM	6,422	141	MINNEAPOLIS, MN	10,338
68	FORT LAUDERDALE, FL	6,427	142	ST. PAUL, MN	10,520
69	LAS CRUCES, NM	6,429	143	MONTPELIER, VT	10,765
70	BOSTON, MA	6,446	144	DES MOINES, IA	10,814
71	TAMPA, FL	6,453	145	GREEN BAY, WI	11,003
72	ST. PETERSBURG, FL	6,467	146	EAGLE RIVER, WI	11,134
73	CAPE COD, MA	6,471	147	PITTSBURGH, PA	11,370
74	TUCSON, AZ	6,495	148	MADISON, WI	11,623
75	OCEAN CITY, MD	6,522	149	MILWAUKEE, WI	12,246

Ranking of Total Tax Burdens for Retirees
Earning $68,098 and Owning a Home Valued at $250,000

Rank	City, State	Total Tax		Rank	City, State	Total Tax
1	ANCHORAGE, AK	$1,329	(TIE)	74	TUCSON, AZ	$7,236
2	JUNEAU, AK	1,701		77	NEW YORK CITY, NY	7,361
3	JACKSON, WY	3,549		78	RICHMOND, VA	7,403
4	CHEYENNE, WY	3,801		79	TOMS RIVER, NJ	7,463
5	FAIRHOPE, AL	4,004		80	BREVARD, NC	7,531
6	GULF SHORES, AL	4,518		81	ST. GEORGE, UT	7,546
7	NAPLES, FL	4,661		82	COLUMBUS, OH	7,591
8	HONOLULU, HI	4,679		83	HENDERSONVILLE, NC	7,615
9	BATON ROUGE, LA	4,707			**AVERAGE**	**7,626**
10	KAHULUI, HI	4,743		84	ALBUQUERQUE, NM	7,661
11	PARIS, TN	4,809		85	CAMDEN, ME	7,727
12	LAS VEGAS, NV	4,951		86	LEXINGTON, KY	7,728
13	NASHVILLE, TN	5,010		87	FORT LAUDERDALE, FL	7,774
14	RENO, NV	5,075		88	ST. PETERSBURG, FL	7,792
15	WILMINGTON, DE	5,248		89	TAMPA, FL	7,813
16	SEATTLE, WA	5,366		90	HARTFORD, CT	7,866
17	COLORADO SPRINGS, CO	5,411		91	CLEVELAND, OH	7,938
18	BLOOMINGTON, IN	5,535		92	GAINESVILLE, FL	8,035
19	DOVER, DE	5,724		93	BEND, OR	8,060
20	FLAGSTAFF, AZ	5,762		94	TULSA, OK	8,099
21	SCOTTSDALE, AZ	5,800		95	ATLANTA, GA	8,101
22	CAPE MAY, NJ	5,822		96	INDIANAPOLIS, IN	8,108
23	CHARLESTON, WV	5,887		97	ASHEVILLE, NC	8,134
24	CARLSBAD, NM	5,904		98	LITTLE ROCK, AR	8,137
25	WENATCHEE, WA	5,948		99	BROWNSVILLE, TX	8,139
26	SANTE FE, NM	5,969		100	SAN ANTONIO, TX	8,240
27	PORT TOWNSEND, WA	6,011		101	FARGO, ND	8,245
28	PRESCOTT, AZ	6,062		102	CHAPEL HILL, NC	8,246
29	CLARKSBURG, WV	6,131		103	PIERRE, SD	8,284
30	PHOENIX, AZ	6,151		104	WICHITA, KS	8,291
31	DALLAS, TX	6,182		105	CINCINNATI, OH	8,305
32	FORT COLLINS, CO	6,186		106	EUGENE, OR	8,341
33	LAKELAND, FL	6,207		107	BOISE, ID	8,484
34	MYRTLE BEACH, SC	6,210		108	LANSING, MI	8,524
35	HOUSTON, TX	6,229		109	SALT LAKE CITY, UT	8,610
36	NEW ORLEANS, LA	6,250		110	PORTLAND, OR	8,613
37	SPOKANE, WA	6,264		111	OKLAHOMA CITY, OK	8,628
38	MONTEREY, CA	6,281		112	BISMARCK, ND	8,661
39	PINEHURST, NC	6,282		113	RAPID CITY, SD	8,666
40	HILTON HEAD, SC	6,286		114	SAVANNAH, GA	8,670
41	ORLANDO, FL	6,417		115	MIAMI, FL	8,689
42	MOUNTAIN HOME, AR	6,435		116	COEUR D'ALENE, ID	8,740
43	CHARLOTTESVILLE, VA	6,439		117	BURLINGTON, VT	8,747
44	OXFORD, MS	6,445		118	HELENA, MT	8,818
45	VIRGINIA BEACH, VA	6,459		119	KANSAS CITY, MO	8,887
46	YUMA, AZ	6,482		120	CONCORD, NH	9,155
(TIE) 47	JACKSONVILLE, FL	6,489		121	DAYTON, OH	9,163
(TIE) 47	FREDERICKSBURG, TX	6,489		122	DECATUR, IL	9,247
49	BOCA RATON, FL	6,500		123	LONG BEACH, NY	9,467
50	MERIDIAN, MS	6,535		124	MISSOULA, MT	9,869
51	ONTARIO, CA	6,607		125	NEWPORT, RI	9,879
52	SARASOTA, FL	6,621		126	AUGUSTA, ME	9,916
53	ROSWELL, NM	6,647		127	PROVIDENCE, RI	9,932
54	PORTSMOUTH, NH	6,653		128	DETROIT, MI	10,028
55	GREENVILLE, SC	6,712		129	TRENTON, NJ	10,039
56	SAN DIEGO, CA	6,716		130	TOPEKA, KS	10,226
57	HOT SPRINGS, AR	6,737		131	BUFFALO, NY	10,260
58	AIKEN, SC	6,743		132	CHICAGO, IL	10,317
59	BARSTOW, CA	6,752		133	CEDAR RAPIDS, IA	10,479
60	WASHINGTON, DC	6,779		134	BALTIMORE, MD	10,507
61	WIMBERLEY, TX	6,785		135	SYRACUSE, NY	10,548
62	AUSTIN, TX	6,801		136	NEW HAVEN, CT	10,649
63	OCALA, FL	6,804		137	OMAHA, NE	10,873
64	LOS ANGELES, CA	6,869		138	LINCOLN, NE	10,932
65	RIO RANCHO, NM	6,882		139	PHILADELPHIA, PA	11,650
66	LAS CRUCES, NM	6,887		140	MINNEAPOLIS, MN	11,754
67	PALM SPRINGS, CA	6,904		141	ITHACA, NY	11,820
68	CAPE COD, MA	7,013		142	ST. PAUL, MN	11,994
69	BRANSON, MO	7,092		143	DES MOINES, IA	12,315
70	SAN FRANCISCO, CA	7,122		144	MONTPELIER, VT	12,465
71	BOSTON, MA	7,139		145	GREEN BAY, WI	12,520
72	OCEAN CITY, MD	7,150		146	EAGLE RIVER, WI	12,633
73	EDENTON, NC	7,176		147	MADISON, WI	13,272
(TIE) 74	TACOMA, WA	7,236		148	PITTSBURGH, PA	13,354
(TIE) 74	MURRAY, KY	7,236		149	MILWAUKEE, WI	14,047

Tax Heaven Or Hell

How do the cities we've profiled stack up against each other tax-wise? The following charts show our 10 tax heavens and hells for each of 9 income/home value categories. Find the category that most closely matches the income and home value you anticipate for yourself in retirement.

If you don't see a city you're interested in, check the full ranking for each income/home value category —from #1 to #149—in the preceeding pages.

Our charts do not take into account cost-of-living factors in the areas we examined. For instance, Honolulu appears in several tax heaven charts, but residents there face very high real estate prices. Our charts rank cities solely by the tax burdens you will incur living there.

You may be surprised to see that not all of our tax heaven slots have been filled by cities from states with

Tax Heavens

$24,281 Income / $50,000 Home

		TAX
1	ANCHORAGE, AK	$ 182
2	JUNEAU, AK	299
3	WILMINGTON, DE	468
4	KAHULUI, HI	588
5	HONOLULU, HI	611
6	DOVER, DE	619
7	BEND, OR	970
8	EUGENE, OR	1,030
9	HOUSTON, TX	1,101
10	PORTLAND, OR	1,138

$24,281 Income / $75,000 Home

		TAX
1	ANCHORAGE, AK	$ 182
2	JUNEAU, AK	299
3	KAHULUI, HI	588
4	HONOLULU, HI	611
5	WILMINGTON, DE	672
6	DOVER, DE	909
7	FAIRHOPE, AL	1,146
8	BATON ROUGE, LA	1,192
9	BEND, OR	1,373
10	CARLSBAD, NM	1,402

$24,281 Income / $100,000 Home

		TAX
1	ANCHORAGE, AK	$ 182
2	JUNEAU, AK	299
3	KAHULUI, HI	598
4	HONOLULU, HI	611
5	WILMINGTON, DE	877
6	FAIRHOPE, AL	1,146
7	DOVER, DE	1,198
8	BATON ROUGE, LA	1,442
9	CARLSBAD, NM	1,533
10	GULF SHORES, AL	1,545

$34,275 Income / $75,000 Home

		TAX
1	ANCHORAGE, AK	$ 182
2	JUNEAU, AK	299
3	KAHULUI, HI	1,253
4	HONOLULU, HI	1,276
5	WILMINGTON, DE	1,324
6	DOVER, DE	1,460
7	BATON ROUGE, LA	1,580
8	CARLSBAD, NM	1,659
9	SANTA FE, NM	1,698
10	DALLAS, TX	1,781

$34,275 Income / $100,000 Home

		TAX
1	ANCHORAGE, AK	$ 182
2	JUNEAU, AK	299
3	KAHULUI, HI	1,263
4	HONOLULU, HI	1,276
5	WILMINGTON, DE	1,528
6	DOVER, DE	1,749
7	CARLSBAD, NM	1,790
8	BATON ROUGE, LA	1,830
9	SANTA FE, NM	1,832
10	FAIRHOPE, AL	1,952

$34,275 Income / $150,000 Home

		TAX
1	ANCHORAGE, AK	$ 182
2	JUNEAU, AK	299
3	HONOLULU, HI	1,348
4	KAHULUI, HI	1,438
5	WILMINGTON, DE	1,936
6	CARLSBAD, NM	2,051
7	SANTA FE, NM	2,099
8	FAIRHOPE, AL	2,132
9	DOVER, DE	2,328
10	BATON ROUGE, LA	2,330

$68,098 Income / $150,000 Home

		TAX
1	ANCHORAGE, AK	$ 182
2	JUNEAU, AK	299
3	JACKSON, WY	2,918
4	CHEYENNE, WY	3,040
5	NAPLES, FL	3,282
6	FAIRHOPE, AL	3,644
7	BATON ROUGE, LA	3,707
8	PARIS, TN	3,797
9	NASHVILLE, TN	3,885
10	LAS VEGAS, NV	3,890

$68,098 Income / $200,000 Home

		TAX
1	ANCHORAGE, AK	$ 756
2	JUNEAU, AK	1,000
3	JACKSON, WY	3,234
4	CHEYENNE, WY	3,421
5	FAIRHOPE, AL	3,824
6	NAPLES, FL	3,972
7	BATON ROUGE, LA	4,207
8	PARIS, TN	4,303
9	GULF SHORES, AL	4,388
10	LAS VEGAS, NV	4,421

$68,098 Income / $250,000 Home

		TAX
1	ANCHORAGE, AK	$1,329
2	JUNEAU, AK	1,701
3	JACKSON, WY	3,549
4	CHEYENNE, WY	3,801
5	FAIRHOPE, AL	4,004
6	GULF SHORES, AL	4,518
7	NAPLES, FL	4,661
8	HONOLULU, HI	4,679
9	BATON ROUGE, LA	4,707
10	KAHULUI, HI	4,743

no state income tax. Florida, the top retirement state, has no state income tax, but only one of the 12 Florida cities we profiled shows up in our tax heavens. Why? Florida levies a hefty sales tax and property taxes in many cities have escalated sharply in recent years. More Florida cities do surface in the top 25 rankings, though.

Across the board, our two top tax heavens are Anchorage and Juneau, AK — although most retirees will think twice about moving there to save on their tax bills.

If you're looking for a warm-weather home, you will be pleased to know that many Sunbelt states are tax-kind to senior citizens. Among the best are Alabama, Florida, Louisiana, Mississippi, Nevada, New Mexico, South Carolina and Texas. Take care to note that there are sometimes sharp differences between cities in these states (particularly true with Florida and Texas).

In general, taxes are highest in the Northeast and Midwest. Our tax hell charts include cities from Connecticut, Illinois, Iowa, Kansas, Minnesota, Nebraska, New Hampshire, New York, Pennsylvania, Rhode Island, Vermont and Wisconsin. Again, some cities in these states fare better than others.

Tax Hells ♆

$24,281 Income / $50,000 Home

		TAX
1	TOPEKA, KS	$3,095
2	PITTSBURGH, PA	3,053
3	PROVIDENCE, RI	2,924
4	DES MOINES, IA	2,772
5	LINCOLN, NE	2,764
6	NEW HAVEN, CT	2,702
7	PHILADELPHIA, PA	2,651
8	ITHACA, NY	2,627
9	OMAHA, NE	2,617
10	MILWAUKEE, WI	2,546

$24,281 Income / $75,000 Home

		TAX
1	PITTSBURGH, PA	$4,045
2	TOPEKA, KS	3,582
3	DES MOINES, IA	3,523
4	MILWAUKEE, WI	3,416
5	PROVIDENCE, RI	3,382
6	LINCOLN, NE	3,380
7	ITHACA, NY	3,369
8	PHILADELPHIA, PA	3,312
9	NEW HAVEN, CT	3,267
10	OMAHA, NE	3,244

$24,281 Income / $100,000 Home

		TAX
1	PITTSBURGH, PA	$5,037
2	MILWAUKEE, WI	4,316
3	DES MOINES, IA	4,273
4	ITHACA, NY	4,112
5	TOPEKA, KS	4,069
6	MADISON, WI	3,997
7	LINCOLN, NE	3,996
8	PHILADELPHIA, PA	3,973
9	OMAHA, NE	3,871
10	CONCORD, NH	3,860

$34,275 Income / $75,000 Home

		TAX
1	PITTSBURGH, PA	$4,589
2	MILWAUKEE, WI	4,290
3	DES MOINES, IA	4,233
4	TOPEKA, KS	4,148
5	PHILADELPHIA, PA	4,104
6	MADISON, WI	4,047
7	ITHACA, NY	3,978
8	PROVIDENCE, RI	3,945
9	LINCOLN, NE	3,942
10	EAGLE RIVER, WI	3,931

$34,275 Income / $100,000 Home

		TAX
1	PITTSBURGH, PA	$5,581
2	MILWAUKEE, WI	5,190
3	DES MOINES, IA	4,983
4	MADISON, WI	4,871
5	PHILADELPHIA, PA	4,765
6	ITHACA, NY	4,742
7	EAGLE RIVER, WI	4,680
8	TOPEKA, KS	4,635
9	LINCOLN, NE	4,558
10	GREEN BAY, WI	4,553

$34,275 Income / $150,000 Home

		TAX
1	PITTSBURGH, PA	$7,564
2	MILWAUKEE, WI	6,991
3	MADISON, WI	6,520
4	DES MOINES, IA	6,485
5	ITHACA, NY	6,270
6	EAGLE RIVER, WI	6,180
7	PHILADELPHIA, PA	6,088
8	GREEN BAY, WI	6,070
9	LINCOLN, NE	5,791
10	CHICAGO, IL	5,751

$68,098 Income / $150,000 Home

		TAX
1	MILWAUKEE, WI	$10,445
2	MADISON, WI	9,974
3	EAGLE RIVER, WI	9,634
4	GREEN BAY, WI	9,486
5	PITTSBURGH, PA	9,386
6	DES MOINES, IA	9,313
7	MONTPELIER, VT	9,065
8	ST. PAUL, MN	9,045
9	PHILADELPHIA, PA	9,006
10	MINNEAPOLIS, MN	8,923

$68,098 Income / $200,000 Home

		TAX
1	MILWAUKEE, WI	$12,246
2	MADISON, WI	11,623
3	PITTSBURGH, PA	11,370
4	EAGLE RIVER, WI	11,134
5	GREEN BAY, WI	11,003
6	DES MOINES, IA	10,814
7	MONTPELIER, VT	10,765
8	ST. PAUL, MN	10,520
9	MINNEAPOLIS, MN	10,338
10	PHILADELPHIA, PA	10,328

$68,098 Income / $250,000 Home

		TAX
1	MILWAUKEE, WI	$14,047
2	PITTSBURGH, PA	13,354
3	MADISON, WI	13,272
4	EAGLE RIVER, WI	12,633
5	GREEN BAY, WI	12,520
6	MONTPELIER, VT	12,465
7	DES MOINES, IA	12,315
8	ST. PAUL, MN	11,994
9	ITHACA, NY	11,820
10	MINNEAPOLIS, MN	11,754

Portland
1

Eugene
1

Bend
1, 2

Jackson
7-9

Cheyenne
7-9

Omaha
1-3

Lincoln
1-6

Topeka
1-5

Las Vegas
7, 8

Santa Fe
4-6

Carlsbad
2-6

Dallas
4

Houston
1

Anchorage
1-9

Juneau
1-9

Honolulu
1-6, 9

Kahului
1-6, 9

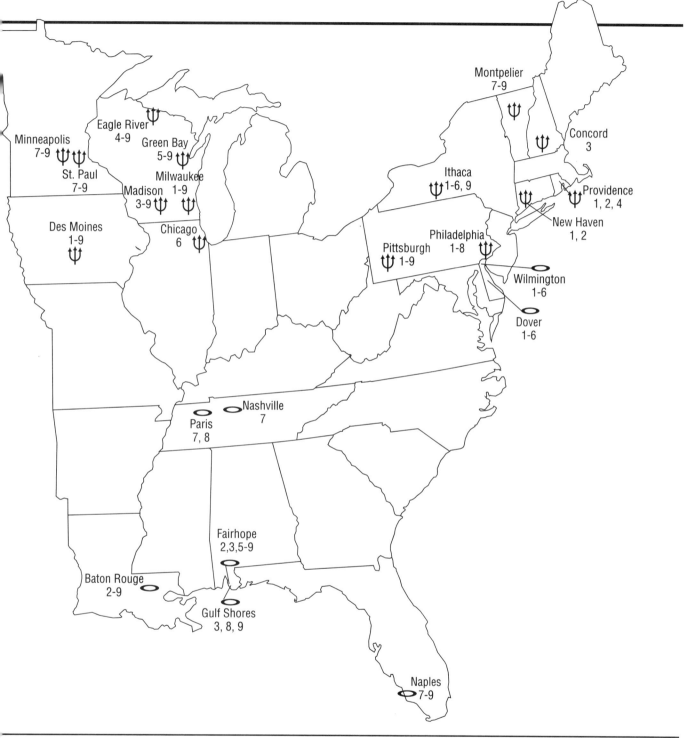

Montpelier
7-9

Concord
3

Minneapolis
7-9

St. Paul
7-9

Eagle River
4-9

Green Bay
5-9

Milwaukee
1-9

Madison
3-9

Des Moines
1-9

Chicago
6

Ithaca
1-6, 9

Providence
1, 2, 4

New Haven
1, 2

Philadelphia
1-8

Pittsburgh
1-9

Wilmington
1-6

Dover
1-6

Nashville
7

Paris
7, 8

Fairhope
2,3,5-9

Baton Rouge
2-9

Gulf Shores
3, 8, 9

Naples
7-9

Key

⬯ Cities qualifying as tax heavens in at least one income/home value category

♆ Cities qualifying as tax hells in at least one income/home value category

The numbers represent income/home value categories as follows:

#1 – $24,281 income and $50,000 home value	#4 – $34,275 income and $75,000 home value	#7 – $68,098 income and $150,000 home value
#2 – $24,281 income and $75,000 home value	#5 – $34,275 income and $100,000 home value	#8 – $68,098 income and $200,000 home value
#3 – $24,281 income and $100,000 home value	#6 – $34,275 income and $150,000 home value	#9 – $68,098 income and $250,000 home value

To make the right retirement relocation, you've got to have all the facts.

And now you can — with limited-edition Special Reports.

You've got to have good information to make a good decision. And if you're wondering where to retire — one of the most important decisions you'll ever make — you need the best information available.

That's why the editors of *Where to Retire* magazine have commissioned this unique and informative series of *Special Reports*. They're practical, in-depth analyses of the most important issues involved in retirement relocation, in an easy-to-read format.

Every *Special Report* is meticulously researched data, hard facts and unbiased reporting. And each is priced at a very manageable $3.95, plus $2.25 total postage and handling no matter how many *Special Reports* you order.

How to Plan and Execute A Successful Retirement Relocation

See what 200 relocated retirees said when asked, "If you could move again, what would you do differently?" You'll save the small price of this report many times over with the first common mistake you avoid. Includes finding and negotiating with a moving company, when to move, what to take, what to leave behind, shutting down at your current address and more.
SR1   48 pages, $3.95

America's Best Neighborhoods for Active Retirees

Many relocated retirees indicate satisfaction with their new town, but disappointment with their particular neighborhood. We present more than 230 top neighborhoods for active retirees, organized in a state-by-state directory. Listings cover location, size of neighborhood, size and price range of homes, age and origin of residents, amenities, and more. Don't buy a home without checking out our top neighborhoods.
SR2   64 pages, $3.95

Should You Retire to a Manufactured Home?

Explore this popular but controversial lifestyle option if you're looking for top value for your housing dollar. We'll tell you how manufactured homes have changed, how they compare to site-built homes and how safe they are from high winds and fire. Covers zoning restrictions, financing options, price appreciation, land-lease and resident-owned communities, home-land packages, purchase, delivery, siting, inspection and consumer protection laws.
SR4   32 pages, $3.95

Retiring Outside the United States

More than 350,000 retired Americans live outside the country, in places like Uruguay, Costa Rica and Portugal. Here's how to determine if you'd be happy retiring abroad, how to find the country and town that suit your lifestyle and how to adjust to everyday life in a new country. Covers eight popular — and economical — foreign retirement spots, plus the most common (and costly) mistakes made in moving abroad and how to avoid them.
SR5   48 pages, $3.95

Discounts for Travelers 50 and Beyond

The older you get, the greater the number of airlines, hotels, rental car companies, theme parks, cruise lines and national parks willing to offer you discounts. We'll tell you where to look and whom to ask. Includes when and how to use discount travel clubs, how to save 50% traveling off-season, how to get a rebate on airline tickets and more.
SR6   48 pages, $3.95